S0-AKN-660

MARKETING
MISTAKES

MARKETING MISTAKES

THIRD EDITION

Robert F. Hartley

Cleveland State University

JOHN WILEY & SONS

New York   Chichester   Brisbane   Toronto   Singapore

Copyright © 1976, 1981, 1986, by John Wiley & Sons, Inc.

All rights reserved. Published simultaneously in Canada.

Reproduction or translation of any part of
this work beyond that permitted by Sections
107 and 108 of the 1976 United States Copyright
Act without the permission of the copyright
owner is unlawful. Requests for permission
or further information should be addressed to
the Permissions Department, John Wiley & Sons.

Library of Congress Cataloging in Publication Data:

Hartley, Robert F.
  Marketing mistakes.

  1. Marketing—United States—Case studies.
I. Title.
HF5415.1.H37 1986   658.8′00973   85-12383
ISBN 0-471-83052-6

Printed in the United States of America

10 9 8 7 6 5 4 3 2 1

Contents

CHAPTER 1

Introduction

These cases, as in the first and second editions, represent classic marketing mistakes, some of which have been widely publicized. For example, the Edsel case is perhaps the most widely known marketing mistake of all time. A variety of firms, industries, problems, and mistakes are presented. Most of the firms are familiar to you—e.g., Gillette, STP Corporation, Adidas, Coors Beer—although the details of their problems may not be. The time span ranges over several decades, although most of the cases involve fairly recent events. Where the mistakes occurred several decades ago—such as the Edsel, and Montgomery Ward's no-growth philosophy—still the circumstances and what can be learned are far from dated.

Our quest here, as in the other editions, is to search for what can be learned from mistakes—what lessons we can come away with that have wider implications: transferable to other firms, other times, other situations.

ORGANIZATION OF CASES

The cases have been specially chosen to bring out certain points or caveats in the art of marketing decision-making. They have been selected to give a balanced view of the spectrum of marketing problems. Some of the mistakes are those of commission, in which wrong actions were taken; other cases involve mistakes of omission, in which no action was taken and the status quo was contentedly embraced amid a changing environment. We have sought to present examples that provide somewhat different learning experiences, where the mistake, or at least certain aspects of it, differs from the other mistakes described in the book.

Mishandling the Public Image

In studying the mistakes, and the successes, of firms over most of the last two decades, I have become more and more convinced that the reputation or public image of a firm—how it is perceived by its various publics—can play a crucial role in success or failure. In this third edition we have consequently included a new section of mistakes: those illustrating serious deficiencies in the handling of the public image.

In light of the importance of public image considerations, Chapter 2 is devoted not to a specific case but to a presentation of the constraints and implications of the public image. The idea is proposed that public image be considered as a fifth "P," an additional element of the marketing mix, controllable by the firm to a considerable degree just as are the recognized four P's of product, price, promotion, and place.

While a number of the mistakes described in the book owe part or most of their problems to a mishandled or misunderstood public image—for example, A & P, Burger Chef, the World Football League, W. T. Grant, among others—we have singled out four where image played a particularly significant role.

The Coors case shows how a great image can be lost through inattention. It is an object lesson on how important marketing really is. Coasting on a mystique that had somehow built up for its brand, Coors had enjoyed great success. But this mystique began fading. With little advertising, a disregard for basic marketing ideas, and aloof public and employee relations, the company's fortunes faltered badly in the face of aggressive competition. The mystique that had been Coors' proved to be ephemeral.

The Nestle case shows the impact of image problems coming from callousness regarding social responsibility. The firm marketed its infant formula in underdeveloped Third World countries that did not have the sanitation necessary to make the product safe. Nestle's stubborn persistence in doing so brought worldwide criticism, and eventually boycotts and profit damage.

Korvette, the star of the early discount-store movement, had supposedly found the magic formula for customer acceptance and unlimited growth opportunity. But ambitions were for more prestige than a discount chain as it attempted to upgrade its image and operation to fashions and higher quality—even a swank Fifth Avenue store. Managerial resources and organizational controls could not keep up with the rapid expansion, and customer acceptance of the new quality image did not materialize. Like a house of cards, the whole enterprise began collapsing. Eventually, the much larger Korvette Company was taken over by a smaller firm. But the problems were never to be fully remedied. The last case in this section, that of the toymaker A. C. Gilbert Company, illustrates practically every mistake imaginable, from not recognizing drastically changing conditions in the industry, to successive rash decisions aimed at correcting the problem. But the most serious mistake, permeating all aspects of the operation, was permitting a quality image, built up over decades, not merely to fade, but to be destroyed, in just a few years. These mistakes caused the 58-year-old company to fail.

Errors of Conservatism

In this section we are exposed to the fallacy of conservatism and examine a major consumer-goods manufacturer and two retail firms that, at important times in their corporate lives, evinced some extreme mistakes of omission. The Gillette Company permitted its dominance in the razor blade industry to be eroded by its stubborn reluctance to introduce its own stainless steel blade (because it thought this might cannibalize or take away sales from its highly profitable Super Blue Blade). Thereby, the door was opened for its smaller, hungry competitors to gain market share they never could have otherwise.

The extreme example of conservatism was Montgomery Ward: it completely shunned any expansion and hoarded its money after World War II in the mistaken belief that a severe depression would occur and that it could expand at much lower cost at that time. As a consequence, Ward lost ground to its major competitors, ground that has not been regained to this day.

The third case in this section is the J. C. Penney Company, which stayed with outmoded merchandising and noncredit policies long after the environment was dictating otherwise. However, in Penney's case, eventually aggressive growth policies replaced conservatism, and much of the lost ground was made up.

Misguided Expansion

Part III deals with firms at the opposite end of the spectrum. The ill-fated World Football League illustrates the fallacy of attempting market entry with an inferior product, in a relatively saturated market, and against a powerful competitor.

The fast-food franchise operation Burger Chef showed unwise expansion, but here under the auspices of a large and seasoned marketer, General Foods. But the irresistible temptation to open hundreds of additional outlets over a few years' time without proper operational fundamentals and a distinctive image forced severe retrenchment. One of the saddest cases in the book is that of W. T. Grant Company, a large and mature firm founded back in 1906. In the early 1970s it went on an expansion binge, far beyond its capabilities. The result was one of the worst business disasters in recent U.S. history.

Specific Errors

Part IV describes specific errors in marketing strategy regarding new products and other aspects of the marketing mix. The Edsel and Corfam cases represent examples of new product introductions that failed mightily. For Edsel and Corfam the losses were a hundred million dollars and more. Yet, careful product planning took place; there was heavy reliance on marketing research, and advertising and other promotional efforts were strongly used. But still the products failed. How could this occur, and what can be learned that might prevent such multi-million dollar mistakes in the future?

The Osborne Computer case represents perhaps the most extreme example of success and failure in the annals of American business. First on the scene with an inexpensive portable computer packaged with an abundance of software, sales rose to $100 million in only 18 months time, only to come plummeting down as the uniqueness of the product and the package was quickly matched and surpassed by competitors.

The A & P case deals with its WEO campaign, in which a price offensive aimed at regaining a faltering market share did little good, cost the firm a $51 million deficit, and forced the omission of dividends for the first time since 1925. This case poses some interesting insights for future marketing strategy decisions.

Finally, the Adidas case. Here was a firm in the catbird seat, having utter market dominance at the beginning of the running boom. But somehow, incredibly, it let its market advantage slip away. And hungry interlopers—Nike, among others—starting from scratch, carved up the burgeoning market among themselves, with Adidas still waiting in the wings for a big piece of the action that was not to be.

Environmental Constraints

The last section deals with two cases where environmental constraints and governmental intervention were operative. In the first, deceptive promotional claims made by the producers of STP were finally challenged by the media and eventually by the Federal Trade Commission. But this was after a useless product (as generally agreed upon by petroleum engineers and automotive experts) had achieved widespread success because of its macho association with racing and race drivers. The second case concerns a conglomerate, Boise Cascade Company, which for a while was the nation's biggest force in recreational land development. However, questionable selling tactics that aroused the resentment of consumer interests, coupled with a disregard for environmental constraints, forced the firm to give up this part of its business altogether, incurring a loss of several hundred million dollars in the process.

RISKS AND REACTIONS

As you know, marketing decisions for the most part represent decision-making under conditions of uncertainty. We can seldom predict with any exactitude the reactions of consumers or the countermoves and retaliations of competitors. Consequently, we think of marketing decision-making as more an art than a science. It seldom lends itself to mathematical model building for solutions to problems. Yet, certain actions or lack of action are more likely to lead to mistakes and should generally be avoided.

In looking at sick and failing companies, and even healthy ones that have experienced marketing failures of certain aspects of their operation, the temptation is to be unduly critical. It is easy to be Monday-morning quarterbacks, to criticize decisions and actions with the benefit of hindsight. Marketing mistakes are probably inevitable, given the present state of marketing knowledge and the dynamic environment in which uncontrollable and sometimes unpredictable factors may be introduced.

Granted that mistakes of omission or commission will occur, alert and aggressive management is characterized by certain actions or reactions:

1. There should be quick recognition of looming problems or present mistakes.
2. The causes of the problem(s) should be carefully determined.
3. Alternative corrective actions should be evaluated in view of the company's resources and constraints.
4. The chosen corrective action or response should be prompt. Sometimes this may require a ruthless axing of the product, the promotional approach, or whatever may be at fault.
5. There should be some learning experience coming from such mistakes; the same mistakes should not be repeated; the future operation should be improved as a result.

In reading these cases, you may want to judge them not only by how the problem or mistake could have been avoided, but also by how alert and aggressive management was in reacting.

Where possible in these cases we have depicted the major personalities involved at the time. We invite you to imagine yourself in their position, confronting the problems and decisions they faced at their point of crisis, or at the time when actions or lack of action led to a subsequent crisis. What would you have done differently, and why? We invite you to participate in the discussion questions and role-playing episodes appearing at the end of each case. We urge you to consider the pros and cons of alternative actions.

For Thought and Discussion

1. Do you agree that it is impossible for a firm to avoid mistakes? Why or why not?
2. How can a firm speed up its awareness of emerging problems so that it can take responsive action? Be as specific as you can.
3. Large firms tend to err more often on the side of conservatism and are slower to take corrective action than smaller firms. Would you speculate as to why this is so?
4. Which do you think is likely to be the more costly to a firm: errors of omission or errors of commission? Why?

One

MISHANDLING THE PUBLIC IMAGE

CHAPTER 2

The Public Image—
An Addition to the
Marketing Strategy

A firm's reputation or public image tends to be taken for granted—until something untoward occurs, and an organization is brought to painful awareness that an image problem exists. Yet, as we will explore in this chapter, the public image for the most part is controllable. It can and should be protected, but it can also provide powerful strategic thrust. It deserves to be considered as one of the elements of the marketing mix: an active tool, not a passive appendage.

THE FOUR "P's" OF THE MARKETING MIX

Marketing strategy has been viewed as manipulating the "four P's," the elements of the so-called marketing mix, in such a way as to best appeal to those customers the firm seeks: i.e., the target market. Subject to certain constraints—of customer acceptance, of competition, of company resources, of governmental regulations, for example—the marketer has been seen as able to control or direct only four variables: the product, its quality level, and particular features; the price to be charged; how it would be promoted; and how it would be distributed or placed in the market.

The four P's are interdependent. Decisions regarding one of the P's will impact on the others. For example, if a product is to be distributed as a prestige item, the pricing must reflect this, as should also the distribution structure and the promotional efforts.

Many alternatives are possible for each of the P's, and they may be mixed or blended in endless combinations. But if the strategy is to be effective, the P's should be *tailored, compatible,* and *coordinated,* as described in the following guidelines:[1]

1. A mix should be specially *tailored* to a product or campaign, keeping in mind particular target markets the firm most wishes to attract.
2. The various elements of the mix must be screened for *compatibility.* If the firm, for example, wants to appeal to those consumers interested in economy, its choice of dealers, prices, promotional efforts, and of course the product itself should be geared to this objective. In this instance, distributing an attractively priced product through discount stores with sufficient advertising to presell customers might seem indicated.
3. Decisions regarding the P's should be *coordinated* and the complete marketing mix strategy made at one time. Some tradeoffs may be desirable. For example, a decision might be made to spend more money on advertising and reduce the sales force because the advertising should make the product easier to sell. If the price is made low enough and if distribution is through discount stores, then sales personnel may also be reduced because these customers have central buying for the entire chain concentrated at their headquarters.

In order to meet these guidelines, the marketing strategy is generally best selected by one person or group, rather than having each element decided independently. Most firms accomplish this by placing authority for all elements of the marketing mix under the control of a marketing manager or marketing vice president.

THE FIFTH "P"

An additional "P," a fifth "P," deserves consideration as another element of the marketing mix. This is the firm's public image, that is, its reputation, how it and its output (products and/or services) are perceived. Figure 2.1 depicts the idea of the public image being added to the other P's and interrelating with them.[2] In the balance of this chapter we will furnish

---

[1]Some of the material to follow has been adapted from my book, *Marketing Fundamentals* (New York: Harper & Row, 1983), pp. 38–41, and 477–501.

[2]A few marketing scholars have begun to question the adequacy of the traditional notion of the four P's. Philip Kotler, for example, has recently proposed that the four P's should be

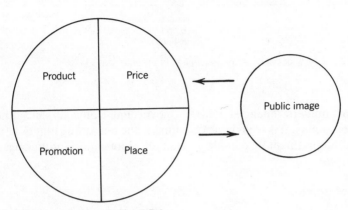

Figure 2.1. A firm's marketing mix (the 5 Ps).

support for the inclusion of the public image as part of the marketing mix, and of the implications of this. But first let us examine the dimensions of the public image.

A public image is a composite of how an organization is viewed by its various publics: its customers, suppliers, employees, stockholders, the financial institutions, the communities in which it dwells, and the various governments, both local and federal. And to these groups must be added the press, which cannot always be relied upon to deliver an objective and unbiased reporting, but is influenced by the firm's reputation.

Two other terms, publicity and public relations, are related to public image development. *Publicity* is communication about the firm, sometimes, but not always, initiated by it, which is disseminated by the media without charge and with little control by the firm. *Public relations* involves a broad set of planned communications about the company, including publicity releases, designed to promote goodwill and a favorable image.

Publicity then is part of public relations when it is initiated by the firm. However, it can also come about through no planned efforts of the firm; in such cases it can be adverse and bring notoriety because of some controversial action or happening. Since public relations involves communications

increased to six P's, by adding Political Power and Public-opinion Formation. ("Kotler: Rethink the Marketing Concept," *Marketing News,* September 14, 1984, pp. 1, 22, and 24.) Public image would seem to be more of an umbrella concept that easily covers these and other controllable factors impacting on a firm's success in the market place.

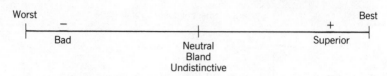

Figure 2.2. Intensity of public image perception of an organization.

with stockholders, financial analysts, government officials, and other non-customer groups, it is usually placed outside the marketing function, perhaps as a staff department or outside consultant reporting to top management.

Types of Images

The general impressions of a firm or organization and of its output, be this product, services, or even future expectations, can range from strongly positive to neutral to strongly negative. The degree or intensity of positive or negative feelings toward it can be depicted on a scale or continuum as shown in Figure 2.2.

Following are some representative images or perceptions that can be categorized as negative, as neutral, and as positive:

Negative Perceptions of Image

A polluter	I just don't like their attitude
Unfriendly	I don't trust them
Junky	Not a sharp operation
Low quality	Inefficient
Poor servicing	Not on top of things
Not a good neighbor	Fading in their industry
Couldn't care less	Too demanding
Stodgy	Bound up in red tape
Always understaffed	Second rate
Insulting advertising	
A dirty store	
Distant	

Neutral and Undistinctive Perceptions of Image

Haven't heard of them	Who?
Just another _____	OK, I guess
Boring ads	An unknown quantity
They haven't proven themselves	

Positive Perceptions of Image	
A good neighbor	An efficient operation
A good place to work	I trust them
Maker of quality products	In the front of the industry
Provides good values	Honest, dependable services
Has the customer's interest in mind	They care
Friendly	Courteous and helpful employees
Interesting and entertaining advertising	A "fun" place

The public image may not necessarily be valid. For example, a firm may be viewed as a polluter despite strenuous and effective efforts to remedy the problem. Furthermore, not all will have the same opinion of an organization and of its output. Perceptions of the firm by its own executives may differ considerably from how its employees, customers, and the general public see it. But even among one group, such as customers, some will be more favorable, others more negative. But if an unfavorable opinion is common, this is a serious problem and needs drastic corrective action. Even if only a few people are negatively inclined, this should not be ignored. Such people are likely to switch to competitors soon—if they have not already done so. And their negative attitudes tend to become contagious as they spread bad word-of-mouth publicity.

How Controllable is the Public Image?

Within certain limits, image is controllable just as the original four P's. (Of course, when a disaster occurs, such as that at Union Carbide's Bhopal, India plant, some would maintain that the resulting poor image is for the most part uncontrollable.) Now skeptics would argue that the public image cannot be changed or manipulated as readily as the other P's, such as promotional efforts and prices. A firm's reputation, after all, would seem rather durable. Therefore, how can image be considered part of the marketing strategy?

Yes, the public image is not quickly changed for the better—although it can be torn down easily enough as we will see in the Gilbert case. But while several of the original four P's are readily changed, others may not be more quickly changed than the public image. For example, the product and place elements of the marketing mix.

Some products take years to develop sufficiently to bring on the market. For example:[3]

Crest fluoride toothpaste—10 years
Hills Brothers instant coffee—22 years
Lustre Creme liquid shampoo—8 years
Minute rice—18 years
Xerox copying machine—15 years
Automatic washer—12 years

Place or channel decisions often are not easily or quickly changed. They involve relationships built up with other members of the channel of distribution and may be broken, but often with hard feelings. Even such huge firms as General Motors would incur severe financial strains and even legal difficulties in changing the distribution: for example, the task of GM in buying out its 18,000 independent dealers or of supporting them in some other endeavor would be monumental.

Consequently, decisions that deal with distribution and with at least some products must be regarded as long-term and capable usually of only gradual modification. And the public image is no different.

Until the last several decades, a firm's public image could more easily be taken for granted as of no major consequence. This, even though the reputation of a firm and its products has affected demand, almost from the beginning of time. In today's skeptical and critical environment, however, few firms can disregard their public image anymore, at least as far as the public relations aspects of it. And this image or reputation can be a strength or a weakness.

Aggressive use of image. The public image as an element of the marketing mix is delimiting if it is viewed—as it often is—only as something to protect and, if necessary, to try to restore. These are defensive moves, reactive and not aggressive. But an image can be used more positively, even aggressively, if it is in good shape, or if it can rather quickly be brought to a favorable public awareness. Take Sears, for example:

Sears has capitalized on its long-established image of dependability and fair dealing by successfully diversifying into a variety of consumer services, such as insurance, investment counseling, even dental clinics.

[3]Lee Adler, "Time Lag in New Product Development," *Journal of Marketing,* January 1966, pp. 17–21.

An example of a most effective building of an image for a new enterprise, and using this as the vital element of the marketing mix, has been Hyatt Legal Clinics:

> Joel Hyatt, in his TV commercials featuring himself as the founder, has conveyed a warm, helpful, and concerned image for his Hyatt Legal Clinics. That this is so different from the general public's impression of law firms and lawyers has enabled the firm, first established in 1978, to grow to the largest law firm in the U.S.

Importance of the Public Image

A firm's public image plays a vital role in the attractiveness of the firm and its products to employees, customers, and to such outsiders as stockholders, suppliers, creditors, government officials, the news media, as well as diverse special groups. In some situations it is impossible to satisfy all the diverse publics: for example, a new highly automated plant may meet the approval of creditors and stockholders, but it will undoubtedly find resistance from employees who see jobs threatened. On the other hand, high-quality products and service standards should bring almost complete approval and pride of association—given that operating costs are competitive—while shoddy products and false claims would be widely decried.

A firm's public image, if it is good, should be cherished and protected. It is a valuable asset that usually is built up over a long and satisfying relationship of a firm with its various publics. If a firm has developed a quality image, this is not easily countered or imitated by competitors. Such an image may enable a firm to charge higher prices, to woo the best distributors and dealers, to attract the best employees, to expect the most favorable creditor relationships and the lowest borrowing costs. It should also enable a firm's stock to command a higher price-earnings ratio than other firms in the same industry not having such a good reputation and public image. All these can give a competitive advantage.

Consequences of a negative image. A bad image hurts a firm with all the different publics with which it deals. All can turn critical and even litigious, depending on the source and extent of the bad image. At best, present and potential customers may simply seek alternative sources for goods and services and switch to competitors wherever possible.

At the worst—the Bhopal disaster, or Love Canal and Agent Orange, or the MGM Grand Hotel fire in Las Vegas—major liability suits can cost hundreds of millions of dollars, bring new governmental regulations, greatly increase the costs of liability insurance, and even spread a badly tarnished

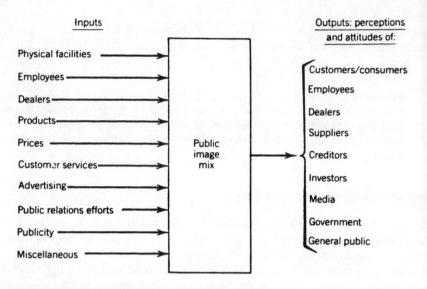

Figure 2.3. Major inputs and outputs of the public image mix.

image to other firms in the industry. Years may be required to mute the negative perceptions, and millions of dollars of advertising may be committed to try to improve public impressions. For example, after Love Canal and Agent Orange triggered a wave of adverse publicity, the chemical industry launched an advertising campaign to try to allay the image. Monsanto alone spent millions on a campaign with the theme, "Without chemicals, life itself would be impossible."

The consequences, of course, of a bad image translates directly to the bottom line, to reduced profits, or worse.

THE PUBLIC IMAGE MIX

Figure 2.3 shows the major inputs in creating an image, and also the outputs or consequences of the resulting image on the various publics. Notice that some of the factors are both inputs and outputs. Employees, for example, they can help foster a negative or a positive image; but they are also affected by their firm's image, with the more able only attracted to the firm with a good reputation. Similarly, dealers both affect image and are affected by it.

So many variables or inputs can be involved that we can hardly identify everything. For example, warranties ("Satisfaction guaranteed or your money back"), and packaging should be included for some firms. Even the brand name conveys an image, although this will generally reflect past actions affecting customer satisfaction or dissatisfaction. However, sometimes the name itself can be instrumental in fashioning an image:

A classic but little known example of this dates back to the late 1800s in England. William Lever, a grocer's son, was a traveling salesman when he entered the soap business with a yellow soap that he called "Sunlight." The name caught on in a dreary, sun-starved England, and in three years the foundation was laid for what was to become one of the largest firms in the world, Unilever, Ltd.[4]

And then there is Cracker Jacks, which built its good reputation with children by "generously" giving a gift in every package.

You can see that most of the inputs or factors that affect the public image are controllable to a considerable extent. A firm certainly can determine its facilities, products, use of advertising, customer service practices, prices relative to competing products, as well as the efforts of public relations and publicity to favorably affect the image. And it can hardly escape blame for such things as poor customer service, or bad publicity about pollution, or disregard for product safety, or poor quality control, which can badly harm the image—despite all the public-relations pronouncements and staged community involvement efforts.

Effect of Facilities on Public Image

The total combination of facilities and the visible accouterments of the firm can create an impression that ranges from positive to neutral to negative. Facilities include trucks, plants, stores, office buildings, the company logo and signs, and any other publicly-visible aspects of the firm.

Factories can be eyesores, unpleasant places to work in, as well as they can be neighbors. They can have a bad environmental impact and can create air and/or water pollution—and worse. Or they can be neatly landscaped, pleasing to the eye, and have strict pollution control. Of course, type of industry plays a major role. Steel mills, paper mills, oil refineries, chemical plants, by their very nature are dirtier, less desirable neighbors than electronics factories or, indeed, factories of most other industries. In any industry, the firm with an old plant may not be able to invest millions to modernize and improve the appearance. But even in heavy industry a firm

---

[4]For more details of the early days of Lever, and a subsequent encounter with Procter & Gamble, see Robert F. Hartley, *Marketing Successes: Historical to Present Day* (New York: Wiley, 1985), pp. 63–72.

can have a good reputation or a bad one, can be a good citizen and neighbor to the community, or a disgrace. As an example of the latter:

Some years ago a paper mill, in attempting to improve its public image, had an advertising campaign showing the clean waters of a river supposedly downstream from its plant. It fell into disgrace when some diligent investigative reporter found that the idyllic scene in the commercials was upstream from the plant.

Where a firm is a dominant employer in a community, the possibility of real public image problems looms very important where layoffs are necessary, whether temporary or permanent. The layoffs of some no-longer competitive steel mills in the Mahoning Valley of northeastern Ohio devastated the cities involved, of which the largest was Youngstown. Regardless of the necessity, the bad publicity emanating from such closings blackened the public image of the entire steel industry. Perhaps one of the worst closings in recent years was that of the Insulite Division of Boise Cascade Corporation in International Falls, Minnesota, a community of 6000 people on the Canadian border.

The announcement of the permanent closing came in a statement December 6, 1984, "The closure affects approximately 500 employees in the International Falls area and another 65 associated with Insulite's sales staff." Workers had about 48 hours to clean out their lockers. There was also a domino effect as another 150 loggers who supplied wood for the siding produced also were out of work. Newspapers throughout the nation picked up on this closing which threw well over 10 percent of the population out of work with no alternative employment opportunities. Headlines such as these appeared: "A Little Town on the Ropes," "Mill Closing a Kick in the Economic Gut," and "Closing Shock: A Child Lies Awake."[5] What made the closing particularly newsworthy, and the public image of Boise Cascade blacker, was the timing: 19 days before Christmas.

If a firm uses its own trucks, this can impact on the image. Retail firms in particular often have their own delivery system, and this can add prestige and advertising for the store, especially if it is well maintained and if the drivers are uniformed. As we noted before, the choice of dealers—their reputations and facilities—will also rub off on the manufacturer's image, and vice versa.

Many major firms, especially those that have widely diversified into unrelated areas, have undertaken corporate identity programs to improve their images through new logos, new signs, and distinctive business forms.

[5]For example, the *Cleveland Plain Dealer*, Dec. 16, 1984, pp. A1 and A10.

lowever, face-lifting alone, without more fundamental changes where there
s a problem, is seldom enough to change an image in a positive fashion.

Effect of Company Employees

Contacts of employees with outsiders, be they customers, suppliers, or
others, convey positive or negative impressions of the firm. Even the way
he telephone is answered casts an impression. Smart firms devote attention
o this aspect of the image. Special employee training may be needed, special
policies established, and some type of follow-up used to ensure that the
ompany's image efforts do not deteriorate. The Bell Telephone Company
vas one of the pioneers in emphasizing this aspect of the public image:

> Servicemen were imbued with the need to leave customers' premises neat, and
> courtesy was stressed. Telephone operators were trained with the objective,
> "Voice with a Smile." Company representatives in business offices learned the
> technicalities of handling many different kinds of customer contacts through
> role playing, and they were judged on the quality of their speech, their
> understanding, explanations, and interested and helpful manner. Periodic
> retraining was used to ensure continuous high quality.[6]

Product Quality and Dependability

The product, its level of quality compared with competing brands, and
particularly its dependability or freedom from defects, is another aspect of
he marketing program that can strongly affect the image. The American
uto industry has long been plagued with product defects, and although
concerted efforts have been made to try to lessen defects in new cars, these
ave not been wholly successful, as most of us know from personal
experience.

In the interests of improving product dependability and freedom from
defects, quality control may have to be improved. Most firms use statistical
quality control which accepts a predictable number of defective units, with
only every *nth* item checked. This is far less expensive than complete quality
control that accepts zero defects. But the latter perhaps ought to be
considered for some items in which serious servicing problems cannot
otherwise be eased. Multiple inspections of critical parts are rejected by
most firms as too costly, but compared to the costs of customer brand
witching and costly callback programs, improved quality control might

[6]Described by Alfred R. Oxenfeldt, *Executive Action in Marketing* (Belmont, Calif.,
Wadsworth, 1966), p. 639.

sometimes offset the increased costs. It would certainly favorably affect the public image.

The intrinsic nature of the products or type of business that a firm handles will also affect the image. For example, consider these extreme examples: diamonds versus prunes; a garbage collection versus air express a salvage store versus a department store. For certain lines of business, the public image will be more negative than for others, not because of the efforts of the personnel involved but because of the nature of the business and of the products or services.

The Price Component

Note in Figure 2.3 that price has a two-way arrow. This reflects that price of a firm's products relative to competing brands tend to be a rather powerful conveyor of image, particularly as to whether the firm is a maker of high-quality or low-quality products, or something in between. A higher price than other brands usually connotes higher quality. Of course, if there is a serious discrepancy between a high price and the realized quality of a product, image is affected adversely.

The perceived image of a firm also helps determine the prices that it can realize for its products. With a favorable image, especially regarding product dependability and customer service, relatively higher prices will be accepted by customers.

> For example, the Maytag Company is located in a small town, Newton, Iowa Compared to its competitors, the likes of General Electric and Whirlpool, it is a small company. But through the years it has achieved and maintained reputation for quality and dependability at a premium price—an image rein forced since 1967 by famous TV commercials showing a forlorn Maytag repairman with nothing to do.

> Lately Maytag has had to worry about its mature appliance market in which the replacement cycle for the industry is 10 to 12 years, and in Maytag's case, often more. Maytag needs to diversify outside the appliance business, and is attempting to do so. It must be careful, however, not to compromise its quality reputation by acquisitions that will not be compatible with its long-established public image.

Importance of Customer Service

Viewed in the broadest sense, customer service includes all offerings to firm's customers beyond the product itself. Repair and warranty service usually receives the most attention (and complaints), but customer service include such diverse things as return-goods privileges extended by retail stores, and conveniences such as delivery, telephone ordering, customer parking, credit, and so on. The effect of a firm's reputation for good service in attracting potential customers and preventing the loss of existing customers is obvious. It results in customer satisfaction, in loyal customers and repeat business, and in word-of-mouth influence, which is potent, if not easily measured. Less obvious is the protection from price competition that a good reputation for service can provide. Although some customers are swayed by a better price, many place a higher value on a firm's reputation for dependable service. Some services, such as extended warranties, are easily imitated. Others, such as prompt and dependable delivery and high-caliber maintenance and repair facilities, are less easily matched, and their effective performance slowly builds reputations.

Indirect benefits can come from a customer service program as a major part of the public image mix. A firm's good reputation for service can make customers easier to sell to. Recruiting salespeople tends to be easier, and higher morale and lower personnel turnover often result from the harmonious customer relations that good service engenders.

Rather than giving customer service the attention it deserves, in many firms executive time is directed elsewhere. Operational crises and problems claim attention, for example, making a decision on promotional scheduling that cannot be delayed, breaking in a salesperson in a new territory, devoting immediate attention to several territories in which planned sales were not reached. And the customers who are antagonized, who are ill treated, whose special requirements are disregarded, who quietly fade away, never to return—all these are overlooked in the pressure of "more important" matters.

A good part of the reason that many firms neglect the customer relations aspect of their business is a lack of awareness of how serious such problems might be. The extent of customer dissatisfaction often cannot be detected by sales and profit figures, at least not until such problems may have assumed major proportions. Moreover, because only a small proportion of total complaints ever reach the ears of responsible executives, expressed dissatisfactions tend to be viewed as involving only a few customers with mostly unjustified complaints.

Procedures should be established for prompt feedback on service problems and customer complaints to responsible executives. Usually some centralized and standardized procedures need to be established both to obtain service feedback and to handle complaints. Some firms have found that "hot lines," toll-free direct lines to company headquarters for customers whose problems are not being handled to their satisfaction, are effective both as a service and a sales tool. Even such a simple thing as keeping customers informed of the status of their orders, especially when shipments will be delayed or reduced as a result of shortages, strikes, or other unforeseen circumstances, can improve the customer-service aspect of the public image.

The Role of Advertising in the Public Image Mix

Advertising can play both a positive and a negative role with a company's image. It can and often does contribute to an existing image, and this may be subtle or more direct. It can also be used to establish a new image.

Contribution to a present image. The type of media used, the message and how it is presented, the TV programs sponsored, the persons who deliver any testimonials, even the repetitiveness of the message—all can affect the image of the company. Advertising can be dignified and in good taste, or it can be petty, raucous, obnoxious, belittling, and insulting to the intelligence. Just as a person is, so is a firm judged by the company it keeps, that is, by the way it advertises and its public display of doing business. For example, we can contrast the dignity of high-quality retail department or specialty store advertising with that of the typical discount store or promotional department store; in the former only one or a few items will be advertised with considerable white space in the ad; the latter will be cluttered and heavy type ads. The situation is similar for TV commercials. We can contrast the Xerox, IBM, and Hallmark-type of advertising with commercials for tooth pastes, detergents, deodorants, and cold remedies.

Defending or establishing a new image. *Institutional advertising* is the main promotional vehicle used to try to influence the company image directly. Institutional advertising is nonproduct advertising that seeks to create a favorable image with the general public.

Some industries and firms have been subjected to considerable criticism by the media, by consumer groups, and by politicians. Particularly during inflationary times, firms that deal with basic necessities and keep raising prices are most vulnerable to criticism, whether justified or not. Thus the oil companies and the public utilities have been castigated. The supermarket and auto industries have also been vulnerable. In order to defend their image and restore some semblance of good public relations, some large firms have turned to advertising to tell their side of the story. This has been termed *advocacy advertising*. Mobil Oil has been particularly aggressive in using advocacy advertising, not only in defending itself, but also in preaching for its point of view in other public and governmental issues.

Image-developing advertising is more common. A firm may find that it s stuck with an image, perhaps that at one time was appropriate and appealing to a substantial target market but now is not, and so wishes to change the image. For example:

Timex for several decades by reason of its advertising had gained the image for watches that "take a licking and keep on ticking." But it found that this formerly successful utilitarian image was wanting in today's watch market dominated by foreign imports. A better image, it seemed to Timex, would be one of more fashion and higher price. To push its image beyond that of a "less expensive brand," Timex in 1981 increased its advertising expenditures some 15 percent.[7]

Whether the efforts of Timex to upgrade its image will be successful is too soon to tell; the task could require a decade. But there is a classic model of success in changing an image; but the image to be changed was not the company's but the activity for which it was gearing its products:

In the late 1950s, the U.S. motorcycle industry was dominated by large high-powered machines. The major producer, Harley–Davidson, had completely captured the market for police and delivery motorcycles and was secure with the other major market segment, the "hard core motorcyclists."

Honda Motor Company started in 1948 as a small Japanese motorcycle manufacturer. As its domestic market was secured, Honda looked to overseas markets and established its first U.S. branch in California in 1959. It correctly assessed market opportunity as existing among first-time riders who wanted a lightweight, inexpensive machine that would solve traffic problems.

An image problem impeded creating such a new market: a mental picture of black leather jackets and *The Wild Ones*. An intensive national advertising campaign sought to win social acceptance for the motorcycle and its rider, and the theme became "You meet the nicest people on a Honda."

Motorcycle registrations jumped from 500,000 in 1960 to nearly 1.9 million in 1966. A survey of Honda owners in 1964 showed that most had never ridden a motorcycle before they bought the Honda. Advertising had changed the image of the motorcycle and made it acceptable.

PUBLIC IMAGE FOR NONPROFIT ORGANIZATIONS

Not only should product oriented firms be concerned and protective of their public image; so too should nonprofit organizations such as schools,

---

[7]For more detail, see "Falling Profit Prompts Timex to Shed its Utilitarian Image," *Wall Street Journal,* September 17, 1981, p. 27.

charitable drives, police departments, hospitals, even politicians. Let us consider here the importance of public image and how it might be improved or built by several nonproduct organizations and persons.

Large city police departments frequently have a poor image among important segments of the population. The need to improve this image is hardly less important than for a manufacturer faced with a deteriorating brand image. A police department can develop a "marketing" campaign to win friends; examples of possible activities aimed at creating a better image are: promoting tours and open houses of police stations, crime laboratories, police lineups, cells, and so forth; speaking at schools; and sponsoring recreation projects, such as a day at the ballpark for youngsters.

Public school systems, faced with taxpayers' revolts toward mounting costs of education and with image damage due to teacher strikes need conscious effort to improve the image in order to obtain more public support and funds.

Many nonbusiness organizations and institutions, such as hospitals, schools, governmental bodies, even labor unions, have grown self-serving, with a bureaucratic mentality dominating, so that perfunctory and callous treatment is the rule and the image is in the pits. Improving the image can only come through a greater emphasis on satisfying customers' or the public's needs.

Building images of political candidates represents the most extensive use of marketing techniques in nonbusiness areas. Two marketing tools are commonly employed: public opinion research and mass media, especially television, advertising. Using these tools, and especially the latter, to win elections almost precludes the candidate without much money from effectively competing. With money, a candidate may bypass political party organizations, challenge entrenched incumbents, in fact manufacture an instant public image.

TYPES OF IMAGE PROBLEMS

Image problems can be categorized as: (1) overcoming a dull image; (2) trying to upgrade an image; (3) combating a fading image; and (4) overcoming a bad image. We will briefly discuss each of these.

Almost three decades ago, this statement was made by an eminent researcher:

> What happens to the retail store that lacks a sharp character, that does not stand for something special to any class of shoppers? It ends up as an alternative store in the customer's mind. The shopper does not head for such a store as the primary place to find what he or she wants. Without certain outstanding

departments and lines of merchandise, without clear attraction for some group, it is like a dull person.[8]

Certainly a dull or innocuous image is a lodestone for any firm and a major competitive drawback. The only thing worse is to have a decidedly negative image. Image is not an easy thing for a firm to improve or change. But efforts certainly need to be made by such a firm.

Sometimes a firm wants to upgrade its image. Perhaps it had originally formulated its niche as a low-price, bargain operation, and now wants to attain more of a quality image. But upgrading an image is not easily done, as described in the Korvette case. Some firms that attempt this fail because they expect results too quickly. But other firms might be better advised to change their name—start afresh, perhaps with a new division—rather than try to upgrade a long-established name and image.

Even mighty Sears, in 1974–1975, attempted to upgrade its image—and its profit margins—with higher-price goods and higher-fashion women's apparel. Its earnings tumbled 28 percent as its traditional price-conscious customers became disillusioned by the emphasis on higher prices. Sears soon abandoned the attempt to change its image, but the damage had been done and sales and profits were slow in recovering.

Combating a fading image would seem easier than upgrading a long-established one. However, aggressive and effective efforts need to be taken to reverse the fading trend, as Coors found out. Reversing an established trend is not easily done, and may never succeed in recouping all the lost ground.

Overcoming a bad image normally is the most difficult problem. This is the extreme position of image illness, and it could even be the death knell. It is far worse than a dull image, an image of low quality, or a formerly good image that is now fading.

A bad image may be formed slowly by a history of questionable practices that have become widely publicized: for example, unsafe products, deceptive advertising, illegal payoffs, callousness toward community relations and employees, and so on.

Occasionally something catastrophic will bring down an image. The calamity of Union Carbide has, of course, been widely publicized. But firms have been known to be more directly involved in their own violent image destruction, as we will examine with the A. C. Gilbert Company case.

[8]Pierre Martineau, "The Personality of the Retail Store," *Harvard Business Review* (January–February 1958), p. 50.

ERRORS IN HANDLING THE PUBLIC IMAGE

Firms can do a great injustice to their image. They may:

1. Blatantly ignore matters that have a probability of affecting it adversely.
2. Disregard the constraining consequences of their image.
3. Abdicate their image-building and image-maintaining efforts to public relations.
4. Not coordinate all aspects of the operation that can affect the image.

Ignoring Possible Negative Image Consequences

Sometimes a firm naively disregards possible negative public reactions:

Columbia Gas of Ohio faces competition for heating homes not only from electric companies but also from cost savers such as heat pumps, solar systems, wood stoves, and kerosene and quartz room heaters. During a period when energy costs were rapidly rising, with much publicity about the need to conserve energy—placing this need even on a patriotic level—Columbia found that all this conservation was resulting in a cut in usage and less revenue. So what did Columbia do? It sought to impose a surcharge on consumers who had heat pumps and other energy-saving devices.

There was immediate public outrage. Responding to public opinion, the Ohio legislature hastened to introduce bills to block surcharges on heat pumps and similar systems. In the face of widespread opposition, Columbia doggedly went ahead and triggered further controversy by trying to block service to homebuilders who planned to install heat pumps in new houses. The Public Utilities Commission finally had to order Columbia to provide service; the firm, now beginning to realize the seriousness of the resentment against it, backed off. As one legislator tersely summarized the situation: "It does not make much sense when the federal government gives tax credits for insulation, to penalize people for doing what we asked them to do, which is conserve."[9]

The Nestle case, described in Chapter 4, also illustrates this unseemly myopia regarding public image.

Why do firms ignore their image, or at least greatly underestimate the consequences of their actions on it? Several factors usually account for this. First, a firm's public image generally makes a nonspecific impact on company performance. The cause and effect relationship of a poor or

[9]Reported in a number of sources across Ohio, of which one example is William Carlson, "Columbia Gas Faces Horde of Challengers," *Cleveland Plain Dealer*, May 24, 1981, p. 27 A.

leteriorating image is virtually impossible to assess, at least until and unless image problems worsen. The inability to be able to point the blame directly o the intangible image results in other areas of performance being given the closer scrutiny and the efforts at corrective action.

Second, an organization's image—how it is perceived by the various publics—is not easily and definitively measured. While some tools are available for tracking public opinion, they tend to be imprecise and of uncertain validity. Consequently image studies are often ignored or given short shrift relative to more quantitative measures of performance.

Third, it is difficult to determine the effectiveness of image-building efforts. While firms may spend thousands, and even millions of dollars, for institutional and image-building advertising, measures of the effectiveness of such expenditures are inexact and also of questionable validity. For example, a survey may be taken of attitudes of a group of people before and after the image-building campaign is run. Presumably if a few more people profess to be favorably disposed toward the company after the campaign than before, this is an indication of its success. But an executive can question how much this really translates into sales and profits.

Disregarding Constraints

A firm's present image ought to be considered and recognized as a factor affecting strategy options. Public image is a resource, just as much so as manpower, facilities, and finances. But it is also a constraint. Most firms do not have unlimited resources, so their planned strategies must be geared to what is realistic and practical. So it is with the image. To expect a Korvette, or a K mart, to be on the same status level as a Neiman Marcus in a few years is unreasonable. As is the expectation that a Volkswagen can soon achieve the status of a Mercedes Benz.

Two generalizations can be made about the constraining influences of a firm's public image:

1. A dull, a negative, or a low-quality image is extremely difficult to upgrade. Massive advertising efforts and years of persistence may be necessary to overcome such an image.
2. A favorable image can be quickly torn down if a firm is careless with its product quality, service, or other aspects subject to public scrutiny.

Abdicating Image Efforts

In many firms a public relations department, either in-house, or through an advertising agency or other outside consultant is responsible for all image related matters.[10] This supposedly places public relations in expert hands, as well as under the control of those who can have the detached objectivity that supposedly no operating executive can have.

Some firms are beginning to move in the direction of greater participation by marketers. This is hardly meeting with the approval of all concerned. Public relations practitioners tend to view such a move as "encroachment,' and the marketers as "carpetbaggers": "Marketing people are making inroads. They are like 'carpetbaggers' . . . who move into an organization then pull out and let PR pick up the pieces."[11]

Yet we know that many other aspects of a firm's operation affect the public image—public relations pronouncements and publicity releases are just one of the factors. A firm that recognizes the importance of its public image, not only as something to be protected, but also as a valuable tool for opening up new opportunities and guiding the marketing strategy would do well not to totally abdicate this important resource to a staff department.

Not Coordinating Internal Image Inputs

From the public image mix we know that a good many aspects of a firm's operation have at least the potential of affecting the firm's public image, for good or for bad. To protect or to build an image, all the various contributors should be in close communication and working with coordination. For example, a sales department's effectiveness is sure to be undermined if servicing of orders or quality control is deficient.

Kotler puts it this way: "Marketers typically think of their jobs as manipulating the 4 P's . . . This is the outside job of the marketer. But marketers also have an inside job to do. That is, they have to make other company departments marketing- and consumer-oriented."[12]

Now we will examine in considerable detail four examples of firms that had image problems, and did a poor—and in one case, even fatal—job of

[10]For a discussion of the relationship between marketing and public relations, see Phili Kotler and William Mindak, "Marketing and Public Relations," *Journal of Marketing*, October 1978, pp. 13–20.
[11]Based on a survey of 4400 PR practitioners released by "pr reporter" newsletter "Twentieth Annual Survey of the Profession," reported in *Marketing News*, December 21 1984, p. 12.
[12]"Kotler: Rethink . . ." p. 24.

coping with them. There is a major learning experience in this: the importance of the public image should not be taken lightly.

For Thought and Discussion

1. "Good customer service doesn't do you much good, but poor customer service can kill you." Evaluate this statement.
2. Evaluate the effectiveness of advertising in enhancing the public image.
3. Give some specific examples of how a firm's public image is both affected by and affects the components of the marketing mix.
4. Discuss the pros and cons of having the public relations function under the control of the marketing department.

Invitation to Role Play

"Our public image is not very good," your boss confides to you one morning. "In a survey our marketing research department just finished, customers rated us below average in service. They also thought we were old-fashioned and not progressive."

"Our appliances still get good ratings for dependability, don't they?" you respond.

"Yes, but that's not enough today. I want you to have on my desk by next Monday a proposal I can present to the board of directors on some concrete ways to improve this image."

Prepare a program to improve the image of a small appliance manufacturer. Also point out what difficulties you would expect in making such an image change.

CHAPTER 3

Coors—A Great Image Can Fade

A tragedy occurred in the winter of 1960 that was to have an impact on the fortunes of the Adolph Coors Company, brewers, some fifteen years later. On the morning of February 9, Adolph Coors III, 44-year-old chairman of the board of the brewing empire, kissed his wife and four children goodbye, and drove off for the plant twelve miles away. He was never seen again, alive.

For months, one of the most intensive manhunts in Colorado history took place. Finally, on September 26, more than seven months later, tattered clothing and scattered bones were accidentally discovered in a desolate, heavily-wooded area of aspen and pine about forty miles southeast of Denver. Apparently, after the body had been dumped, the remains were scattered by coyotes or hogs. Dental charts confirmed the identification of Coors.

THE GOLDEN YEARS

Adolph Coors III had been sharing leadership responsibilities with his father, Adolph Coors II. After the murder, the father again assumed the sole leadership mantle even though his official title was treasurer, until he died in 1970 at the age of 86. The elder of the two surviving sons, William H. Coors, is the chairman and chief executive; the other son, Joseph, is president. There are no formal lines of authority, although Bill generally handles the technical side of brewing and Joe the financial and administrative functions.

Both Bill and Joe (employees call them by their first names) are lean and tall and rugged outdoorsmen. In fact, they regard physical fitness and athletic recreation as so important for their employees that executives and workers are sent to outdoor-survival schools. Golf is subsidized for employees. Ski trips are underwritten. But Bill and Joe are concerned with more than the therapeutic benefits of fresh air for their employees: they insist that employees must not only participate in these programs but also must compete. "If you can't fight competition, you don't need to survive," Bill Coors asserts.[1]

Sensational Growth

By 1970, the accomplishments of Coors in the brewing industry were awesome—all the more so in light of the nonconformity of Coors to existing industry practices. The company produced only one kind of beer, and this in a single brewery, albeit the largest in the world. It sold its beer in only eleven Western states, most of these the most sparsely populated areas of the United States. It refused to build branch plants, and had not expanded its territory in twenty-two years. The one brewery in Golden, Colorado, was not even close to its biggest market, California—indeed, the average barrel of Coors traveled over 900 miles. Finally, its ads featuring rushing mountain streams, and the slogan "Brewed with pure Rocky Mountain spring water" had not been changed in thirty-three years.

Yet, this little regional brewery of Bill and Joe Coors had moved up to the big time. With a 19 percent increase in production in 1969 over 1968, it moved into fourth place in the national beer rankings, the only regional brewer to come close to the national brewers. In 1969, the production of the top four breweries was as follows:

Anheuser-Busch	18.8 million barrels
Joseph Schlitz	13.7 million
Pabst	10.2 million
Coors	6.4 million

Furthermore, in nine of the eleven states where it had distribution, Coors topped all other brands in sales. Among the full eleven states, the market share of Coors was 30 percent. In California, by 1973 it had 41 percent of the market, compared with only 18 percent for the industry leader, Anheuser–Busch; in Oklahoma almost 70 percent of all the beer sold was

---

[1]"Colorado's Coors Family Has Built an Empire on One Brand of Beer," *Wall Street Journal,* October 26, 1973, p. 1.

Coors. Overall demand was so outstripping supply that the company was forced to ration its product among distributors.

In compiling this performance record, the brothers eschewed a marketing orientation. Bill Coors stated this succinctly: "Our top management

---

INFORMATION SIDELIGHT

THE MARKETING CONCEPT

A marketing orientation, commonly known as the marketing concept, is a well-known philosophy of marketing—almost every basic marketing text devotes an early chapter to this. Yet many firms still disregard it—as Coors did for most of its corporate life—under the belief that their products will sell themselves. For a wanted product of exceptional quality that is unique from competing products, such a production orientation may succeed, for a while. But competitively, the firm having the marketing concept will usually win out over the longer period.

We can define the marketing concept or orientation as:

An integration of marketing activities directed toward customer satisfaction.

Essentially this is a change in emphasis within a firm to a customer-oriented type of thinking: finding out consumers' needs and preferences, how these might be changing, how they can be better served. The marketing concept has these basic components:

1. Customer orientation
2. Integrated marketing
3. Marketing research
4. Long-range planning and new-product development

Organizational realignment has sometimes been the most tangible evidence that a firm has adopted the concept. All business functions related to marketing—e.g., sales, advertising, product planning, physical distribution—are integrated under a top marketing executive for coordination and a unified objective. A consumer orientation almost necessitates marketing research in order to keep up with customers' wants, attitudes, and buying patterns. A more formal role for long-range planning is also needed to coordinate a firm's efforts as well as to pursue a vigorous program of new-product development.

---

thrust is on engineering and production . . . we're production-oriented. Nobody knows more about production than I do."[2] Emphasis was on making a quality beer in terms of processing and raw materials. The product was a mild, light-bodied beer, scientifically tested and brewed, using hops, rice, Rocky Mountain spring water, and a specially developed strain of barley grown by contract farmers. Great pains were taken to preserve the flavor. Pasteurization, which would add greatly to the ease of preserving, was shunned, since it would slightly affect the taste. Eliminating pasteurization greatly increased the logistical problems. The beer had to be canned at near-freezing temperatures and shipped under refrigeration to refrigerated warehouses—otherwise, the natural taste could not be maintained. To further assure perfection of taste, distributors were required to pull Coors cans off the shelves in thirty days, lest there be some fading of the flavor.

Coors had become the beer of celebrities; from President Ford, who packed Coors on Air Force One, to Henry Kissinger, as well as such actors as Paul Newman (who in an *Esquire* interview claimed, "The best domestic beer, bar none, is Coors") and Clint Eastwood. In these years, the famous, as well as the rank and file, all were contributing to the Coors "mystique." Some 300,000 Coors fans a year toured the brewery; others made "pilgrimages" to a waterfall near Grand Lake, Colorado, which was supposed to be the one pictured on Coors bottles and cans. T-shirts and sweatshirts emblazoned with "Coors—Breakfast of Champions" were being sold by entrepreneurs hoping to cash in on the Coors mystique. And in the East, where Coors was not directly distributed, it could sell for three times the regular price.

Besides the product, the company was unique from the rest of the industry in certain other respects. In the heady years of the 1960s and early 1970s, Bill and Joe shunned outside expertise. Advertising and promotion were handled by inside staff, and total expenditures averaged only one-quarter those of major competitors. Construction at the brewery was done by Coors' own construction crews. Company engineers designed machinery for the can plant. Management talent was developed and promoted from within the organization, rather than brought in from outside.

The guiding philosophy of the company since it was founded by a German orphan who stowed away on a U.S.-bound ship to avoid conscription into the German army—the first Adolph Coors, in 1873—was to refuse to go to a bank for a loan. Such fiscal conservation led the company to reject some seemingly attractive expansion possibilities. For example, the company's can-manufacturing subsidiary, Coors Container Company, was

[2]"The Brewery That Breaks All the Rules," *Business Week,* August 22, 1970, p. 60.

instrumental in developing the technical process for making a two-piece aluminum can. Coors, however, sold the process to Continental Can Company and American Can Company: "We could have dominated the industry, but we would have had to borrow from the banks, and Coors doesn't do that."[3] Between 1970 and 1974, in order to keep up with the burgeoning demand for Coors beer, some $276 million was spent on plant expansion. And how was this financed? All of it from cash flow.

How Come the Mystique?

What was the magic of Coors? How durable was this magic or mystique likely to be? Perhaps part of the mystique was accidental and fortuitous: being a Western-made brew at a time when the freedom and environmental purity of the West—emphasized by Coors' slogan, "Pure Rocky Mountain Spring Water"—was seen by many consumers as contrasting sharply with the degradation of the industrial centers of population. But was it a better beer—better tasting, higher quality? There were many who said it was. Whether real or imagined, Coors offered a "unique selling proposition" that distinguished it from other beers. One could claim that coming from a single brewery insured better quality control and uniformity of ingredients and flavor. The company liked to boast that Coors was the most expensively brewed beer in the world, even though it sold in the popular price range. A plant geneticist was employed full-time to develop improved strains of barley for malting. Most hops were imported from Germany. And, as noted before, great pains were taken to prevent any deterioration of the flavor in shipping and handling.

Undoubtedly, part of the mystique came from the contagion generated by the aficionados, those famous and not so famous. A Western image conveying the out-of-doors and environmental purity, a light tasting beer . . . perhaps the timing could not have been better in the 1960s and early 1970s. (In the cigarette industry, Marlboro rose to become the top seller on a somewhat similar advertising and image thrust: the Marlboro man.)

It hardly seemed to Bill and Joe that the golden image of their beer could in the span of just a few years fade drastically. How could it help but be enduring?

Going Public

For 103 years, ever since the first Adolph Coors opened his brewery on the trail to the Colorado gold camps, the company stayed private—talks of

---

[3]"Colorado's Coors Family," p. 27.

having public or outside shareholders were anathema to the Coors family. And it seemed that the company could indeed finance large-scale capital expenditures internally. Throughout the decade of the 1960s its average rate of growth was over 10 percent, all this without turning to outside stock ownership or borrowing. In 1975, Coors had only $2 million in long-term debt on its books, against $375 million in equity.

But in 1975 the proud family tradition had to be abandoned. With the death of the parents of Bill and Joe, the Internal Revenue Service presented a bill for $50 million in inheritance taxes. While many companies would have solved such a problem by going into debt, Bill and Joe decided to go public as the lesser of two evils. In order not to risk relinquishing control of the company to outsiders, they would offer only nonvoting shares. Furthermore, to avoid diluting the equity, no more than 5 percent of net income would be paid as dividends.

The time for such a stock offering was not very propitious. The Dow Jones Industrial Average was then moving between 620 and 690, and many were the investors who thought it would go still lower. Added to a sick stock market, the restrictions placed on this new stock venture were hardly likely to appeal to many investors. Since the shares would be nonvoting, this precluded listing on the New York Stock Exchange, as well as being offered for sale in many states, including California, where Coors' stock could otherwise have had a warm reception. The nonvoting feature would also make the stock offering unattractive to many large institutional investors.

In the end, Coors lucked out. When the offering finally reached the market, the stock market was beginning to rebound. Coors' investment bankers found so much interest in the stock in the last days before the offering that they raised the price to $31 a share. And it was a sellout the first afternoon. Not only was the $50 million raised to pay off the inheritance taxes, but an additional $77 million went into the company coffers. This $127 million offering was the first major new stock issue to come to market since 1973 and the fourth largest offering by industrial companies in the previous ten years. The mystique of the company and its beer mitigated all the negative factors impinging on demand.

Geographical Expansion

Now Bill Coors turned his attention to geographical expansion. The first target was eastern and southern Texas. Prior to this the only Texas inroads were in the northern part of the state around Dallas, and the western part.

Eager to jump on a lucrative bandwagon, potential distributors lined up like beauty queen candidates, vying for selection by Coors. The contest,

however, was hardly for the weak or poorly-financed, since Coors' distributors had to build refrigerated warehouses so that Coors' unpasteurized beer
could be kept under 40 degrees until opened by customers. From 4000
"panting" contestants, Coors selected 29 distributors for the eastern Texas
expansion.

By 1976, Coors was also invading Montana, and looking closely at
expanding into Washington state, Arkansas, Nebraska, and Missouri, the
latter state being the home base of Anheuser–Busch, the largest brewer. Bill
Coors was also laying plans for expanding to the heavily populated Eastern
market: "I think we've got a good enough beer—the beer that won the
West—to assure ourselves 20 percent to 25 percent of the nationwide
market," he told *Forbes'* reporters in the summer of 1976.[4] A bold statement
this, with Anheuser holding 24 percent of the total market, while Coors had
only 8.2 percent, although admittedly on far less than national distribution,
in fact on only 20 percent of the total national distribution.

The question of whether expansion could still be handled out of the one
brewery in Golden seemed not particularly troublesome to Bill. While the
Golden brewery was already at an annual capacity of 12.3 million barrels,
about one million barrels of capacity was being added a year, and Bill was
aiming for a total of 25 million. "Eventually we might build other breweries," he said. "But if you take a circle up around from where we already ship
to in Northern California, you hit Atlanta, Georgia."[5]

The growth and profitability picture—and the highly successful public
stock offering—should have been cause for heady optimism and great
satisfaction for the Coors brothers. Sales for 1975 were $520 million, up from
$350 million just four years before. Operating margin on net sales had
reached 28 percent, the highest in the industry. Profit per barrel averaged
almost $9, about double that of Anheuser. But there were some ominous
portents on the horizon.

STORM SIGNALS FOR COORS, 1975–1976

While the successful public stock float spurred new ambitions, trouble was
brewing in the California market—a key market that accounted for almost 40
percent of all Coors' sales. In a bitter dispute with Coors' Oakland
distributor, the California Teamsters called for a statewide boycott of the

[4]"Off Coors," *Forbes,* June 1, 1976, p. 60.
[5]Ibid., p. 61.

beer. At the same time, Anheuser was bringing on line a new 3.75 million barrel brewery in Northern California. As a result, in this key market, Coors' sales dropped about 10 percent in 1975, while market share fell 4 percent to 36 percent. Anheuser picked up most of this, gaining 3 percent to a 23.2 percent share of the California market. Perhaps another contributor to the market share losses in California was a hefty price hike made in 1974 without first warning retailers.

Several other aggravations were also being encountered. The Federal Trade Commission in January 1975 was upheld by the Supreme Court in its efforts to loosen the tight grip Coors had held on its 167 distributors. Then the Equal Opportunities Commission filed a suit against Coors alleging discrimination against minorities in hiring and in promotions. And the Colorado Health Department charged Coors with polluting Clear Creek, in the very same valley where the "Rocky Mountain Spring Water" rises.

Finally, brother Joe was embarrassed as the Senate Commerce Committee vetoed his nomination to the board of the Corporation for Public Broadcasting, citing Coors' ownership of a right-wing television news service as a conflict of interest. Joe had long been known locally as an arch-conservative, but his political views came to national attention in 1975 when the *Washington Post* ran four lengthy stories about his right-wing efforts in allegedly using Television News, Inc., a broadcast news agency subsidiary of the Coors Company, to further his own political views. This publicity, as well as the fact that the news subsidiary was losing money, induced the company to close down the TV news service. Whatever negative effect might have emanated from the hardly-favorable publicity could not be gauged.

Some dangers could be seen in the decision to push East, even though such a move, if successful, would greatly increase the sales of Coors as well as lessen the risks inherent in relying on only a few markets—such as the California one—for maintenance of growth and even viability. To attempt to enter the Eastern markets would bring Coors face-to-face with entrenched major brewers: with Schlitz, Pabst, and Philip Morris's Miller, in addition to Anheuser–Busch. Miller, in particular, looked like a most formidable competitor: it had become the nation's fastest-growing major beer company, and by the beginning of 1976 had moved to third place in the U.S. beer market, moving ahead of Coors in the process. Undoubtedly Coors moving into the East would necessitate massive additional advertising expenditures. While sales might be increased by such expansion efforts, more questionable was what effect such would have on profits. Furthermore, despite optimism by Bill Coors about their one brewery being adequate to supply their entire national market, rather serious logistical problems could be expected.

Table 3.1   Relative Sales of Top Five U.S. Brewers, 1973–1977

	Sales (millions of dollars)				
	1973	1974	1975	1976	1977
Anheuser Busch	1109.7	1413.1	1645.0	1441.2	1838.0
Miller	275.9	403.6	658.3	982.8	1327.6
Schlitz	703.0	814.5	923.0	1000.0	937.4
Pabst	355.4	431.3	525.0	600.5	582.9
Coors	378.8	467.8	520.0	593.6	593.1

Source: Company annual reports.

THE BREWING INDUSTRY

Concentration has increasingly characterized the brewing industry. In the last several decades the number of beer firms dropped from 900 to 50. The smaller local and regional brewers just could not match the economies of scale of the big brewers, nor could they match their aggresssive marketing efforts. In the span of only eight years, from 1970 to 1978, the combined market share of the five largest brewers increased from 49 percent to 74 percent of total industry sales.

The hottest product in the brewing industry by the mid-1970s had become light beer, or low caloric beer. Almost 10 percent of industry sales were accounted for by lights, and 30 percent of Miller's, with the trend rising rapidly. Initial introductions of low-caloric beers had failed because they were marketed as diet drinks to consumers who did not drink much beer in the first place. Miller changed the thrust by positioning its Lite to heavy drinkers, with the theme that they could drink as much beer as before without feeling so filled (a subtle inference was that they thereby could consume more beer). Profitably speaking, the lights are good business: they sell for more than premium beers, and they cost less to make.

The other growth area is super premium beers, so called because they sell for higher prices. For years, Anheuser's Michelob had the market almost to itself, with its only real competition coming from imported beers. Miller was the first to intrude on Michelob's market niche by arranging first to import Lowenbrau from Germany, and then to produce a domestic version of Lowenbrau.

Table 3.1 shows the relative sales of the big five of the brewing industry from 1973 through 1977; Table 3.2 shows the relative profit performance for this period. Notice particularly the major burst of Miller both in sales and profits.

Anheuser–Busch, the industry leader, makes Budweiser, Budweiser malt liquor, Michelob, and Busch Bavarian. As Tables 3.1 and 3.2 show, its

Table 3.2   Relative Profits of Top Five U.S. Brewers, 1973–1977

	Net Profits (millions of dollars)				
	1973	1974	1975	1976	1977
Anheuser-Busch	65.6	64.0	84.7	55.4	91.9
Miller	(2.4)	6.3	28.6	76.1	106.5
Schlitz	55.2	49.0	30.9	50.0	17.8
Pabst	23.8	18.3	20.7	32.4	21.8
Coors	47.5	41.5	59.5	76.5	67.7

Source: Company annual reports.

business has been booming. It has ten breweries operating full blast, yet can hardly keep up with demand. However, the meteoric rise of Miller has to cause concern. Yet, Anheuser should have the marketing muscle and financial resources to more than match Miller's marketing efforts and building plans.

Miller Brewing Company makes Miller High Life, Miller malt liquor, Miller Lite, and Lowenbrau. Miller was a sickly company run by an aging management when it was acquired by Philip Morris, the tobacco company, in 1969. Philip Morris moved its tobacco executives in to run the brewing operations, and found that beer and cigarettes have a great deal in common, both being low-priced, pleasurable products processed and packaged on high-speed machinery, while they can be advertised and distributed similarly to many of the same end-use customers. With aggressive marketing efforts, Miller moved up from eighth to second place among U.S. brewers by 1977, and is trying hard to catch Anheuser. Its Lite beer, introduced in January 1975 with a blitz advertising campaign, was a marketing coup, and by 1978 Miller was selling 10 million barrels of Lite, equal to its entire beer sales only four years before.

Joseph Schlitz Brewing Company—maker of Schlitz, Schlitz malt liquor, Old Milwaukee, Promo, and Schlitz Light—has staggered badly, both in sales and especially in profits, as Table 3.2 shows. After fifteen years of uninterrupted growth, it lost second place to Miller in 1977. The product mix has proven weak of late, with sales of premium and light beers—the more profitable items in the line—falling off more than its lower-priced beers. In addition, Schlitz has had problems coming up with a super premium beer to compete with Michelob and Lowenbrau.

Pabst makes Pabst Blue Ribbon, Pabst Extra Light, and Andeker of America. It has found it impossible to keep pace with Anheuser–Busch and Miller. Because of intense competition it has been forced to spend more and more for advertising, but volume continues to slide. Pabst Blue Ribbon has lost considerable ground in certain major midwestern markets; Pabst's light beer and Andeker, its super premium beer, are both weak contenders.

TARNISH ON THE GOLDEN PROSPECTS, 1977–1978

In 1977 the boom lowered. While Tables 3.1 and 3.2 show Coors as faltering considerably less than Schlitz and Pabst in sales and profits, still 1977 marked a serious trend reversal after the heady years of growth. Furthermore, the reversal appeared to be not short-lived, but rather symptomatic of serious underlying problems.

In 1977 Coors earned $1.92 a share, down 12 percent from 1976. It shipped 12.8 million barrels of beer, down 5 percent from 1976. It lost market share in many of the sixteen Western states where it had the bulk of its distribution. The problems continued into 1978. For the first half of 1978, barrelage was down another 12 percent, per-share earnings were down from $1.02 the year before to 56 cents, and in California, which had accounted for 39 percent of its sales, it had been surpassed by Anheuser–Busch. Coors' stock, which had been subscribed for $31 in 1975, was now hovering around $16, a loss of about 50 percent for the first public stockholders. Only a few years before, Coors had been selling its beer by allocation only; now, suddenly, it had to cut back production. Bill Coors was forced to admit: "Making the best beer we can make is no longer enough."[6]

The Eastern markets no longer beckoned, either. They were heavily saturated with strong, well-entrenched competitors. In fact the big Eastern brewers were moving West because of this. Anheuser had built a new plant in California. Miller was building one. Schlitz had expanded its capacity in the West. Coors, with its single plant in the mountains of Colorado, faced exorbitant transportation costs in trying to reach the Eastern markets, all the more so because its beer had to be shipped under refrigeration to maintain quality. Unfortunately, the quality image of the beer had suffered from bootleggers bringing it into the East with careless handling and selling it at black market prices. Coors had even been forced to take out newspaper ads in some Eastern cities advising beer drinkers not to drink Coors. But a negative image had been created in the minds of many Eastern beer drinkers.

Labor Problems

Labor problems exacerbated a deteriorating situation. On April 5, 1977, the brewery workers at the Golden, Colorado plant walked out. A week after the

---

[6]"A Test for the Coors Dynasty," *Business Week,* May 8, 1978, p. 69.

walkout, the AFL–CIO approved a nationwide boycott of the company's beer.

The company was unyielding, and now raised the issue that all prospective employees take lie-detector tests. The idea of polygraph testing hearkens back to the kidnapping of Adolph Coors III and the family fears that this could happen again. Eventually more than 1000 of the 1472 workers who walked out returned, while the rest were replaced. The strike lasted fifteen months, and eventually the union was rejected by the employees. But the wrath of labor was incurred in the process and Coors now ranked with J. P. Stevens Company on union hate lists.

Opinions differ as to the effects the union boycott had on Coors' sales and profits: how much of the decline was due to labor boycotting, and how much was due to intensified competition? Bill Coors blamed most on the union boycott: "It was a shock for us to find that, as far as the union is concerned, anything goes. No lie is too great to tell if it accomplishes their boycott objectives. We view the boycott as a monument to immorality and dishonesty."[7]

The mystique of Coors, the image it had gloried in and which seemed to give it a competitive edge over all other brews, was gone, abruptly, bewilderingly. Just perhaps, the ultraconservative policies spawned by the tragedy of a brother's kidnapping and murder, over a decade-and-a-half previously, had blinded the company to a changing environment.

Competition

As evident from Table 3.1, the aggressive marketing efforts of Anheuser and Miller were having detrimental effects on the other members of the big five, not to mention the smaller regional brewers. The erosion of Coors' market share in California, its biggest market, where previously it had a 40 percent market share, was particularly worrisome, especially as it hinted at a greater erosion to come. In the first six months of 1978, Anheuser took over first place with a 35 percent share, with Coors dropping to 25 percent. Even more threatening was the threat of the surging Miller. While number two nationally, Miller was still a poor third in California with less than 10 percent of the market. But Miller was building a brewery there and Coors certainly had to expect that once its production facilities were established at a sufficiently high level, Miller's aggressive marketing efforts would be leveled at California. Coors would be placed in the more vulnerable position in attempting to

[7]"Coors Beer: What Hit Us?" *Forbes*, October 16, 1978, p. 71.

match the expenditures and the expertise of Miller and Anheuser in a hotly contested market.

DEFENSIVE REACTIONS

Bill and Joe turned to market research to determine where they had gone wrong. The answer was quite definitive. The beer industry was growing at only 3 percent a year, but almost all the growth was coming from two products: light or low-caloric beer, and super premium beer. Coors offered neither of these, relying still on its traditional one kind of beer. Furthermore, research revealed that four out of every ten new light-beer drinkers had switched from Coors. In addition to the lack of a responsive and aggressive product mix vis-a-vis competitors, Coors also had a hard-to-open press tab can that hardly met consumers' desire for convenience and ease of operation.

Coors finally moved to rectify the product deficiencies of a single-beer strategy, and in the spring of 1978 introduced its first new product in 20 years, Coors Light. The company also began developing a super premium beer, planning market tests in early 1980. It was considering naming this Herman Joseph's, after Coors founder Adolph Herman Joseph Coors, thereby emphasizing family name and tradition.[8] Coors' reluctance in expanding the product line is understandable, if not recommendable: producing different kinds of beer in the same brewery poses serious production problems and results in sharply higher costs than where there is an infinitely long and unchanging production line.

Coors now began directing its geographical expansion to the central states and those parts of the West it had not previously served. In 1978 it began distribution in Missouri, Iowa, and in parts of Washington state. In early 1979 it announced plans to begin distribution in Arkansas, which would bring to seventeen the number of states in which it was now marketing its beer. The Coors brothers were reaching some painful conclusions, among them that the company must abandon its comfortable role as a regional brewer and emerge as a national power. "There'll be fewer than ten breweries left in the United States in ten years," predicted Bill Coors. "I don't say we have to be number one, but we do have to stay in the top five to survive."[9]

---

[8]"New Coors Brand Nears Test Stage," *Advertising Age,* December 10, 1979, pp. 2 and 86.

[9]As quoted in "Men at Coors Beer Find the Old Ways Don't Work Anymore," *Wall Street Journal,* January 19, 1979, pp. 1 and 24.

Table 3.3   Relative Advertising Expenditures for Top Eight Brewers, 1973–1976*

	Expenditures (millions of dollars)			
	1973	1974	1975	1976
Anheuser-Busch	20.5	17.8	27.4	28.5
Jos. Schlitz	19.7	20.9	26.5	34.1
Miller	10.9	13.6	21.3	29.1
Pabst	7.2	8.4	9.6	9.7
Coors	1.4	1.6	1.2	2.0
Olympia	3.3	3.9	5.8	5.7
Stroh	4.5	4.4	4.0	5.0
F. & M. Schaefer	4.4	4.3	2.7	2.5

* These expenditures are understated since they do not include the large sums typically spent by brewers on point of purchase materials and other nonmeasured media.
Source: Advertising Age, September 26, 1977, p. 112.

Coors' promotional expenditures had been lagging far behind those of its major competitors, and even of some of the much smaller regional brewers. See Table 3.3. Accordingly, in 1976 Coors had hired J. Walter Thompson agency to enhance its corporate image, and in 1978 budgeted a whopping increase in the advertising budget to $15 million.

For the full year of 1978, Coors registered a small sales gain to $624.8 million. However, profits again declined to $54.8 million, almost 20 percent below 1977 profits and almost 29 percent under the peak year of 1976. Even back in 1975, profits had been higher. And Coors' stock had now declined to less than $14 a share by early 1978.

The question at this point is whether Coors waited far too long to awaken to a changing and much more aggressive marketplace. Deeply imbedded policies of conservatism, the misplaced confidence in the everlasting appeal of a beer and of an image that thereby dispelled the need for any aggressive or even conventional marketing efforts, and finally a confrontation philosophy with union employees—all these factors may have brought the venerable Coors brewery to a point of no return—not that the viability of the company is in jeopardy, but perhaps the golden, glory years are over for all time.

WHAT CAN BE LEARNED?

The Coors case evinces a classical disregard for marketing techniques, at least until great damage had been done to a company's market share and future promise. It shows the consequences of deemphasizing marketing in a production orientation. It is a prime example of "marketing myopia."[10]

The problem was not that the company was not growth minded; it was— if increasing the productive capacity of the single brewery and venturing into other geographical regions can be construed as growth minded. However, this philosophy or policy of growth gáve no recognition to changes in the environment and especially in the competitive picture—changes that necessitated adjustments and modification in business and marketing strategy. But alas, it is so tempting when things are going well, when a product is receiving accolades not only of the common man but of the famous, to be lulled into a sense of unrelieved complacency, to envision nothing going wrong, to see a favorable image as insulating the company and its brand from all competition and adversity. Such a perception of the environment tends to provoke less than desirable consequences. It tends to make a firm arbitrary and dictatorial in its dealings with dealers, with employees, and even with customers—in other words, it promotes a "take it or leave it" attitude. It can also induce a company to regard its situation as a "cash cow"[11] from which the profits can be fully milked while investments in advertising, in new product planning, and other marketing activities are kept at a minimum. Certainly, as Table 3.3 reveals, Coors' expenditures for advertising were woefully below those of other brewers, even those much smaller than Coors.

We can also see from this Coors example the sad but nonetheless to-be-recognized fact of the impermanence of a good image. It is difficult to develop an image of quality and of great desirability; even more difficult and time-consuming is the cultivation of a mystique. While such an image can be a company's biggest asset while it is operational, it can be a fleeting thing. Coors' image of quality and great taste was lost in the Eastern markets because of difficulties in maintaining required refrigeration during transportation and far-flung distribution; as a result, a negative image was quickly incurred in these markets. But also we see that consumer wants can be fickle and can change drastically: the sought-after image of today may not necessarily be that of next year. The new sought-after image of beer became light or low-caloric beer, and super premium beer. The brand image of Coors was left in the dust—not completely, of course, but enough to mute the growth of the company.

A firm should not beguile itself into minimizing the threat of competition, both present and potential. Coors was guilty of this, under the illusion of the invincibility of their product vis-a-vis competing brands. Yet, we can

---

[10]This famous phrase was coined by Theodore Levitt in "Marketing Myopia," *Harvard Business Review*, July-August, 1960, pp. 24–47.

[11]The term "cash cow" was perhaps first used by the Boston Consulting Group.

see how easily such an entrapment could occur: during the heady days of the early 1970s, they dominated every market they were in. But the reality was soon to impose itself that without greatly increased marketing expenditures and probably the establishment of additional breweries closer to the market, there could be little chance of cracking the Eastern market against entrenched and powerful competitors. Furthermore, even Coors' captive and cherished Western markets—particularly the important California market—were vulnerable to the aggressive efforts of major competitors.

A firm has to be adaptable; it cannot expect the status quo to endure. It has to be prepared to adjust to a changing environment. But ideally such a firm should anticipate changes, and should make needed adjustments before they are forced on it. Otherwise, an initial advantage can be lost, and never be regained.

This suggests the need not to take an image for granted, but to continually monitor its standing in the marketplace, and how this may be changing. Clues of change can come from many sources: industry publications, dealer comments, attitude surveys of consumers, sales force feedback, and competitive activities and inroads.

Update

By 1981, Coors was budgeting some $87 million for advertising and promotion. This was nearly double what the company spent two years before, and compares with a bare $1.2 million spent back in 1975. Coors Light was running neck and neck with Miller's nationally dominant Lite in the 20 states in which Coors was now selling. But its problems were hardly solved.

Both barrelage and income were down. Coors' share of the California market had dropped to 20 percent in 1981. Anheuser was invading the Coors stronghold of Texas, and its Bud Light gained 3 percent of the total market in one month. And Coors was still undecided whether to begin total distribution of its Herman Joseph's 1868, which it had been test marketing for a year without making inroads against Anheuser's Michelob.

By 1984, however, Coors appeared to have honed its marketing strategy. It moved aggressively into the Southeast in 1983 and captured some 11 percent of the market, with a good coordination of advertising, point-of-sale materials, and wholesaler incentives. However, Coors was still struggling to combat market-share erosion in its original Western markets. In California, its market share had fallen to 16.1 percent by 1983; in this state with the highest beer consumption in the nation it had had a 37.8 percent market share in 1972.

By 1984 Coors was in 26 states with its Coors Premium and Light brands. But it was still testing Herman Joseph's 1868, which had been in and out of test since May 1980, and was also testing another potential premium beer, Golden Lager, with the results not suggesting a strong "go." Coors was still clinging to its fifth place among all brewers, and had a 7.6 percent market share, exactly the same as it had had in 1978 with a much smaller geographic distribution.

For Thought and Discussion

1. How do you account for the fact that Coors beer achieved such a success despite the company's lack of a marketing orientation?
2. Do you think the company's fortunes would have remained strong and growing if advertising expenditures had been doubled or tripled during the late 1960s and early 1970s?
3. Is it likely that Coor's labor disputes had any serious effect on its fortunes? Why or why not?
4. At this time 1986, should Coors plan to go national? Examine as many pros and cons as possible.

Invitation to Role Play

1. Place yourself in the role of Peter Coors, the 32-year-old, $94,000-a-year senior vice president for sales and marketing. How would you attempt now (as of 1980) to reverse the company's fading performance? Be as specific as you can; also consider and identify any constraints to a corporate strategy that should be recognized. You might also want to consider how a mystique might again be built up for the Coors brand.
2. Place yourself in the role of a staff analyst. You have been asked to evaluate the desirability of opening another brewery in the East—perhaps in Virginia. Consider as many pros and cons as you can (you will, of course, have to make some assumptions, especially regarding construction costs). Develop a recommendation for a go/no go decision, and be prepared to defend it before a top management committee.

4

Nestle's Infant Formula— The Consequences of Spurning the Public Image

When a firm is a huge international conglomerate, with diversifications into many product lines, bad publicity and negative public reactions about a single product seemingly should be no particular cause for alarm. The inclination is to ignore such a "minor" problem and it should go away.

But the expectations of Nestle went awry. The attitudes of the general public toward the firm continued to worsen, exacerbated certainly by a negative press and vocal protestors. Far from diminishing over a few weeks and a few months, the situation worsened over years. And far from affecting only the particular product involved—infant formula marketed to underdeveloped countries—other products and other divisions of the company became the object of virulent protests. Nestle had for too long ignored assaults on its public image, and now the road back to public acceptance was slow and rocky.

BACKGROUND

The Trouble Begins

By the early 1970s, suspicions were arising that powdered infant formula manufacturers were contributing to the high rates of infant mortality in less developed Third World countries by their aggressive marketing efforts directed to people unable to read the instructions or use the product properly due to their living conditions. The possible linkage between infant formulas and mortality through product misuse began to be discussed by medical professionals, industry representatives, and government officials at a number of international conferences. But public awareness of the problem had not surfaced as yet.

Then in 1974, A British charity organization, War on Want, published a 28-page pamphlet, *The Baby Killer*. In it, two multinationals, Nestle of Switzerland, and Unigate of Britain, were criticized as engaging in ill-advised marketing efforts in Africa. With the printing of this short publication the general public became not only aware of the problem, but increasingly concerned.

This concern was to intensify less than a year later. A German-based Third World Working Group reissued a German translation of *The Baby Killer*, but with a few changes. While the British version criticized the entire infant formula industry, the German activists singled out Nestle for "unethical and immoral behavior" and retitled their version to *Nestle Kills Babies*.

The accusation enraged executives at Nestle headquarters and they sued the activists for defamation. The trial lasted two years and focused worldwide attention on the issue. Though Nestle won the lawsuit, the court advised the firm to review its current marketing practices. "We won the legal case, but it was a public-relations disaster," one Nestle official admitted. "The baby-killing accusation was a natural for antiwar groups and others looking for a cause. The company was dealing with the situation on a scientific and nutritional level, but the protestors were dealing on an emotional and political level.[1]

The Nestle Company

The Nestle Company, formally known as Nestle Alimentana, S.A., is headquartered in Vevey, Switzerland. It is a giant, worldwide corporation with sales of $12.5 billion in 1983. It owns or controls extensive interests in numerous companies of the food and cosmetics industries in various parts of the world. Products include instant drinks (coffee and tea), dairy products, cosmetics, frozen foods, chocolate, and pharmaceutical products. In addition it holds interests in catering services, as well as restaurant and hotel operations such as the Stouffer Corporation, which was acquired in 1973. By 1980, Nestle was marketing its products in Europe, Africa, North America,

[1]"Infant Formula Protest Teaches Nestle a Tactical Lesson," *Marketing News*, June 10, 1983, p. 1.

.atin American, the Caribbean, Asia, and Oceania. Its three top product
.roups were dairy products, instant drinks, and culinary/sundry products.
nfant foods, including the controversial infant formula, and dietetic prod-
.cts accounted for considerably less than 10 percent of total conglomerate
ales.

Nestle's appetite for acquisitions has continued unabated in recent
'ears. In 1975 it purchased food processor Libby, McNeill & Libby. In 1979
t acquired Beech-Nut, the baby-food producer. Other purchases of note
nclude CooperVision, a contact-lens maker, such well-known candy brands
.s Chunky, Bit-O-Honey, Raisinettes, Oh Henry, Goobers, and Sno Caps,
.nd most recently Hills Bros. Coffee Company and Carnation.

The Infant Formula Industry

Nestle first developed and marketed a milk food used to nourish premature
nfants in 1867. This was in response to an urgent need of a premature infant
vho was unable to take any food. Borden also introduced a similar
sweetened and condensed milk.

Infant formula foods are somewhat more recent, being developed in the
:arly 1920s as an alternative to breast feeding. Infant formula is a specially
orepared food for infants (under 6 months) and is based on cow's milk. It is
scientifically formulated to approximate the most perfect of all infant foods,
1uman breast milk. Today a number of different artificial milk products are
1vailable for infants, and these range in nutritional value from very high
humanized infant formula) to very low (various powdered, evaporated, and
sweetened condensed milks).

Sales of infant formula had increased sharply after World War II and hit
1 peak in 1957, with 4.3 million births in developed countries. From this
ooint on births started a decline that continued into the 1970s. The result was
1 steep downturn in baby formula sales and profits. Therefore, the industry
oegan searching for new business. This was found in the Third World
countries where the population was still increasing: the less developed
countries of Africa, South America, and the Far East.

Total industry sales for infant formula alone, excluding all other
commercial milk products, is about $1.5 billion. Of this, an estimated $600
million comes from the less developed countries. Hence this market segment
comprises a significant total market potential.

Nestle maintained a strong market share—some 40 to 50 percent of the
Third World market for baby formula. Competitors included three U.S.
firms, American Home Products, Bristol Myers, and Abbott Labs, which
shared 20 percent of the market. Foreign firms accounted for the remainder.

In 1981 the market was estimated to be growing at 15 to 20 percent per year.[2]

THE ISSUE: MISUSE OF THE PRODUCT, AND MARKETING PRACTICES

> If your lives were embittered as mine is, by seeing day after day this massacre of the innocents by unsuitable feeding, then I believe you would feel as I do that misguided propaganda on infant feeding should be punished as the most criminal form of sedition, and that these deaths should be regarded as murder.[3]

This lone indictment from a doctor back in 1939 evolved from a single cry into a crescendo of protest against the infant formula industry.

Incapability of the Market to Use the Product Correctly

A large number of Third World consumers live in poverty, have poor sanitation, receive inadequate health care, and are illiterate. Therefore, the misuse of the infant formula would seem inevitable. Water is obtained from polluted rivers or a common well and is brought back in contaminated containers. A refrigerator is considered a luxury item, and fuel is very expensive.

Consequently the powdered formula may be mixed with contaminated water and put into unsterilized bottles and nipples. In addition, the mothers are tempted to dilute the formula with excess water so that it will last longer. An example was cited by one physician at a Jamaican hospital of the malnutrition to two exclusively bottle-fed siblings, 4 months and 18 months old respectively. A can of formula would adequately feed a 4-month old baby just under 3 days. However, this mother so diluted the formula as to feed the 2 infants for 14 days. This mother was poor and illiterate, had no running water or electricity, and had 12 other children.[4]

Studies have given three reasons for the trend to less nursing and more bottle feeding in the less developed countries.[5]

---

[2]Kurt Anderson, "The Battle of the Bottle," *Time,* June 1, 1981, p. 26.

[3]As quoted in Cicely D. Williams, "The Marketing of Malnutrition," *Business and Society Review,* Spring 1980–81, p. 66.

[4]U.S. Congress, Senate, Committee on Human Resources, Subcommittee on Health and Scientific Research, *Marketing and Promotion of Infant Formula in the Developing Nations,* Hearing, 95th Congress, 2nd Session, May 23, 1978 (Washington, D. C.: Government Printing Office, 1978), p. 6.

[5]Prakash Sethi and James E. Post, "Public Consequences of Private Action: The

First, a changing sociocultural environment. This consists of urbanization, changing social mores, and increased mobility in employment. Infant formula was seen as representing social mobility and a symbol of the highly regarded modern products and medical expertise. The smiling white babies pictured on the fronts of formula tins suggested that rich, white mothers feed their babies this product and that therefore it must be better. The high-income consumers in these less developed countries were the first to use infant formula in imitation of western practices. Bottle feeding was looked upon as a high status practice, and the lower income groups readily followed along.

Second, the health care professional. Many hospitals and clinics endorsed the use of infant formula. A mother's first experience with a hospital may be to deliver a baby. Therefore, any products or gifts received there carry medical endorsement. Also, hospital practices are perceived as better and deserving of emulation. Babies are routinely separated from their mothers for 12 to 48 hours and are bottle fed whether or not the mothers plan to breast feed.

Third, the marketing and promotional practices of the infant formula manufacturers, which we will discuss shortly.

In 1951, approximately 80 percent of all 3-month old babies in Singapore were being breast fed; by 1971, only 5 percent were. In 1966, 40 percent fewer mothers in Mexico nursed 6-month old babies than had done so six years earlier. In Chile in 1973 there were three times as many deaths among infants who were bottle fed before 3 months of age than among wholly breast-fed infants. Other statistics of increased illnesses and higher death rates of bottle-fed infants were plentiful.[6]

Quality Control Problems

Nestle had some serious quality-control problems in its production of the formula in its far-flung plants:

In April 1977, the Colombian General Hospital encountered an increase in mortality at the premature ward. Bacteria was traced back to a Nestle factory. But 25 deaths occurred before the cause was found.

Also in 1977, the Australian Department of Health reported that 134 infants had fallen seriously ill as a result of being fed contaminated infant milk formulas produced by Nestle. Government officials estimated 20 million

---

Marketing of Infant Formula in Less Developed Countries," *California Management Review,* Summer 1979, pp. 35–48.

[6]For more such statistics, see Leah Margulies, "Bottle Babies: Death and Business Get Their Market," *Business and Society Review,* Spring 1978, pp. 43–49.

pounds of contaminated milk had been exported to the Southeast Asian countries. The Australian story started in 1976. The Nestle Tongala plant noticed an increase in bacterial counts in samples of infant milk powder. Inspection revealed cracks in the spray drier used to turn liquid milk into powder form. The bacteria was found to be a variant of salmonella that causes severe gastroenteritis. The State Health Department was not informed, and Nestle attempted sterilizing the equipment without halting production, but the bacteria continued to be discovered. The drier was kept in operation for a full 8 months after the contaminates were found.[7]

Perspective of Criticisms of Misuse

In fairness to Nestle, the critics who condemned the company and other infant food manufacturers for even attempting to market in the underdeveloped countries disregard any benefits of such products over the alternatives. The problem of water contamination also affects the alternatives to the commercial infant foods, which are various "native" cereal gruels of millet/rice used as weaning foods. The nutritional quality of these gruels tends to be low, and this deficiency is in addition to contamination of the water and containers used to cook the material. Furthermore, the millet/flour often has microbiological contamination. While it is true that infant formula mixed with contaminated water and containers presents dangers, the commercial formulas are more nutritious than local foods and are closer to breast milk than native weaning foods and are therefore easier to digest. A further rebuttal to the critics is that not all people of the less developed countries face water contamination. Millions can safely mix powdered formula with local water without water contamination.[8]

Criticisms of Nestle's Marketing Practices

Nestle has undoubtedly been an aggressive marketer in many Third World countries. Its promotional efforts have been directed to physicians and other medical personnel as well as consumers. Direct consumer promotion of infant formula has taken many forms. Media have included radio, newspapers, magazines, and billboards—and even vans with loudspeakers have been used. It has widely distributed free samples, bottles, nipples, and measuring spoons. In some countries direct customer contacts have been

[7]Reported in Douglas Clement, "Nestle's Latest Killing in Bottle Baby Market," *Business and Society Review,* Summer 1978, pp. 60–64.
[8]John Sparks, "The Nestle Controversy—Anatomy of a Boycott," Public Policy Education Fund, Inc., June 1981.

made through "milk nurses," and these have been the subject of particular criticism. Nestle employed about 200 women who were registered nurses, nutritionists, or midwives. These professionals were often nicknamed, "milk nurses." Critics maintained that these milk nurses were actually sales personnel in disguise who visit mothers and give product samples in an attempt to persuade mothers to stop breast feeding. With their uniforms giving them great credibility, this practice was condemned as being too persuasive for naive consumers.

Promotion to physicians and other medical personnel has also been controversial. This type of promotion has generally involved the use of detail people who discuss product quality and characteristics with pediatricians, pediatric nurses, and other related medical personnel. (The use of detail people, who are a type of missionary sales representative, is common practice, as we will describe in the accompanying "Information Sidelight.") Materials such as posters, charts, and free samples were made available to physicians, hospitals, and clinics without charge. Physicians and other hospital personnel have also received company-sponsored travel to medical meetings.

Critics felt that the promotion of infant formula had been too aggressive and had contributed to the decline in breast feeding. Despite increased criticisms, however, sales of infant formula in poor countries continued to escalate. It had become the third most advertised product in the Third

---

INFORMATION SIDELIGHT

THE USE OF MISSIONARY SALESPEOPLE (DETAIL PEOPLE)

Missionary salespeople—these are called detail people in the drug industry—are commonly used by many firms to provide specialized services and cultivate customer goodwill. They generally do not try to secure orders.

Missionary salespeople are employed by manufacturers to work with their dealers. They may put up point-of-purchase displays, train dealer salespeople, provide better communication between distributor and manufacturer, and in general try to have their brand more aggressively promoted by the dealer. In the drug industry the detail people leave samples, and explain research information about new products to the medical professionals so as to encourage prescriptions and recommendations for their brands.

World, after tobacco and soap. And it was generally recognized that nev
mothers in such countries were most susceptible to advertising. A 196
study of 120 mothers in Barbados found that 82 percent of the ones give
free samples later purchased the same brand—this, whether the sample
were received from the hospital or at home.[9]
In summary, the criticisms of promotional practices were:

- Bottle feeding contributes to infant mortality in less develope
  countries.
- Baby booklets ignore or de-emphasize breast feeding.
- Media promotions are misleading in encouraging poor and illiterat
  mothers to bottle feed rather than breast feed their infants.
- Advertising portrays breast feeding as primitive and inconvenient.
- Free gifts and samples are direct inducement to bottle-feed infants
- Posters and pamphlets in hospitals, and milk nurses are viewed a
  "endorsement by association," or "manipulation by assistance."
- The prices of formulas at the milk banks are still too expensive fo
  many consumers who are tempted then to dilute the formula.

THE SITUATION WORSENS FOR NESTLE

With the publication of the two articles, *The Baby Killer,* and *Nestle Kill.
Babies,* and the subsequent lawsuit by Nestle which received worldwid
publicity, two groups were formed and solidified their opposition that wa
eventually to lead to boycotting Nestle products and services: The Interfait
Center on Corporate Responsibility, and the Infant Formula Action Coali
tion (INFACT).

Since the early 1970s, various agencies had been trying to reduce th
promotion and advertising practices of the infant formula companies. Thes
agencies included the Protein Advisory Group in 1970 and 1973, the Worlc
Health Assembly in 1974, and the World Health Organization (WHO) i
1978.

As a by-product of the growing condemnation of the industry, Nestl
and other firms began to make some changes in their promotional practices
at least on paper. The changes were brought about through the auspices o
the International Council of Infant Food Industries (ICIFI), which wa:
formed in 1975 by nine infant food manufacturers, including Nestle. Th
changes included: product information would always recognize breast mil
as best; infant formulas would be advertised as supplementary, and tha

---

[9]Reported in "A Boycott Over Infant Formula," *Business Week,* April 23, 1979, pp
137–140.

professional advice should be sought; nurse uniforms would be worn only by professional nurses.

But the self regulation apparently did not work sufficiently to allay the criticisms. Documentation by the International Baby Food Action Network confirmed over 1000 violations of the "code" since 1977. Some critics compared "asking for self regulation was like asking Colonel Sanders to babysit your chickens."[10]

With continued reported violations, a boycott was organized in the United States in July 1977, and soon spread to nine other countries. It was to last until January 26, 1982 in the United States and Canada, with other countries following suit over the next two years.

Nestle was singled out as the sole object of the boycott due to its 50 percent worldwide market share along with the adverse publicity that had centered on it more than other firms who were engaged in the same marketing practices.

The demands of INFACT and the boycotters were:

1. Stop altogether the use of milk nurses.
2. Stop distributing all free samples.
3. Stop promoting infant formula to the health care industry.
4. Stop consumer promotion and advertising of infant formula.

The boycott soon had the support of over 450 local and religious groups across America, and proponents claimed it was the largest non-union boycott in U.S. history. Boycott activity was strongest in Boston, Baltimore, and Chicago, where INFACT established an office with five full-time staffers. Thousands of signatures were gathered on various petitions urging removal of Nestle products from supermarket shelves. Some grocers acquiesced, agreeing to remove such products as Taster's Choice from their shelves. The boycott also hit college campuses. With the slogan, "Crunch Nestle," boycotts were encouraged on products ranging from milk chocolate to tea, coffee, and hot chocolate. The college boycott reportedly began at Wellesley College and soon spread to others, such as Colgate, Yale, and the University of Minnesota.

This boycotting undoubtedly was effective, not only directly in causing lost business and profits for the company, but also indirectly in crystallizing public opinion against the company, and in invoking governmental response. For example:

The government of New Guinea enacted stringent laws to curb the

---

[10]"Killer in a Bottle," *The Economist,* May 9, 1981, p. 50; and Douglas Clement, pp. 60–64.

artificial feeding of babies in the summer of 1979. Bottles and nipple
now could only by obtained by prescription. Other countries also bega
introducing legislation to reduce the marketing and advertising o
breast-milk substitutes.

The World Health Organization (WHO) in May 1981 adopted a restric
tive ad code that applied only to the infant food industry. A portion o
Article 5 of the Code states, "There shall be no advertising or othe
forms of promotion to the general public of products within the scope o
this code."[11] The products covered were infant food formulas and othe
weaning foods.

The European Parliament in France voted overwhelmingly for stric
enforcement of the WHO Code throughout the 10-nation Commo
Market. The European Parliament also placed responsibility on com
mon market firms for the actions of their subsidiaries abroad i
observing the WHO code.

NESTLE FIGHTS BACK

Nestle's first efforts to combat vituperative accusations resulted in mor
harm than good, as we have seen. As its public image continued to worsen
the worldwide boycott finally surfaced in 1977. Now Nestle could no longe
ignore the protests and hope they would go away. Obviously they were no
going to go away. Initial strategy at this point was to treat the boycott an
widespread protests as a public-relations problem. The public relation
department of the firm was upgraded into the Office of Corporate Respon
sibility. The world's largest public relations firm, Hill & Knowlton, wa
hired to assist. Over 300,000 packets of information were mailed by Nestl
to U.S. clergymen, informing them that they were wrong in their denunci
ations of Nestle. Finally, Daniel J. Edelmon, a renowned public-relation
specialist, was hired. He advised the company to keep a low profile and t
try to get third party endorsements of its actions.

Finally, in 1981 after failing to improve its image and mute the critica
cries against it, Nestle dismissed its two public-relations firms, and took o
itself the task of reestablishing its reputation. Ignoring the situation had no
helped; public outcries, rather than lessening, had increased. And efforts t
angrily denounce the critics had only exacerbated the situation. Now th
firm was ready to try a new tack in efforts to establish its credibility as
humane and responsible corporate citizen.

---

[11]"World Health Organization Drafts Restrictive Ad Code," *Editor & Publisher*, April 1
1981, p. 8.

One of the first steps was to endorse the World Health Organization's Code of Marketing for Breast Milk Substitutes—a step three other U.S. manufacturers did not make until two years later. The code, which imposed only voluntary compliance, banned advertising to the general public, as well as banning distribution of samples to mothers.

Next, Nestle sought an ethical group to work with in vouching for its compliance with the code, and found it in the Methodist Task Force on Infant Formula.

Nestle's relations with the press had been abysmal. For example, in the first six months of 1981, the *Washington Post* published 91 articles critical of Nestle. In the company's multi-faceted attempt to rebuild its image, the policy dealing with the media was changed to an "open-door, candid approach."[12]

The most effective restorative strategy finally adopted was the establishment of a ten-member panel of medical experts, clergymen, civic leaders, and experts in international policy to publicly monitor Nestle's compliance with the WHO code and to investigate complaints against its marketing practices. This Nestle Infant Formula Audit Commission (NIFAC) gained credibility with the acceptance of the chairmanship by Edmund S. Muskie, former Secretary of State, vice-presidential candidate, and Democratic senator from Maine. The Commission was established in May 1982.

This so-called Muskie Commission worked with representatives of WHO, International Nestle Boycott Committee (INBC), and UNICEF to resolve conflicts in four areas of the WHO code. Points of contention were educational materials, labels, gifts to medical and health professionals, and free or subsidized supplies to hospitals. These were resolved, and Nestle agreed that, on educational material it intended to distribute, the social and health aspects of formula vs. breast feeding would be addressed. Its infant formula labels would clearly state the dangers of using contaminated water and the superiority of mother's milk. Personal gifts to health officials (which smacked of bribery and seeking of preferential treatment) were banned. Finally, free samples of formula distributed to hospitals were to be limited to supplies that go to mothers incapable of breast-feeding their children.

At last, after years of an adversarial posture, which had only resulted in a growing crescendo of criticisms and boycotts, with bitter accusations that the company was causing the deaths of millions of Third World babies because of its marketing practices, the situation was improving. "We have all learned a lesson . . . ," said Rafael D. Pagan Jr., president of the Nestle Coordination Center for Nutrition. "Companies should be sensitive and

[12]"Fighting a Boycott," *Industry Week,* January 23, 1984, p. 54.

listen carefully to what consumers and members of the general public ar
saying. When problems surface, they should seek a dialogue with responsi
ble leaders and try to work out the problems together."[13]

After a decade of confrontation with protestors and seven years o
boycotting, early in 1984 most groups agreed to a suspension of thei
boycott. While some diehards refused to accept the conciliatory efforts o
Nestle, several large groups—for example, the American Federation o
Teachers, the American Federation of Churches, the Federation of Nurse
& Health Professionals, the United Methodist Church, and the Church of th
Brethren—had either withdrawn from the boycott or decided not to join it

The company admitted, however, that perhaps 20 obdurate boycot
leaders and 50,000 followers in the U.S. may never stop ostracizing th
company no matter what Nestle does.[14]

The results in lost business for Nestle of the infant food controversy ar
difficult to pinpoint. Company estimates ranged up to $40 million in los
profits as direct results of the boycotts. However, lost business wa
probably far greater than this, with some coming in the years before th
boycotts began as consumers turned to alternative brands from firms wit
better reputations. Even during the years of boycotts, not all consumer
were militant protestors; but they could certainly take their busines
elsewhere, as sort of a silent protest. Admittedly, infant food busines
accounted for only 3 percent of total Nestle sales worldwide. But othe
Nestle products were blackened to an unknown degree by the destroye
public image of this one minor part of the total business. One of the mos
obvious negative consequences of the boycotts was the loss of meetings an
convention business at Stouffer facilities, with some planners opting t
schedule at other locations as a means of avoiding any association wit
negative publicity.

Table 4.1 shows the sales and profits for the Nestle conglomerate durin
some of these years. It shows profits declining from the years before th
protests had become so pronounced. But we really cannot measure hov
much is the direct effect of the confrontation; more important, we can onl
guess at the extent of unrealized potential.

WHAT CAN BE LEARNED?

The Nestle debacle should be sobering for many firms. It should raise som
real concerns about the possibility of damage to the public image, damag

---

[13]"Nestle Gains Formula Accord: Product Boycott is Suspended," *Marketing New*
Feb. 17, 1984, p. 5.
[14]"Fighting a Boycott," p. 55.

Table 4.1   Nestle Sales and Profits, 1974–1980 (In thousands of Swiss Francs)

Years	Sales	Profits
1974	16,624,000	742,000
1975	18,286,000	799,000
1976	19,063,000	872,000
1977	20,095,000	830,000
1978	20,266,000	739,000
1979	21,639,000	816,000
1980	24,479,000	638,000

Sources: Company annual reports.

that can be difficult to rebuild. Specifically, these are major points to be learned from this experience:

• The vulnerability of the public image. A reputable image, or at least one that is neutral and not negative, can be quickly besmirched. A firm should not underestimate the power of social awareness and activist groups. Furthermore, the large firm is the most vulnerable—even if other firms in the industry are engaged in the same practices—and is the most desirable target for activist groups. Size brings with it greater visibility and public recognition than is the case with smaller competitors. This makes it the target of choice: to bring down the giant. And public sentiment—whether on the athletic field, in business, or whatever—is not on the side of the big and powerful.

• The power of a hostile press. A bad press can both arouse and intensify negative public opinion. It can fan the flames. A firm cannot plan on the press being objective and unbiased in such reporting. The press tends to be eager to find a "fault object," and when this is a large and rather impersonal firm, the likelihood is all the greater that bad actions or the negatives of a particular situation will be emphasized far more than the positive and helpful side of the issue. While infant formulas had many benefits and were a very positive health influence in many situations, still publicity focused almost exclusively on alleged marketing abuses and customer misuses.

• The longevity of a besmirched reputation. Nestle's expectations that the controversy would die out were certainly squashed by the duration and increasing virulence of the protest movement. Without constructive efforts by Nestle in the early 1980s, the gathering strength of the protest movement probably would have resulted in ever-greater boycotting, and most likely in restrictive legislation by many countries. Thus, a tarnished reputation is not suddenly going to become bright and shiny just because of the passage of time Some sort of strong positive efforts must be made by the firm to try to restore its image. Or it will not be improved.

- Public relations deficiencies. Public relations is not the answer when certain aspects of a firm's operation are the focal points of criticism. The act must be cleared up first. The public relations efforts of Nestle were notoriously impotent, despite hiring two of the largest and most expensive public-relations firms in the world. Without improving the operations under question, no amount of public-relations statements—even mailing to clergy some 300,000 pamphlets propagandizing Nestle's position—is likely to produce positive and lasting results.

- The potential of marketing efforts to impact on the public image. We maintain that marketing inputs (see Figure 2.3 in Chapter 2) have the greatest potential for affecting the public image, positively or negatively. Here, all the problems of Nestle emanated from its marketing efforts in the Third World countries. Normally such marketing efforts would be viewed as effective; under different circumstances they could well have been lauded as models for the effective use of marketing for a new and improved product. Alas, of course, the marketing efforts were seen as far too effective—too aggressive in swaying a naive population in not wholly desirable directions. A firm's marketing efforts are the most visible aspects of its operation. This visibility can be a curse sometimes, as it was with Nestle. The caveat is to consider marketing efforts as part of the important public-image mix, and be guided accordingly.

Suggested Reactions with a Darkening Public Image

The Nestle example gives us helpful insights as to how best to react to smears and protests. Ignoring the problem seems ill-advised, if the protests are severe enough and if the issue is inflammatory enough. And certainly alleged culpable loss of life—whether from chemical dumps or spills, or from the ill-advised use of infant formula—is usually inflammatory enough.

Direct confrontation and an adversarial stand is seldom effective either. As Nestle found out the hard way, its court case, even though won by Nestle, only increased the negative publicity and fueled the protestations. Even if the weight of evidence is on the firm's side, the propaganda and one-side criticisms of the opposition will likely win over the general public.

So it seems more prudent for the firm that unwittingly falls into the snare of public image problems regarding its social role to approach the situation with a spirit of cooperation and constructive participation with opposing groups. This, despite some diehard activists who may refuse all efforts at conciliation. We cannot fault the efforts of Nestle in 1981-1983 in working with the more reasonable critics. But we can severely fault the company for waiting so long to take such constructive actions.

Many firms need a greater sensitivity to potential problem areas involving corporate social performance. They need to try to anticipate potential problems and nip them quickly. Failing this, an organization should strive to resolve as many of the objections as it can—even if this means assuming the burden of an inequitable compromise position. The consequence otherwise may be a gradually deteriorating image problem, even if the negative public perceptions are not fully based on facts.

A firm doing business in sensitive areas needs to prove that it is a responsible corporate citizen and not an insensitive giant organization. More attention to the public image mix may well prevent the type of image problems that bedeviled Nestle for years.

For Thought and Discussion

1. Faced with activist protestors, do you think a firm has any recourse but to yield to their complete demands? Is there any room for an aggressive stance?
2. Could the public relations efforts of Nestle have been used more effectively?
3. Do you think Nestle was unfairly picked on? Why or why not?

Invitation to Role Play

1. As the staff assistant to the CEO of Nestle, you have been asked to develop a position paper as to the desirability of withdrawing infant formula from the market in Third World countries. Discuss the pros and cons of such a move, and then make your recommendations and support them as persuasively as you can.
2. You are the manager of a Stouffer hotel. A delegation of clergy and lay people have approached you with the threat of boycotting your premises. Be as persuasive as you can in trying to dissuade them from doing so.

CHAPTER 5

Korvette—Inability to Handle Growth and Upgrade an Image

The Korvette chain of discount department stores represented the classic American success story. Its rise was the story of one man, Eugene Ferkauf who started in 1948 with a tiny luggage shop one flight up on East 46th Street in Manhattan. With a simple strategy of undercutting department stores 10 to 40 percent on appliances and other hard goods, his corporation grew to over $700 million in sales by 1965. In the process, he revolutionized merchandising and profoundly altered the policies of conventional retailers. Malcolm McNair, Harvard's famous professor of retailing, rated Ferkauf as one of the six greatest merchants in the United States, alongside men like Frank Woolworth, John Wanamaker, and J. C. Penney. But, somehow, the heady success story began to change, dramatically and irrevocably. An inability to cope with large size, coupled with a misguided attempt to change a successful image—to upgrade to a higher status one—led to the downfall. And a few years later, McNair was to retract his assessment of Ferkauf.

THE DREAM THAT WAS KORVETTE

Gene Ferkauf began his retail career in his father's luggage store. However, he was visionary and eager to grasp opportunities as he saw them. He disagreed with his father's traditional philosophy of merchandising, which was to sell goods at list or manufacturers' suggested prices and reap the rewards of good profit per unit sale. He dreamed that maybe only a small profit per unit sale might yield the greater total profit, *if sales volume could greatly be increased by so doing.* Accordingly, Ferkauf struck out on his own, opening a luggage shop in a second-floor loft on an offstreet of Manhattan. The name of the business he chose rather arbitrarily: E. J. Korvette. The E stands for Eugene, his first name; the J for Joseph Blumenberg, his friend who became treasurer of the company; and "Korvette" was the name of a Canadian subchaser in the first world war that was spelled with a C but was changed to a K.) While the basic stock was luggage, as an accommodation to his customers Ferkauf began selling appliances at just about cost. Soon he branched out into fountain pens and photography equipment. In the early days, Ferkauf sold all appliances for $10 over the wholesale cost: "If a guy came in to buy stereo equipment that cost the firm $1000, we would just mark it up ten bucks and he took it home."[1]

And people began lining up on the sidewalk outside and down the block to get into the store to purchase such bargains. Ferkauf found he was making money with the appliances and was operating at a million-dollar-a-year rate. By the end of 1951 he had moved his store to street level and opened a branch in Westchester. Sales climbed to $9.7 million in 1953.

Gene Ferkauf was a quiet man; he shunned the public limelight. At stockholder meetings he liked to sit mute. He even absented himself from a reception celebrating the new quarters for Yeshiva University's Ferkauf School of Social Work. He believed in casual clothes, had a contempt for formality, and spurned an office and other executive amenities. But he believed in friends.

In the early 1950s, a group of thirty-eight men, almost all Brooklyn high school pals of Ferkauf, ran the company. They were called the "open-shirt crowd" or "the boys." Korvette's management operated from a dingy old building with Ferkauf presiding at a beat-up desk in one corner. And the company grew, incredibly, from $55 million to $750 million in sales within ten years, thereby becoming one of the fastest growing companies in the history of retailing. In the early 1960s, the company was opening huge new stores on the average of one every seven weeks.

In the 1950s and early 1960s, Korvette led the discount revolution that was sweeping the country. The American consumer relished the idea of low prices, of items priced up to 40 percent less than department stores' prices. Korvette profits and stock seemed headed for the stratosphere. And the business philosophy was so simple: if you have sales volume, even with a low markup, you are going to make a profit. To do so, however, Korvette

---

[1]"Korvettes Tries for a Little Chic," *Business Week*, May 12, 1973, p. 124.

and the other discounters operated with austere surroundings. Stores and fixtures were simple, even pipe racks were used for hanging garments; no services such as credit or delivery were offered at first; and self-service was the rule in order to cut down on salary expense. Just as important as paring costs, lean stocks of merchandise were offered—a narrow selection of best selling sizes and styles—to maximize merchandise turnover and thereby increase the return on investment.

As the company persisted in its discounting policies, it came up against state fair trade laws, which permitted manufacturers to set the minimum prices for which their goods could be sold by retailers. Some of the major manufacturers, including General Electric, wanted to maintain an image of quality and to protect their regular dealers from price cutting. Korvette, by selling below the fair-traded prices, was vulnerable to lawsuits by such manufacturers. At the time the company went public in 1955, thirty-four fair-trade lawsuits were pending against it. This was not as bad as might seem, however. Enforcement of fair trade rested with the manufacturer who wanted it for his products. And in 1956, Korvette received a legal boost when a New York court threw out a suit brought by the Parker Pen Company on the grounds that Parker was not sufficiently enforcing its fair-trade program. Many manufacturers were finding enforcement difficult amid the spate of discount stores. In addition, the lack of severe penalties prescribed by the courts for violating fair trade (in many cases, only court costs were levied against the offending discounter) further limited its effectiveness as a deterrent to price cutting by Korvette and others. Actually, fair trade and list prices aided discount stores since customers could readily see the base price from which the item was discounted.

In his growth policies, Ferkauf had the theory that it was better to open a cluster of stores in a metropolitan area, to saturate an area, rather than spread out more thinly nationwide. Where three or four or more stores were located in one metropolitan area, advertising costs could be shared, as could warehousing, servicing, and certain other expenses. Customer acceptance could be gained more quickly from the massive presentation of stores and promotional efforts. Following this strategy, by 1966 Korvette had ten stores in the New York metropolitan area, five in Philadelphia, four in Baltimore–Washington. Between 1963 and 1965, five large stores had been opened in metropolitan Chicago, three in Detroit, and two in St. Louis.

But by 1966, the company was in trouble, and could not handle its growth nor digest its accumulated size.

TROUBLE!

In the four years between 1962 and 1966, store space and sales volume more than tripled. But "genius though Ferkauf might be at minding the store he

INFORMATION SIDELIGHT

IMPORTANCE OF TURNOVER IN PROFITABILITY

Consider the following comparison of a department store operation and a similar size discount store for an example of the effect of higher turnover on profitability:

Department Store

Sales	$12,000,000
Net profit percent	5
Net profit dollars	$600,000
Stock turnover	4
Average stock	
(12,000,000 ÷ 4)*	$3,000,000
Return on investment	
(without considering	
investment in store	$\dfrac{600,000}{3,000,000} = 20\%$
and fixtures)	

*To simplify this example, inventory investment is figured at retail price, rather than cost, which would technically be more correct. However, the significance of increasing turnover is more easily seen here.

A similar size discount store might have a turnover of 8, while net profit percentage might be only 3%:

Discount Store

Sales	$12,000,000
Net profit percent	3
Net profit dollars	$360,000
Stock turnover	8
Average stock	
(12,000,000 ÷ 8)	$1,500,000
Return on	$\dfrac{360,000}{1,500,000} = 24\%$
investment	

Thus, the discount store can be more profitable than the comparable department store (as measured by the true measure of profitability, the return on investment), even though the net profit is less. Furthermore, the discount store not only has a lower investment in inventory to produce the same amount of sales, but also has less invested in store and fixtures.

had neither the temperament nor the desire to mind the office."[2] When Korvette had no more than a dozen outlets, Ferkauf, on "foot patrol," could give on-the-scene guidance. But his organization failed to provide any serious substitute for the diminishing face-to-face supervision of Ferkauf and his home-office executives. The constant addition of stores placed enormous pressures on management. There was enough work and problems in running existing operations, much less having to simultaneously bring on the additional operations. Buyers who were busy filling the needs of the old stores had to somehow provide for the new stores as well. Advancement, of course, was fast. Section and department managers moved quickly into jobs as store managers and less experienced people took their places. But there was little time either to develop top-notch management people or to be selective in screening for the best.

Along with the sheer number of new stores opening, the doubling and tripling of floor space, and merchandise and management, problems, several other factors were destined to create trouble for Korvette by the mid-1960s. One was the geographical aspect of the expansion. As long as new stores were added in the East, and particularly around metropolitan New York City, the close contact of stores with Ferkauf and the home office could still be maintained. However, expansion to Detroit, to Chicago, and to St. Louis practically negated this close personal guidance and control.

There were difficulties in lining up enough good management people to run these distant operations, and profits outside New York generally ran behind. But Ferkauf had the dream of becoming a national company, and his cluster philosophy seemed well-geared to tapping other metropolitan markets. However, sound though it was in theory, there were drawbacks. Invading a market area with not just one, but several stores, induced the strongest kind of competitive reaction from established merchants. In Chicago, for example, Sears and other retailers reacted vigorously to Korvette's entry with heavy price reductions and promotional efforts. This blunted the efforts of Korvette to gain solid market position.

With all this, major strains were caused by an attempt to upgrade the image. In addition now to more elaborate stores and more costly services, this meant bringing in higher priced goods and also giving a greater emphasis to clothing and fashion merchandise. Ferkauf, as most discounters, started out discounting so-called hard goods: refrigerators, washing machines, TV and stereo equipment, small appliances such as irons, toasters, blenders, etc., and photo equipment. But the route to an upgraded image brought

Korvette into clothing and other soft goods, which offered higher profit margins. However, the risks of markdowns and unsalable inventories due to fashion and seasonal obsolescence were high, and the demands on management greater than for the more staple hard goods. Eventually, Korvette's inability to handle the soft goods and fashion end of the business and to generate enough customer acceptance led to Korvette merging with Spartans Industries, an apparel conglomerate that specialized both in manufacturing and retailing low-end fashion goods.

Food merchandising also harassed Ferkauf. In 1961, Korvette had two supermarkets. Then the firm started adding supermarkets, winding up with twenty-two, six of these in Detroit and Chicago, unfamiliar territory to an eastern retailer inexperienced in the local purchase of meat and produce in these areas. There was good rationale for expanding with supermarkets: consumers generally stock up with groceries weekly; by building supermarkets adjacent to discount stores, heavier and more constant customer traffic can be realized.

Unfortunately, the basic tenet of discount merchandising, high turnover, was disregarded with the food operation. These food stores were opened without warehousing, which meant they had to stock more goods if out-of-stocks were to be minimized. But a heavy inventory was not compatible with lean fast-moving stocks and high turnover. Furthermore, competition in the supermarket industry was increasing about this time, and losses from this operation reached $12 million by 1964. Ferkauf was forced to turn to the outside for help.

Hill Supermarkets, a 42 store chain on Long Island, seemed the answer. Hilliard J. Coan, Hill's chief executive, ran a profitable operation with net of $1,036,000 from sales of $119 million in 1964. He also had a warehouse on Long Island big enough to supply both Hill's needs and Korvette's in the east. Ferkauf persuaded Hill to merge with Korvette, and Coan became the executive in charge of the $200 million food division. Meantime, the food stores in Chicago and Detroit were leased to a local operator.

But the merger with Hill was not to solve the food problems. Shop-Rite, an efficient supermarket chain, began aggressively promoting with low prices on Long Island. This drastically affected Hill's profits at the very time it was trying to assume operation of the Korvette food division. In 1968, after several years of frustration, quits was finally called on the food operation, and Hill–Korvette Supermarket Division was sold for cash.

The final problem plaguing Korvette was its furniture department. This was a leased operation by the H. L. Klion Company. However, the lessee was undercapitalized, and serious management and inventory problems were emerging by 1963, the time when Korvette was undertaking its greatest expansion efforts. Inventory controls, accounting, and deliveries broke down, and the furniture departments in the newer stores never made it into the black. To add to the problems, two strikes hit Klion in 1964 and nondeliveries caused customers to cancel $2 million worth of orders. With the strikes finally settled, much of this merchandise in specially-ordered colors and fabrics—odds and ends for which little demand existed—jammed stores and had to be heavily marked down.

While the furniture operation was leased, customers were unaware of this. So Korvette bore the brunt of complaints about service and delivery, and its reputation was being badly affected. In 1964–65, Klion lost $2,667,000 and was approaching bankruptcy. Supplying some financial help was not enough, and Korvette was forced to take over the Klion Company and underwrite its heavy losses in order to try to preserve the Korvette reputation. Along with Klion, Korvette acquired the Federal Carpet Company, a lessee that had a profit of $700,000 in 1964 and that shared space with Klion in the furniture department. Federal Carpet executives were given responsibility for running the combined carpet-and-furniture division. But it continued to be a profit drain, and the confidence of customers was slow to be rebuilt.

There was another, smaller, ill-fated venture about this time. The success of Avon in selling cosmetics door-to-door prompted Korvette to try something similar. However, losses were so heavy that this was soon discontinued.

1966, THE YEAR OF DECISION

The strains in the Korvette operation were beginning to show clearly by 1966. While net sales for the last six months of fiscal 1965 were more than 10 percent ahead of the same period the year before, earnings declined from $16,634,000 to $13,877,000. Then, for the generally unprofitable first quarter of the year, Korvette saw the deficit grow from $1,124,000 in 1965 to $4,452,000 in 1966. There were other indications of trouble, as well. Inventory turnover was down by one-third from 1961. Sales per square foot had also fallen by one-third. And Korvette stock had dropped from a peak of 50½ in May 1965, to 13 by the beginning of 1966.

While the substantial losses experienced in the furniture division contributed to this worsening picture, food still was not doing well, and now even the main-store departments of the older stores were experiencing declining sales. In 1966, Hilliard Coan, the former president of Hill Supermarkets, became president of Korvette. He tried to tighten the loose organization by clarifying executive duties and making work loads more equitable. Additional experienced merchandising executives were hired, and the company moved to install its own data processing. A new warehouse to serve as the first distribution center was built in northern New Jersey, thereby being rather centrally located for the eastern stores. This permitted the company to buy more expeditiously, supply store needs for certain items more quickly, and also eliminate some wholesalers. At last the expansion policies were being toned down. Only three new stores were opened in 1966, and attention was turned to the existing stores and efforts made to increase their customer traffic.

Rather unexpectedly, on September 25, 1966, Korvette merged with Spartans Industries. Charles Bassine, the chairman of Spartans, had his own chain of Spartans discount stores and had also acquired the Atlantic Thrift chain of forty-six discount stores. Spartans had only $375 million in sales compared with $719 million for Korvette in 1965. However, Ferkauf was eased out of active management, left Spartans in 1968 to develop his own boutique chain, and faded from the limelight. Bassine turned his attention to developing tighter controls for the Korvette operations: controls over merchandise, costs, markups, markdowns, shrinkage and expense—the aim, a much tighter ship.

AFTER 1966

Despite the stronger management that Spartans provided, the Korvette operation could not regain its previous strength. An attempt was made to raise Korvette's profit margins by upgrading the merchandise with higher price lines, but this served to drive away many of the old bargain-hunting customers. While sales of Spartans Industries were now over a billion dollars, there was a continual fight to generate profits. Bassine tried to unload the unprofitable parts of his operation, such as the supermarkets, but profits were little improved. Then in 1970, the apparel business was hit by a flood of cheaper foreign imports, and a recession hurt retail sales. In 1970, the Korvette division lost $3.7 million.

In 1971, a "third rebirth"[3] took place, as Spartans merged with Arlen Realty & Development Corporation, a big real estate developer. Arlen was run by the son-in-law of Bassine and had participated in the building of some of the Korvette stores in the late 1950s and 1960s. Besides bringing younger blood into the top management, the merger enabled Korvettes (an "s" was added at this time, and the "E.J." dropped) to cut its tax bill with the help of Arlen's big tax shelter, property depreciation.[4]

[3]"Will the Store Be Minded?" *Forbes*, August 15, 1971, p. 44.
[4]"Korvettes Tries for a Little Chic," *Business Week*, May 12, 1973, p. 124, 125.

POSTMORTEM

Both internal and external factors contributed to the faltering of Korvette. Competition was changing, becoming keener than it had been. Not only Korvette, but many other early discounters were also faltering or had succumbed at this time. Internal factors undermined the firm and made it less able to cope effectively with the stronger competition.

Internal Factors

Vigorous expansion creates problems and stresses for any organization. In Korvette's case, the expansion came from a rather small base of nine stores; suddenly there were twenty-five. Supervision and control, which formerly could be handled on a face-to-face basis, moved away from this possibility.

Korvette until the middle 1960s did not have the kind of controls needed for the size of operation it was attaining—controls coming from well-defined policies, objectives and plans for the various aspects of the operation, such as for markups, markdowns, merchandise turnover, and the various categories of expenses. The business was run rather informally, with little advance planning and coordination at a time when size precluded the effectiveness of this. The growth was too fast; there was not sufficient time for digestion and for developing sound policies for coping with such growth.

There were not enough trained executives at all levels, from home office buyers and store managers to department and section managers. While promotion was necessarily fast, ill-trained and marginal people were thrust into responsible positions; bodies had to be found to fill certain spots. Korvette could have gone outside the organization to fill important slots and began doing so in the 1960s for some of the top home office positions. But at middle and lower management levels, discount stores often lacked the prestige to attract top-notch people.

Part of the problem in recruiting top-notch poeple stemmed from the organizational policies of Ferkauf. Management was highly centralized; the home office dictated all merchandising and other policies, and store managers and other store executives were not given much authority. But if rapid growth was to be achieved in an absence of tight controls, decentralization giving more authority and responsibility to store executives would have helped. This would have meant both higher paid and more carefully chosen store executives.

There is contagion in expanding rapidly, in opening massive new stores every six or seven weeks—everyone from top management on down becomes preoccupied with the new units coming on the scene. Older, established stores tended to be overlooked until they were faltering badly, at which point effective solutions were sometimes no longer possible. Furthermore, while communications poured from the home office, good communications upward from the stores were lacking since store executives carried little authority, and no procedures had been established for systematically providing such feedback. Consequently, worsening situations went unnoticed.

The cluster strategy of entering metropolitan areas with a number of stores as simultaneously as possible was splendid in theory as a means of creating massive promotional impact while apportioning advertising expenditures among a number of stores. However, as we noted earlier, this sometimes aroused severe competitive reactions, and at some point the cluster concept could be carried too far: new Korvette stores began to hurt older Korvette stores in the same metropolitan area.

Another major troublesome factor was the image of Korvette: Ferkauf was not content with it. In the early golden days of the chain, the discount image—bare-bones prices—had great customer appeal. However, as Korvette expanded with more stores and into soft goods and fashion items, Ferkauf's conception of the company changed. He saw it no longer as a discount store, but rather as a promotional department store. In line with this, he opened a store on Fifth Avenue in Manhattan, only a few blocks from some of the most fashionable stores in the world, such as Bonwit Teller and Lord & Taylor. A massive chandelier was placed in the lobby, indicative of the disavowal with the "sordid discount" image. "We have Cadillacs that pull up to the store, the women get out and enjoy, as everybody enjoys, being able to buy something a little bit cheaper than they normally would. We have some of the most famous people come in to our stores."[5] Alas, Ferkauf's dreams were short-lived.

Management problems began surfacing as the company tried to upgrade. Korvette had started from a hard-goods base. Ferkauf and his associates had no experience in merchandising soft lines and fashion goods, and they were slow in recruiting people who had. As this upgrading of merchandise proceeded, markups rose strikingly: from less than 8 percent in 1950 to some 33 percent in 1965. The problem was, if Korvette was to escape the discount image, how could they do so and yet keep their old customers. Korvette was becoming similar to the basement operations of department stores—that is, carrying standard markup items supplemented by loss leaders used for promotional purposes. As merchandise was upgraded, as new stores were more elaborate, as services such as credit began to be offered, higher overhead was the result. The uniqueness, the particular

---

[5]Per an interview with Murray Beilenson, secretary and general merchandise manager, as reported in Robert Drew-Bear, *Mass Merchandise: Revolution and Evolution* (New York: Fairchild Publications, 1970), p. 124.

customer segment that had been so effectively appealed to, began to be lost. Gradually Korvette was moving toward the expense structure of traditional retailers, but without quite the same level of expertise that department and specialty stores possessed in the way of quality and fashion merchandising.

External Factors

With Korvette leading the way, the onslaught of discounters onto the conventional retail scene in the 1950s and early 1960s was traumatic; some called it the revolution in retailing. However, by the mid-1960s, other retailers had been exposed to discount competition for some ten years. Many were beginning to counter it, and even to act aggressively against discounters. Department stores and appliance retailers had blunted the initial competitive advantage of discounters either by matching them price for price on identical goods, or else by stocking their own private branded appliances and other items that prevented price comparisons. Many retailers had shifted parts of their operations to self service and had eliminated some of the frills that made their operations high cost. And the major advantage that discounters had of relying on high merchandise turnover to yield a good return on investment despite low markups was being copied to some extent by other retailers. Meantime, average costs and markups were rising for all discounters. The result, predictably, was that customers no longer streamed to just any discount store. Discount firms such as Tower Marts International, Grayson–Robinson Stores, Marrud, John's Bargain Stores, and smaller firms that expanded too rapidly were in financial jeopardy.

As the discount-store industry began maturing in the 1960s, other kinds of discounters came on the scene: well-financed, well-managed companies who swept away marginal competitors. K-mart, the discount subsidiary of S. S. Kresge Company, began what was to become the world's largest discount operation, tightly run, having highly paid store management, a carefully supervised training program (recruiting college graduates), and with solid financial resources behind it. Major department-store corporations, such as Dayton–Hudson, L. S. Ayres, Federated, and Allied Stores, opened discount subsidiaries, again carefully run with well-trained, high-caliber personnel, and with definitive policies. These latter discount stores had the advantage of years of experience with apparel and fashion merchandising due to their mother firms. And they were content to be discount stores. They grew slowly, carefully, testing the water, experimenting to find the best way.

WHAT CAN BE LEARNED?

The dilemma that confronted Korvette was not unique by any means among the discounters of the day. Rising on a wave of consumer enchantment with lower prices (and the self-service and parking convenience of the discount stores), many small chain owners found themselves with a few successful stores and developed grandiose plans for expansion. Many thus overextended themselves, financially and managerially, and were in trouble. The difference with Korvette was that the attained size was much greater than most of its contemporaries before problems began to overwhelm it. Largely, this is a credit to the work load of a peripatetic Ferkauf, who was able to directly supervise a rather large number of stores before it became too much for him.

But the experience of Korvette and the smaller discount store casualties points to the need for *controlled growth*. Usually this means a slower, more carefully planned growth. Objectives, policies, and management and financial controls should be well defined. In particular, lines of authority and performance measures should be specified—who is responsible for what, and how is performance to be measured?

Only when there is controlled growth is it likely that a seasoned and strong management team can be available so that experienced merchandising, buying, shipping, and accounting departments can function smoothly. In developing the most effective operation, some testing usually is necessary so that adjustments and modifications can be made where needed. Without time to sit back and analyze past successes and failures, a firm really is proceeding with a blind expansion. Faults are undetected in time and are uncorrected; strengths or areas of potential opportunity are not pinpointed and acted upon. For example, a well-run discount operation needs strong and well thought-out policies regarding store security (since with self-service and fewer employees per customer than traditional stores, shoplifting and employee theft are more tempting) and the control of waste and shrinkage.

For an organization desiring the most rapid expansion, there are strong arguments for a decentralized management. Most discounters, such as Zayre, Spartans, and Korvette, were centralized with home office executives having major authority for most policies and decisions regarding store operation and merchandise. In the most extreme cases, the store manager only "carries the keys"; that is, he is responsible for opening and closing the store, seeing that adequate workers are on hand, store maintenance, and display and other dictates of the home office. He has little opportunity to exert initiative and accordingly is neither well paid nor very high caliber.

One of the most successful examples of rapid growth in retailing was that of the J. C. Penney Company. As described in chapter nine, Penney's achieved this fantastic growth without sacrificing either operational effectiveness or strong managerial resources through one of the strongest uses of decentralized management in the history of retailing.

A few discount firms, notably K-mart, decentralized and gave their store managers much more authority over operations and merchandising. These managers were well trained (seven to ten years before becoming K-mart managers, versus one to two years for some discount chains) and well paid.

Upgrading an image to one of more prestige and quality is never easily done, and can rarely be accomplished without a commitment to perhaps years of costly effort. Such efforts for a retailer will necessarily involve heavy advertising, costly refurbishing, heavy investment in inventory, and a willingness to endure sizable markdowns—all these a drain on profits in the not-at-all-assured expectation that in years to come profits will be the greater.

In addition to the cost constraints, two other problems lurk for the retailer attempting to upgrade. More than likely the present staff will not be able adequately to merchandise the higher quality efforts. New people will be needed to provide the expertise required. This can present recruiting problems as well as increasing staffing costs. So, this brings more drain on profits for the indefinite future.

But a further caveat is in order. In trying to upgrade, a firm may lose the old bargain-conscious customers without gaining significantly from other customer segments. Hence, a firm must weigh the risks versus the rewards in such a strategy change. This is a decision of no small moment, be the firm a retailer or a manufacturer.

Update

Did the Arlen's acquisition of Korvette from Spartans bring the discount chain back to the marketplace as an aggressive and progressive factor? Sadly, not at all. Its momentum had been lost, never to be regained. Under Arlen's, Korvettes continued trying to convince customers that it was no longer a discount chain but rather a "quality promotional department store." It succeeded only in confusing customers about its identity.[6] In the years after the Arlen's acquisition, Korvettes either lost money or barely broke even. Eventually, Arlen had to pick up a $7.7 million tab for the Korvette loss sustained in closing its furniture and carpet departments.

In early 1979, Korvettes experienced its third transfer of control. Arlen was able to sell a majority 51 percent interest in the Korvettes 50-unit chain to a French retail and manufacturing group, Agache–Willot, for $30 million. The new ownership expressed its approval of a policy of changing the image

----

[6]For more detail, see "Arlen's Dream Versus Korvettes' Reality," *Forbes*, April 15, 1977, p. 85–93.

of the Korvettes operation from just low prices to fashion quality at reasonable prices.[7] The approval and satisfaction of Agache–Willot with their acquisition was not long-lasting. Continued losses and cash crises plagued the retailer and bankruptcy was threatened in 1980 before the French parent agreed to restructure $55 million of debt to institutional lenders. The decision was made to gradually liquidate the company, and by the middle of 1981 only twelve stores were still owned and they were in the process of being sold. Now Korvette, the pioneer discounter, is little more than a memory.

In contrast, K-mart, which had caught the discount ball repudiated by Korvette and was running with it, had climbed to become the number two nonfood retailer in the United States, behind only Sears.

For Thought and Discussion

1. Why did Korvette have such difficulty competing with fashion goods when it was so successful with appliances and other hard goods?
2. We have noted that one of the serious problems Korvette faced during its rapid growth was a lack of adequate systems and procedures, particularly regarding feedback and controls from the stores. What controls or performance measures would you want to have established in this situation?
3. Personal supervision by Ferkauf was possible when he had only a small number of stores in a limited area. With steady expansion, such personal supervision was no longer possible. What might have been done at this point to assure adequate supervision of stores?
4. What image do you think Korvette should have tried to develop, and what was the best way to do this? Critically evaluate the various alternatives.

Invitation to Role Play

1. Place yourself in the role of Eugene Ferkauf, a tremendous innovator and leader of the discount movement. You have just been proclaimed by famed educator Malcolm McNair as one of the six greatest merchants in U.S. history. You are humble, yet ecstatic at this honor. Now to prove it. How? Be as specific as possible.
2. Place yourself in the role of assistant store manager of one of the Chicago-area Korvette stores. Your particular responsibility is the fashion division of the store: women's dresses, coats, sportswear, and accessories. To date, despite an adequate stock of popular fashions (these are mostly lower-priced replicas of

---

[7]"Arlen Realty Says It Agrees to sell 51% of Korvettes," *Wall Street Journal*, October 26, 1978, p. 18.

expensive styles), this merchandise is just not selling. Develop a recommendation for what you think it would take to make this division most successful. Then, recognizing the constraints of selling fashion merchandise in a discount store, develop modified recommendations that are more likely to be practical and acceptable to higher management.

CHAPTER 6

A. C. Gilbert Company— Tearing Down a Quality Image

A. C. Gilbert Company was not a youngster, having had some fifty-eight years of toymaking experience at the time it failed. For years its products had filled a definite market niche. Its name was respected, well known, and signified quality.

In a few years all this was to end. Almost incredibly, bad marketing replaced the solid achievements of the past. Changing market conditions were ignored for too long. Then rash, frantic decisions were substituted for a well-planned, corrective marketing strategy that would build on the strengths of the company. The result was self-destruction of the public image, and shortly, dissolution of the company.

BACKGROUND

The A. C. Gilbert Company was the product of one imaginative man's inventiveness and the willingness to back his ideas himself rather than selling out. Alfred Carlton Gilbert, after graduating from Yale, established the Mysto Manufacturing Company in 1909 to make the Erector set, which he had perfected. In 1916 this company became the A. C. Gilbert Company. In time, the son, A. C. Jr., joined the company as assistant to his father, and became president in 1954. In 1961 the senior Gilbert died, and the son became chairman of the board. Gilbert Jr. was a respected figure in the toy industry, serving as president of the Toys Manufacturers of the U.S.A. in 1962–1963.

While the company never became a large firm, it was firmly in the top ten of toy manufacturers in the 1950s, with sales reaching over $17 million. It was strong in science toys—chemistry sets, microscopes, and Erector "engineering" sets—at a time when science was becoming important as a national priority. Gilbert had the reputation of a quality toymaker, and its American Flyer trains and Erector sets were known by generations of boys and their fathers.

This was the situation as the company entered the 1960s. However, the environment of toy marketing was changing. The 1960s, with their attendant prosperity, brought a booming toy market. But it was different from what Gilbert was familiar with. A new promotional medium, television, had become important for toy marketing and was superseding catalogs and window displays. But television was expensive and made the breakeven point on toy sales much higher. It also enabled many items, from hula hoops to Batmobiles, to attain quick popularity. The market was fast changing, and a firm had to be nimble to tap the sales potential and not be caught with too heavy an inventory when demand was superseded by another fad item.

The toy market was also changing in that the traditional toy stores, hobby shops, and department stores were being bypassed for self-service, high-volume supermarkets and discount stores. These new dealers were mainly interested in low-priced, heavily advertised toys with attractive packages that could act as selling tools.

So the old successful, well-entrenched company entered the 1960s rather complacent and content with the status quo.

PROBLEMS

Anson Isaacson, president of Gilbert, had a desperate task before him. In April of 1966 he was searching frantically among financial circles to raise the money needed to operate another year, after suffering losses of $2.9 million in 1965.

Mr. Isaacson had assumed the presidency in June 1964, after A. C. Gilbert Jr. died. He was a former vice president of Ideal Toy Company, a larger toymaker, and had been brought into the company to straighten out serious sales and profit problems that had been getting worse since 1961.

After three weeks of scouring for financial aid, Anson Isaacson was successful. Pledging most of the remaining unpledged assets of the company, he was able to obtain a loan of $6.25 million, of which he himself put up $250,000 to show creditors his faith in the company and his confidence in his ability to straighten out the problems. There was one frightening stipulation in the loan agreement, however. The loan was contingent on the company's making a profit in 1966. If Gilbert failed to do so, the loan would be called and the assets liquidated to satisfy the indebtedness. Isaacson was not bargaining from a position of strength and had to accept the condition. Although he did feel that under his management the condition would not pose a particular problem, still it lurked in the background, ominous and threatening.

PRELUDE

Now let us examine how Gilbert got into his mess. The company did not really recognize a problem until the end of 1961, at which time sales dropped from $12.6 million in 1960 to $11.6 million. In 1961 the company counted a mere $20,011 in profits. Now the company was obviously facing serious problems, and a program was hastily devised to correct the situation.

In early 1962, with stock prices down, the company became attractive to Jack Wrather, president of a West Coast holding company that owned the "Lassie" and "Lone Ranger" television programs, the Disneyland Hotel, Muzak Corporation (piped-in music), and a boatyard. He acquired a 52 percent interest in the Gilbert Company for some $4 million. He then replaced Gilbert top executives with his own men. While A. C. Gilbert Jr. remained as board chairman, his power was substantially lessened.

The 1961 sales drop was attributed to two factors: insufficient new products and insufficient advertising. Plans were formulated to boost sales to $20 million with the addition of new, "hot items." The sales staff was increased 50 percent, since more aggressive selling and more frequent contacts with retailers were assumed to be directly correlated with increasing sales. With an expanded sales staff, a new general sales manager and a new director of international sales were appointed.

But this marketing strategy proved of no avail. In 1962, sales dropped to $10.9 million, with a $281,000 loss. This loss was attributed to the cost of preparing the new, greatly expanded 1963 line and the scrapping of obsolete materials. The company was pinning its great expectations on the 1963 selling season. A major effort had been made to expand the line. For the first time, the company was offering toys for pre-school children, and for girls in the six-to-fourteen-year-old bracket in addition to boys, who had been the traditional market segment. More than 50 new items boosted the line to 307 items, by far the largest in the company's history. The ambitious expansion program seemed fully justified and badly needed; now the market was 35 million boys and girls, instead of just 9 million boys.

Modern Packaging magazine hailed the package revitalization program in 1963.[1] Upwards of $1 million was spent to repackage the entire line. Packages for Erector sets and the other long-established toys had been virtually unchanged for many years; now they were given an "exciting" new full-color pictorial treatment illustrating the models in action.

The future looked bright at this time, and such an aggressive marketing approach was viewed as badly overdue in an old, conservatively-managed family business. Officials confidently predicted record sales and earnings.

It must have been a bitter pill when sales results finally came in (in the toy business, the Christmas selling season is crucial for the year's performance: until the results of this business season are tabulated late in the year, no one really knows how successful a year has been). Incredibly, sales continued to slide in 1963, to $10.7 million; worse, instead of a profit, there was a whopping $5.7 million loss, stemming mostly from huge returns of low-priced toys shipped on a guaranteed sale basis to supermarkets. After Christmas, Gilbert had an inventory of almost $3.5 million of unsold toys.

Corrective Efforts

At this point, Jack Wrather decided that a toymaking company needed more expert toymaking experience. He fired most of the top management he had brought in nearly two years before. A. C. Gilbert Jr. reassumed the presidency, but Anson Isaacson, former Ideal Toy Company vice president, was brought in as chief operating officer and chairman of the executive committee.

In two years, losses had reached almost $6 million. This was a terrible drain on a firm whose revenues were not much more than $10 million a year. But loans were renegotiated at higher interest rates, and major creditors agreed to a delay in payment over a three-year period. After the last several years of profligate expansion of sales staff and product lines, Isaacson began a strong economy drive.

He made a major change in the selling mechanism. In place of company salesmen, he fired the sales staff and switched to manufacturers' representatives. Manufacturers' representatives are independent sales representatives who handle a number of noncompeting lines of various manufacturers and charge a fixed commission, usually 5 or 6 percent on all sales made. They are somewhat less expensive than a company sales force and should be able to contact more dealers. Gilbert had less control over them, however, and their customer service for Gilbert could be erratic. In addition, major

---

[1]"Saving a $500,000 Investment," *Modern Packaging*, August 1963, pp 97–98.

cuts were made in factory personnel with the result that administrative and operating expenses were reduced from $10 million to $4.7 million for 1964. In June of 1964, A. C. Gilbert Jr. died, and Mr. Wrather became chairman of the board and Mr. Isaacson president.

For the 1964 Christmas season, 20 new toys were added to the depleted line. Encouragingly, sales picked up almost 7 percent, to $11.4 million. The company would have registered a profit for the year, but Isaacson insisted on dumping excess inventory in order to enhance future years' profits, so a loss was registered of $1,900,000.

The expectations of Isaacson and the Gilbert Company now rested on the fall and Christmas selling season of 1965. This was to be the year the company turned around and reached for its new potential. To this end, the product line was again revamped and a heavy advertising and point-of-purchase display program budgeted. Television advertising centered on a 52-week schedule of Saturday morning Beatles cartoon shows, and $2 million was committed for this. In addition, the Gilbert Company furnished some 65,000 animated displays free to dealers at a cost of $1 million.

Early indications for 1965 were favorable. By July, Isaacson predicted a net profit for the year. The order backlog was $12 million in July, and losses for the first six months of the year (toymakers characteristically incur losses through most of the year until the peak Christmas business is realized) were only half those for the same period in 1964.

Isaacson's optimistic prediction, however, proved wrong. The heavy promotional expenditures did bring sales of $14.9 million, the best since the early 1950s, and a 30 percent increase over the preceding year. However, losses were up to $2.9 million, mostly due to heavy returns on a 007 auto racing set, which was then handled exclusively by Sears, as well as other racing sets. These racing sets turned out to be poorly engineered and constructed, poorly packaged, and overpriced.

As the company's financial condition continued to worsen, Anson Isaacson began his rounds to find the financing necessary to keep the company alive. The multi-million dollar rescue loan that he finally obtained made virtually all the assets subject to liens to secure such indebtedness and was contingent on the company's making a profit in 1966.

It did not make a profit in 1966. Instead, the announced loss was $12,872,000. The once proud A. C. Gilbert Company went out of business in February 1967. Gabriel Industries acquired certain of Gilbert's assets, including erector sets and chemistry sets, for about $17 million. This was paid to the financial institutions holding Gilbert's indebtedness.

Figure 6.1 depicts Gilbert's last six years.

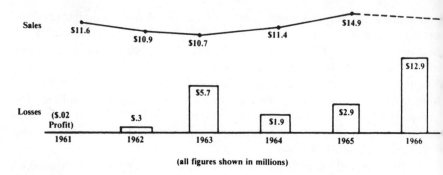

(all figures shown in millions)

Figure 6.1.

HOW DID IT HAPPEN?

We can group the mistakes that Gilbert made into two broad categories: lack of recognition of the problem until late, and frantic reactions once the problem was recognized, resulting in successive mistakes until the end. Each of these will be discussed in more detail, and the specific mistakes under these categories identified.

Gilbert failed to recognize that the toy environment was changing, and that the changes were causing an ever-worsening problem. Diminishing sales from the peak years of the 1950s apparently did not alert the company that there was a problem needing investigation and some adjustment in marketing strategy.

We have previously noted how major changes in advertising and distribution of toys were occurring and were only belatedly recognized by Gilbert. One change in toy demand that should have been quickly detected was that table-top slot-car auto racing sets, almost unknown ten years before, were now outselling toy trains. Gilbert should have been in this market near the outset. Instead, not until the mid-1960s were its racing sets introduced. And these were poorly engineered, fragile, and overpriced, and their returns in 1965 practically scuttled the company.

Apparently not until the end of the 1961 selling season, when the company barely made a profit, was there any awareness of a possible problem. At this point, frantic and poorly thought-out actions were commenced. With the serious loss of 1962, there was no longer any doubt that there was a problem.

Frantic actions took place with the product line. This had remained relatively unchanged for decades. Suddenly in one year the line was greatly expanded—more than fifty new toys were added, not only directed to the traditional target market of six-to-fourteen-year-old boys, but now also for girls and for pre-school children. Furthermore, the toys were different from what the company had been used to making—lower priced, lower quality, and geared to large-volume sales. This placed great strains on the company's engineering and production capabilities. The almost inevitable result was poorly designed toys of not very good quality and of disappointing customer appeal. More than this, the company's unique niche as a quality toy-maker of high-level educational toys was abandoned, and the company flung itself into the fiercely competitive marketplace against better experienced and mostly larger competitors.

Subsequent actions did nothing to restore the image of the reputable toymaker. A company and brand image is precious; a good image is not easily developed but can be torn down rather quickly.

Toy buyers were critical of the company's product changes and of its packaging:

> Gilbert had a natural in its Erector sets. Instead they neglected it. They used to offer sets up to $75 packaged in metal boxes. Now the most expensive is only $20, the parts are flimsy, and it's in an oversized cardboard box. They did the same thing to their chemistry sets. You can't store anything in those oversize see-through packages.[2]

Gilbert had high hopes for its new All Aboard series, consisting of landscaped panels that fit together to form a tabletop train layout. But:

> It's a real good idea, but the quality is poor. The locomotive and cars are cheap and lack detail.[3]

Gilbert's doll series was overpriced, poorly made, and incomplete because no changes of clothes were offered. This was at the time when additional wardrobes were the major appeal of many dolls, as well as a source of extra profits.

Incredibly poor timing was the lot of the company in attempting to compete with fad items. For example, in 1965, spy items were especially popular, with spy and secret agent movies and television series having high audience ratings. So Gilbert introduced such spy figures as Man from U.N.C.L.E., James Bond, and Honey West. The only trouble was that they did not reach the market until after Christmas Day in 1965, obviously too late for the selling season. While such timing was inexcusable and reflected

---

[2]"Toymaker A. C. Gilbert Co., Poor Loser?" *Sales Management,* May 1, 1966, p. 27.
[3]Ibid., p. 28.

drastic problems in the planning and operations of the company, the ground
was laid for this situation in 1964.

Successive errors were piled on each other. After the ill-conceived
product line expansion of 1963 that resulted in $5.7 million in losses, an

---

INFORMATION SIDELIGHT

USE OF MANUFACTURERS' REPRESENTATIVES vs.
A COMPANY SALES FORCE

While the switching of Gilbert to manufacturers' reps is cited as a
drawback, we should recognize that such independent representives pose
some specific advantages to a firm over having its own sales force.

These independent reps are paid on a straight commission for sales,
often 6 percent. This makes selling costs entirely variable, rising or falling
with revenue. In contrast, a company-owned sales force has such fixed
costs as sales managers' salaries, home and branch office overhead, and
base salaries of salespeople, in addition to travel and entertainment
expenses. These costs remain constant whether sales are up or down;
commissions and bonuses would, of course, be variable.

Independent representatives also give a company considerable flexibility. During periods of rising sales, more reps can be used; during
periods of falling sales, retrenchment is easier than with a company-
owned sales force. Furthermore, when there are seasonal differences in
demand for a firm's products, reps are a logical preference, since a
company's sales force may not be effectively utilized during slack
periods.

Some argue that independent sales reps can actually provide better
sales production than company salespeople. Since they contact the same
customers with products of a number of manufacturers, sales calls are
more economical; the cost is spread over several products. These reps
may also have more stature in the eyes of their customers because of the
breadth of their lines and the fact that they may handle several important
product lines for the customer. Generally, these reps tend to be experienced and competent salespeople. Of course, a firm has less control over
such independent operators; but control is not altogether lacking, since
the threat to take away a well-received line of merchandise unless
performance improves is seldom taken lightly by the independent rep.
However, if the product line or brand does not sell well, then such a threat
would receive little attention.

austerity campaign was put in effect in 1964, with major cutbacks made in engineering and production—expenses were consequently reduced more han 50 percent for 1964. But such austerity hardly led to the planning and production efficiencies needed for the quick introduction of fad items. Other aspects of the austerity were less obvious but consequential. The company switched from having its own sales force to contracting for independent manufacturers' representatives to handle its selling efforts. While this move was expected to increase dealer coverage while not adding to the cost of selling, dealers did not like the new arrangement: "It used to be that you could call a Gilbert salesman and get service on a problem. Now he reps just want to get the order," disgruntled dealers were saying.[4]

In attempting to widen its distribution to supermarkets, discount stores, and other aggressive promotional retailers, Gilbert made certain concessions that were to cost dearly, such as guaranteeing the sales of its products to some of these demanding outlets. By guaranteeing sales, the company assumed the burden of poor selling efforts, markdowns, and product write-offs of anything unsold after the Christmas season. Guaranteeing sales is usually a last ditch effort by a new manufacturer trying to gain entry in the marketplace. Offering an unknown brand, such a supplier is totally dependent on retailers and may be forced to accept the conditions demanded by some. Gilbert was not a small unknown firm trying to crack the marketplace. In 1963, it still had a quality image, was widely known, and had good distribution, even though not as wide as desired.

A final dramatic mistake came in 1965. After the austerity of 1964, the spigots were reopened and with a vengeance. More new toys were added. Of more significance, a massive television advertising campaign and point-of-purchase display program were instituted. Here was a company with sales of just over $11 million facing the specter of insolvency; yet almost 30 percent of sales was budgeted for a massive promotion effort. The lack of success, due to poor judgment of products, of distribution, and of timing, laid the groundwork for the demise of the company. The image of a reliable producer of high-quality toys had been lost. The $6.25 million last-resort financing that Isaacson managed to come up with in 1966 could no longer support the company's efforts to regain a viable niche in the market.

WHAT CAN BE LEARNED?

Perhaps the first thing to be learned from the experience of Gilbert is that it does not take long for a supposedly healthy and long-experienced company

[4]Ibid.

to come to its end. A series of successive bad decisions coming in the space
of a few years can destroy all the gains built up by decades of successful
marketing. And the inexcusable self-destruction of the quality image paved
the way. We are left to shudder at how quickly a good reputation can be lost
can be torn down, while we know from the Korvette case the difficulty of
building up an image. These should be sobering thoughts for any organiza
tion.

Certainly the need for better attention to and sensoring of the market
place is evident. While marketing research could have been of help to the
Gilbert Company in better assessing changing conditions both in consumer
demand and in competitive actions, this probably was not essential. What
was needed was alert and cognizant executives working with certain control
or measuring tools such as market share analysis. The changes occurring
were not difficult to detect; they were obvious to all, consumers, retailers
manufacturers alike. But Gilbert continued to operate as if the status quo
could be maintained, as if the market were unchanging. If nothing else, this
case should point out the need to be constantly alert and responsive to
change.

But a firm must also beware of reacting too quickly, without careful
analysis of alternatives. Problems need to be carefully identified, and
probable solutions or adjustments to them weighed in view of the particular
strengths and resources of the firm. In Gilbert's case, hasty actions only
compounded past mistakes. To be specific, the major strength of the firm
was its quality image; this should not have been sacrificed to hastily bring
out a proliferation of "cheap" new products similar to competitors'. By
expanding hastily with new products, the capabilities of the company were
disregarded, and a flood of poorly made products resulted.

Mistakes on top of mistakes; frantic actions leading to more frantic
actions and to disastrous decisions. Few company have made as many
successive bad decisions as those evinced by Gilbert.

Update

While the Gilbert Company has folded, never to return to life, happily we
can note that the Erector set has survived. As described earlier, Gabriel
Industries, a large toy manufacturer that also makes Tinker Toys, acquired
the Erector asset at the liquidation of Gilbert. In 1977, nearly 600,000
Erector sets, ranging in price from $1 for a 45-piece pocket set to $40 for a
deluxe 450-piece set, were sold around the world.

In August of 1978, Gabriel and its Erector set subsidiary were pur
chased by CBS for $27.1 million. The senior vice president of Gabriel

predicted: "A hundred years from now, I think you'll still be able to buy an Erector set . . . long after everyone here is gone."[5]

For Thought and Discussion

1. What controls should Gilbert have had to remain alert to changing market conditions? What research would have helped?
2. Do you think Gilbert was right in expanding its target market in 1963? Why or why not?
3. Evaluate the advertising efforts of 1965. The point-of-purchase display expenditures.
4. Discuss the pros and cons of changing management quickly when adversity sets in.

Invitation to Role Play

1. As an assistant to the president, what would you have advised Gilbert to do at the end of 1961 when the first drastic decline in profit (to a $20,011 profit) occurred?
2. As a management consultant, what would you have advised at the end of 1963?

[5]"The Nuts and Bolts of Erector Set Firm," *Cleveland lain Dealer*, September 10, 1978, Sec. 2-1.

Two

FALLACY OF CONSERVATISM

CHAPTER 7

The Gillette Company— Painful Procrastination, 1962–1963

Even firms whose past performances have been beyond reproach, and whose profits are the envy of American industry, can succumb to mistakes and leave themselves vulnerable to competitive inroads, inroads that need never have happened. In the early 1960s, venerable Gillette erred in assessing the impact of a new product in its industry: the stainless steel blade. It was reluctant to cannibalize (take sales away from) the major product in its line, the Super Blue blade, and procrastinated in introducing its own stainless steel blade. It thereby gave competitors the opportunity to wrest away some of its dominance. The result was a loss in market share never to be fully regained. How could such a thing happen to a shrewd and aggressive firm, a marketing specialist?

THE PROFIT MACHINE, 1962

Through the years, the Gillette Company had compiled one of the best profit records in American industry. In 1962, the company racked up its fourth consecutive record year, with sales of $276 million and net earnings of $45 million–a profit margin of 16.4 percent. This was the fourth best return on sales of all corporations on *Fortune*'s list of the 500 largest industrial corporations. Even more noteworthy, Gillette was number one in return on invested capital, with a whopping 40 percent—no other major firm in the U.S. could claim such profitability.

In its primary business of manufacturing and selling razor blades Gillette dominated the market. In 1962 it had 70 percent of the $175 million retail blade market, up from 40 percent of an $86 million blade market in 1946. Of the total razor blade market, single-edge and injector blades accounted for 25 percent, while the double-edge segment was 75 percent of the market. And in this important double-edge segment, Gillette was ever more dominant, holding an awesome 90 percent share of the market.

It is not surprising, then, that as a result of this market share and profit performance the company had no debt of any kind. About 30 percent of its assets, some $56 million, were in cash and marketable securities. With highly automated machinery, efficiency and production costs continued to improve. For example, in 1952, 850 blades per man-hour were produced; by 1961, Gillette improved to 3100 blades per man-hour. A sharp eye was also

---

INFORMATION SIDELIGHT

THE KEY INDICATOR OF PROFITABILITY: RETURN ON INVESTMENT

The true measure of the profitability of any investment is the return—the interest, dividends, or profits—we get for the money invested. This is true whether the money is in a savings and loan association paying 5½ percent interest or in a business, where it may realize more. But note that in the examples below return on investment is not the same as net profit percentage of sales.

	Firm A	Firm B
Sales	$100,000,000	$100,000,000
Investment in plant and equipment, inventories, etc.	30,000,000	90,000,000
Net profit %	10%	12%
Net profit dollars	10,000,000	12,000,000
Return on investment (profit divided by investment)	33%	13/33%

In this example, Firm A is much the more profitable despite its lower net profit as compared with Firm B, since the money needed to be invested in the plant, equipment, raw materials and other inventories, etc., is so much less than that required for Firm B.

kept on other costs, such as packaging costs, which accounted for about half the factory costs of blades—all this while maintaining rigid quality control. The Super Blue blade was the heart of the Gillette blade line, the top of the line, by far the biggest profit maker, and the one most sought after by consumers. The more economy-minded customers used the Thin or the Blue blade, both of which had been on the market much longer. The Super Blue was introduced in 1960 after five years of laboratory research aimed at developing a silicone coating that would prevent hair molecules from clinging to the blade and thereby impeding the cutting. The much easier shaving with the Super Blue resulted in its immediate success, even though it was priced 40 percent higher than the old Blue blade. Despite the silicone coating and some necessary heat treatment, the production costs of the Super Blue were not appreciably higher than for the other blades. The Super Blue soon had a major impact on Gillette's profits. In 1962 it contributed some $15 million in profits, more than one-third of the company's total net profit.

As we come into the 1960s, two men were in charge of the company. Carl Gilbert had been chief executive since 1956. Silver-haired, genial, calm and thoughtful, his areas of specialization were manufacturing and finance. The second man was Boone Gross, direct descendant of Daniel Boone; he was a West Point graduate, and president of the company. He had joined Gillette in 1946 as general sales manager, at which time he had launched a program that tripled the sales force and increased sales of blades 150 percent in three years. In contrast to Gilbert, he was dark-haired, aggressive, and restless, with expertise in sales and management.

EARLY HISTORY OF THE GILLETTE COMPANY

In the winter of 1901, a salesman named King C. Gillette and several associates rented a room over a fish market in Boston where they could make a shaving device invented by Gillette: a safety razor with thin replaceable blades. This was a far handier shaving tool than the old straight-edge razor that could even be used as a weapon. However, the results that first year were not very encouraging; only 51 razors and 163 blades were sold. But things slowly improved, until by 1917 annual razor sales were over one million with 120 million blades being sold a year.

Then the United States entered World War I. Now almost the entire output of the Boston factory went to the Armed Forces. Men who had never heard of a safety razor were issued a Gillette, and began to shave regularly. Most continued with the practice when they returned home after the war, rather than going back to their straight-edge razors or professional shaves by a barber. World War II introduced Gillette and self-shaving to millions more By 1961, the shaving population was 61 million people in the United States with 1.7 million new shavers entering the market every year. Four hundred twenty-six million dollars a year was being spent for razors, blades, electric shavers, shaving creams, lotions, and talcums. This did not include the rapidly growing overseas market, where rising living standards and populations suggested greater potential markets for shaving products than in the United States.

As the Gillette Company grew in size and industry dominance, it expanded its research and development activities. By 1960, over 80 scientists and technicians were engaged in fundamental and applied research. Out of the research program had come the blade dispenser, developed at the close of World War II, which did away with paper-wrapped blades and permitted insertion of the blade directly into the razor, thus eliminating most of the danger of being accidentally cut while handling a razor blade. The adjustable razor was brought out in 1957 and contributed to shaving comfort by permitting easy adjustment of blade angle and exposure to suit any combination of skin and beard. Then, in 1960, came the Super Blue blade. This was the company's first new blade product in twenty-one years and represented a major improvement in shaving ease (though not in blade longevity), by requiring 60 percent less cutting force for the average shaver than ordinary blades. Its edge was 750 times thinner than a page from a newspaper, so thin that it had to be measured by an electron microscope.

For decades the company's product line had been limited to safety razors, double-edged blades, and shaving cream. Then in 1948 it acquired the Toni Company, a leading manufacturer of women's hair preparations. Other acquisitions followed, most notably the Paper Mate Corporation in 1955. Although Gillette had marketed a brushless shaving cream in a tube for many years, it made a major thrust into the toiletries business with the introduction of Foamy Shave Cream in 1954, and Right Guard Deodorant in 1960.

In the heady days as the company moved into the 1960s, it could look ahead with complete optimism. With a new plant in Boston and facilities abroad, it had all the capacity it would need for razor blade production for years to come. Its market seemed secure, unless the whiskered look should suddenly become the universal mode, or unless some depilatory should be invented that would banish the need for razors and blades—and no depilatory was on the horizon that could remove whiskers without damage to sensitive facial skin tissue.

THE STAINLESS STEEL BLADE

Wilkinson: Just a Gnat

Wilkinson Sword, LTD, headquartered in Chiswick, a London suburb, was a family-owned firm of swordsmiths, some 190 years old in 1961. While the company made ceremonial swords, its principal interest was a line of expensive garden tools (for example, a pair of its pruning shears retailed for $12.75, and this was in the days before inflation). Almost incidentally, Wilkinson began making a stainless steel razor blade, the Super Sword-Edge. Properly manufactured, the stainless blade is sharp, corrosion-free, and long-lasting—some men were getting more than 15 shaves per blade, versus about 3½ shaves average for the regular carbon blades.

Of course, stainless steel blades cost more. Carbon steel strips, from which most double-edge blades were made, cost about $1900 a ton; the steel used for stainless blades about $3700 a ton. The manufacturing process itself was also more expensive. Grinding, stropping, special heat-treating, and quality control added to the costs and tended to limit production. Consequently, the Wilkinson blade was selling for 15 cents, versus about 6.9 cents for a Gillette Super Blue, 5 cents for the Blue, and 3.5 cents for the Thin.

In the summer of 1961, Wilkinson began marketing its tools in the United States. However, getting distribution for an unknown line that sold

---

INFORMATION SIDELIGHT

DIFFICULTY IN GAINING MARKET ENTRY

A new firm, or an established firm attempting to market a new, unrelated line of products, frequently faces problems in getting dealers to handle its goods. The more aggressive dealers already have strong relationships with established producers, and are naturally reluctant to take on distribution for a competitive brand, and an unknown one at that. The manufacturer in such a dilemma may be forced to offer such inducements as consignment (which Wilkinson did) or guaranteed sales:

Consignment—the manufacturer keeps title of the goods until they are sold by the dealer, thereby bearing all the risks and inventory costs.

Guaranteed sales—similar to consignment in that anything unsold or selling too slowly in the opinion of the dealer can be returned to the vendor. The difference is that the dealer takes title or ownership when the goods are placed in his stock, thereby committing funds for inventory and assuming such risks as fire and flood damage.

for two to three times American prices was difficult, at best. Wilkinson finally convinced some dealers and distributors to stock its products by placing the tools in garden shops on consignment. In November 1961, the Wilkinson U.S. sales subsidiary got the first trickle of stainless steel razor blades from England. These were mentioned in promotional letters to the dealers, and there was an immediate reaction. By the spring of 1962, dealers were clamoring for more blades. Some were giving them away one at a time to customers for promotional purposes; others were selling them as fast as they could get them. About this time, a few small entrepreneurs who supplied sundries to tobacconists and druggists wandered into the cramped New York City sales office and cajoled a few cartons of blades for resale. Macy's also heard about the blade and took six cartons a week.

As the blades moved irresistibly into distribution, word-of-mouth spread. Retail stocks were soon exhausted. Now a new distribution policy was instituted. Blades henceforth were to be available only through authorized dealers, and to be authorized a dealer had to also stock the Wilkinson garden tool line. Consequently, garden supply shops and suburban hardware stores remained practically the only "authorized dealers" of Wilkinson blades. These stainless steel blades, then, in the midst of an insatiable demand, became the supreme promotional leader: customers were drawn to the garden shops—the only places they could get the blades—and they were sold the garden tools. As Wilkinson admitted, the profit on the blades was not very large; on the other hand, the tools were very profitable indeed.[1]

So, Wilkinson introduced the superior shaving product, stainless steel razor blades, to the market. By late 1962 it already had gained 15 percent of the British blade market, which Gillette previously had practically owned with a 75 percent market share. Now, almost in spite of itself, the U.S. market was practically begging for this scarce item. But Wilkinson was such a gnat. In fact, in 1962 it exported about seven million blades to the United States, less than one day's output of Gillette. It had limited blade manufacturing capacity and was without the necessary mass distribution channels. While Wilkinson intended to increase production, in no way was it in a position to match horns with the behemoth Gillette—nor, apparently, was it interested in doing so. But there were others who were!

U.S. Competitors: Hungry and Aggressive

While Wilkinson, despite its heavily-demanded new product, could hardly be depicted as either an aggressive competitor or a serious challenge to Gillette, the publicity the Wilkinson blade engendered was not lost on

[1]"Cheek by Trowel," *Business Week,* December 22, 1962, p. 82.

Gillette's smaller and relatively unprosperous U.S. competitors. Indeed, the lack of interest by Gillette gave them the opening wedge they needed: a chance to bring out a stainless steel blade before Gillette. Little Eversharp, Inc., with assets of $20 million, was already exploiting the opening. On January 26, 1963, it began marketing a stainless steel blade, priced at five for 79 cents, under its Schick "Krona Plus" label in New York City and eleven western states. "We're in heavy production," said its chairman, Patrick J. Frawley, Jr., "and we've already started shipping"[2] With 1962 sales of only $24.5 million against Gillette's sales of $276 million, this would hardly seem a formidable competitor. But . . .

Another competitor out to exploit the stainless steel breakthrough was the American Safety Razor division of Philip Morris. Its plans were to introduce its Personna, a stainless steel blade, in the early spring. "This will give us entry into the double-edge blade business which we have never been in before. We expect a tremendous improvement," proclaimed its president.[3]

Gillette's Position re Stainless Steel Blades, 1962–1963

So, where were Gillette's stainless blades? Why were its competitors given this opportunity? Boone Gross, Gillette's president, stoutly stated "We are not inclined to use crash programs."[4] Technological reasons, particularly the production problems in getting a stainless steel blade into the kind of mass production Gillette needed, were cited for the delay. The company claimed, for instance, that it was much harder to get a proper cutting edge on a stainless steel blade than on a carbon steel blade, and that the rejection rate would consequently be considerably higher.

Chairman Gilbert admitted that the company did not particularly like having to put a stainless blade on the market at that time: "We're doing it primarily as a response. When other people come in, we have to join. But we wouldn't have chosen this route."[5] Part of the bearish thinking came from the fear that the Gillette stainless blade, although priced higher than the company's other blades, would yield so many more good shaves that the customer would end up spending less per shave—buying far less blades—

---

[2]"Close Shave," *Forbes,* February 1, 1963, p. 14.
[3]Ibid., p. 15.
[4]"Women! God Bless 'Em," *Forbes,* May 15, 1965, p. 26.
[5]Walter Guzzardi, Jr., "Gillette Faces the Stainless Steel Dragon," *Fortune,* July 1963, p. 240.

thereby bringing Gillette's profits down. There was particular fear that the highly profitable Super Blue blade would be adversely affected—that its sales would be cannibalized.

Gillette's analysis of the situation involved three considerations other than the production and technological problems in starting up the mass production of the new blades:[6]

1. Cost to Gillette of the stainless blade, relative to the price it could obtain.
2. Durability of the blade.
3. Kind of customer most attracted to the stainless blade.

Undoubtedly there would be substantially higher costs in producing the new stainless steel blade. Not only would stainless steel costs be twice as much as carbon steel, but new production lines would have to be installed and there would have to be considerable training of technicians for the new process. However, some of these costs would be nonrecurring. The only cost that should continue to go higher would be the cost of the raw material the new type of steel. At the same time the raw material costs would be increased, packaging costs would decline somewhat. By packaging the new stainless blades in the same kind of dispenser now used for the Super Blue blade, fewer packages would be needed to put a year's blade supply in the hands of the consumer. With the selling price two to four times the price of Gillette's other blades, the profit per blade should be higher.

A somewhat more difficult estimate to make was the durability of the blade—i.e., how many shaves the average user would get from one stainless blade. If the average man used the blade for about eight shaves, which was twice as many as the average shaver got from a carbon-steel blade, then Gillette would fare well. It would be offering a new blade that would last twice as long as the Super Blue, that was priced twice as high, but that cost less than twice as much to make. On the other hand, if the average switcher from the Super Blue to the stainless blade used it for sixteen shaves—four times as many as the Super Blue—then Gillette's profits would drop by as much as 25 percent. Table 7.1 shows the effects of cannibalization on Gillette profits for several different rates of usage for the stainless blade. Gross and Gilbert could hardly be unconcerned, knowing that some of the early users were getting more than fifteen shaves from each blade, with some even gloating as to how many shaves they could eke out of a single blade, even to the point of sacrificing some comfort. Were these to be typical?

The final unknown facing Gillette in the decision to go with the stainless

[6]Ibid., p. 242.

Table 7.1   Cannibalization: Possible Consequences of the Stainless Steel Blade on Gillette Profits

	Stainless	Super Blue
Retail selling price	15¢	7¢
Markup percent for retailers	33%	33%
Gillette's revenue per blade	10¢	4⅔¢
Estimated cost to Gillette	4¢	2¢
Gross margin per blade	6¢	2⅔¢
Average use of blade	unknown, but probably between 7 and 16 shaves	3⅓ shaves
Approximate number of blades used in a year		100
If 8 shave average	45	
If 12 shave average	30	
If 16 shave average	22	
Profit margin per customer per year		$2.67
With 8 shave average	$2.70	
With 12 shave average	$1.80	
With 16 shave average	$1.32	

steel blade was what type of customer would be most attracted to it. If this were the Super Blue blade user—if the stainless blade were to cannibalize Gillette's most valuable property—then the firm should be reluctant to embrace the new product. As we see in Table 7.1, only if a former Super Blue user were to average eight shaves or less with the stainless blade would the profit be maintained or improved, and this was by no means a certainty.

Yet, the company had some reason to hope the new blade would not cause many Super Blue users to switch. Laboratory tests had shown that the stainless steel blade, while it gave better third and fourth shaves than the Super Blue, did not give as good a first shave: stainless steel blades required one and a half pounds of pressure to make the same cut as one pound by the Super Blue. Gillette, furthermore, based on some early sales data in England, had reason to believe that once the initial glamour wore off, the man most interested in the stainless blade would be the economy-minded customer who wanted the cheapest shave possible, even at some sacrifice of comfort. This would be the man who used the Gillette Thin or the Blue, and not the Super Blue customer. While Gillette then might experience some loss in sales, the switch to the stainless steel would mean higher profit margins per blade, and as much or more profit. And the Super Blue blade, the real profit-maker for Gillette, would be left unperiled.

Such reasoning finally assuaged some of Gillette's fears and hesitation in starting production on its own stainless blades. However, there still were enough unknowns that Gillette procrastinated and entered the market months after its competitors had moved aggressively.

Gillette finally brought its own version of the stainless steel blade to market in the fall of 1963, a good six months after Eversharp and American Safety Razor had introduced theirs. Once the decision to market the stainless blade was made, Gillette moved with its customary aggressiveness. First introduced in the New York and Philadelphia markets in early September, by October nationwide distribution had been achieved to over 500,000 retail outlets. The blades were competitively priced at six for 89 cents.

Gillette supported its new production with $4 million of promotional and advertising funds. About 80 percent of the budget was diverted from other Gillette blade lines, notably from the Super Blue blade, which previously had received most of Gillette's promotional push. Because of the market-by-market introduction, the advertising campaign included intensive television spot (local) advertising. The exposure was soon broadened to include the traditional Gillette-sponsored telecasts of the World Series, Fight of the Week, American Football League games, Wide World of Sports, and the Rose Bowl.

The Result

During the next few years Gillette paid the price of being the last company to the market with the stainless blade. Profits declined badly in 1963 and 1964. See Table 7.2. The effect on profitability is even more striking when we consider the return on investment (the real measure of profitability). Table 7.3 shows how the lofty 40 percent that made Gillette the most profitable of all U.S. firms dropped precipitously to below 30 percent by 1964, and was not regained.

But more damaging by far was the loss of market share. This fell from 70 percent of the wet shaving market to 55 percent, while share of the double-edge blade market declined from 90 percent to 70 percent. With the situation stabilized as of October 1965, Gillette had obtained about 45 percent of the stainless blade market. However, Schick could claim 35 percent, American Safety Razor 15 percent, and little Wilkinson had about 5 percent of the market.

Table 7.2   Gillette Company Sales and Profits, 1955–1964

Year	Net Sales	Net Income (after taxes)
1955	$176,928,594	$28,378,393
1956	200,714,707	28,726,938
1957	194,929,175	23,312,315
1958	193,865,095	25,593,990
1959	209,276,635	31,151,623
1960	224,737,000	37,123,000
1961	253,502,000	42,761,000
1962	276,159,000	45,274,000
1963	295,700,000	41,545,000
1964	298,956,000	37,673,000

Source: Published company records.

ANALYSIS OF GILLETTE'S DELAY WITH THE STAINLESS STEEL BLADE

Perhaps this was a "small" mistake. Certainly the viability of the company was not jeopardized, nor was the mistake to result in monumental cost write-offs, as experienced by some of the other firms in this book. Rather, here we have only a hesitation, a missed step perhaps, resulting in a somewhat lower profit showing for a few years than might otherwise have been the case. What is so bad about this, you might ask, to merit its being included in a book of classic mistakes?

But here we are exposed to the importance of market share, something

Table 7.3   Gillette's Return on Investment, 1960–1967

Year	(1) Stockholders' Equity (000)	(2) Net Income (000)	(3) Return on Investment (2) ÷ (1)
1960	$ 94,436	$37,123	39.3%
1961	106,601	42,761	40.1
1962	113,065	45,274	40.0
1963	121,918	41,545	34.1
1964	126,265	37,673	29.8
1965	136,346	42,330	31.0
1966	153,145	49,866	32.6
1967	186,721	56,615	30,3

Source: Calculated from published company records.

that ought to be zealously guarded and maintained, even though the slippage of a few percentage points may not always seem so crucial, especially if sales and profits are still maintained at comfortable levels. But market share erosion means a shifting of customers to competitors. These customers may not easily be regained—perhaps never. There's the rub, and the critical importance of market share.

Whatever its reasons, Gillette tarried too long in introducing the stainless steel blade. In so doing, competitors were given a chance to gain a niche they otherwise probably could not have gained; the precious market share was ill-protected. Now, it can be argued that there really was no mistake. Hesitating to introduce the new blade can be supported as a calculated effort to let competitors face the risks inherent in bringing out a new product, and only if it turned out to be successful would Gillette then step in.

Charitably, we can find rationale for hesitating with the stainless steel blade. The procrastination of Gillette's management can be supported. But, can a reluctance to embrace innovation really be condoned? For any firm or organization? Whatever the rationale, Gillette erred in taking a back seat with this promising innovation in shaving. Gillette was the industry leader, and it should have led with this. Sure, it misjudged the eagerness and the effectiveness with which its smaller competitors were able to develop their production capabilities. But, in whatever industry, when the dominant firm is willing to take a back seat, to let some other firm gain a initiative . . . this is hardly the mark of aggressive and effective management.

WHAT CAN BE LEARNED?

Successful management is alert to opportunities, is quick to note them, quick to pursue them. Of course, not all innovations will be successful. But there is usually less risk in trying an innovation only to have it fail, than in not trying and then finding another firm with a roaring success and a consequent competitive advantage.

There is the serious temptation for the dominant and successful firm in an industry to rest on its laurels, to be content with the status quo, to view significantly different products or marketing techniques as disruptive and potentially cannibalizing, and therefore not worthy of support. There is also the temptation for the dominant firm to underestimate its competitors and what they are capable of doing: ''. . . after all, they have not come close to matching our performance; they have proven themselves second rate; they are no threat.'' But such perceptions, comfortable though they may be, are often misleading since downtrodden competitors tend to be more hungry, more willing to take risks, and more flexible in action than the large, complacent, and typically conservative industry leader.

In one sense, Gillette can be lauded for recognizing the error before much time had elapsed, and strenuously trying to correct it. Decisive action and aggressive marketing efforts were finally instituted by the fall of 1963. But the crucial delay and abdicating the initiative to other firms was a serious marketing mistake, a classical one of a dominant firm's unreceptivity to innovation. There are lessons for all marketers to be gained from this.

After the Mistake

After 1962 and 1963, as men began deserting Gillette in droves with the inevitable profit consequences, Gillette's fortunes began improving. The reason for this was not so much that men were returning to Gillette as that women were coming to its rescue. By 1965, over one-third of Gillette's U.S. sales were to women. Gillette's Toni division, acquired in 1948, had for a number of years achieved only a so-so performance because of the decline of home permanents caused by the popularity of softer hair styles. Now it was becoming highly profitable with its Adorn hair spray, White Rain shampoo, Tame creme rinse, and Deep Magic facial cleansing lotion. In 1965, Toni contributed $10 million of Gillette's total profit of $42 million for that year. Even more spectacular was the success of Right Guard deodorant, again thanks to women. Right Guard had been introduced as a man's deodorant in 1960. But marketing surveys showed it to be very popular with women also. Subsequently, Gillette used two cities as tests for an advertising theme of Right Guard as a family deodorant, rather than a man's deodorant. Sales doubled in those two cities in four months. By 1965, marketed as a family deodorant, Right Guard had become the number one deodorant in the United States, with sales over $17 million. (Later advertising for Right Guard, however, returned to the original target of men.)

In 1965, the double-edge blade accounted for 75 percent of the $200 million razor blade market; single-edge and injector blades accounted for the other 25 percent of the market. Within the important double-edge segment, 50 percent of the dollar volume had now been captured by the stainless steel blade since its introduction less than three years before; carbon steel blades accounted for the other half of this market. The stainless steel blade was being used for an average of ten shaves, and continued to be retailed at 15 cents each, versus 4 cents for regular carbon steel blades and 7 cents for Gillette's Super Blue.[7]

By 1965, Gillette's stainless steel blade had captured over half the stainless market. But Schick and Personna had firmly established their stainless steel blades in a way they never could with their regular blades.

[7]"Close Shave," p. 26.

Table 7.4   Gillette Company Sales and Profits, 1965–1970

Year	Net Sales	Net Income (after taxes)
1965	$339,064,000	$42,330,000
1966	396,190,000	49,866,000
1967	428,357,000	56,615,000
1968	553,174,000	62,278,000
1969	609,557,000	65,532,000
1970	672,669,000	66,075,000

Source: Published company records.

While its diversification kept its profits from sinking abysmally, still Gillette's overall earnings declined for two years, and not until 1966 were they to equal the net income of 1962. Table 7.4 shows the sales and profit performance for 1965 through 1970.

Update

In the 1970s, sales and profits marched inexorably ahead—the stainless steel blade miscalculation had seemingly long since been shrugged off. By 1973, Gillette's worldwide corporate net sales exceeded the billion dollar mark for the first time, reaching $1,064,427,000. Net profits were $86,665,000, also the highest in the company's history.

By 1980, sales were $2,315,294,000 with profits of $123,977,000. Return on investment (of equity), however, lagged behind the 30 percent to 40 percent returns in the decade of the 1960s, as shown in Table 7.3. The five-year average ending in 1983 was 18.7 percent.

For Thought and Discussion

1. Using an analysis similar to that of Table 7.1, calculate the effect on profits of cannibalization of the Gillette Thin blades, assuming that the selling price is 4 cents, the retail markup is 33 percent, and the cost to Gillette is 1¾ cents. What do you conclude from this analysis as to the desirability of marketing the stainless steel blade?
2. Critique the Wilkinson marketing strategy with its stainless steel blade. What rationale can you give for its nonaggressive efforts with its blade?
3. In what other ways than consignment and guaranteed sales can a small and relatively unknown manufacturer induce dealers to stock his goods?

Invitation to Role Play

Assume the role of vocal and critical stockholder at the annual meeting of the Gillette Company in early 1963. What arguments would you introduce for the company to proceed to bring out its own stainless steel blade without delay? How would you counter contrary arguments from Messrs. Gross and Gilbert?

CHAPTER 8

Montgomery Ward— Effect of a No-Growth Policy

Firms can pursue diametrically opposite strategies to their detriment. Major errors that have brought firms to the edge of bankruptcy and beyond have come from overly ambitious expansion efforts. W. T. Grant Company in recent years followed such a course of action; profitability diminished and debts rose to the disaster level. Some discount chains expanded too fast and could neither effectively manage their additional operations nor adequately finance them. Certain fast-food franchisers expanded with ill-defined policies, careless selection procedures, and weak controls, and quickly faltered as competition intensified.

There are fewer examples of firms that made mistakes at the other end of the spectrum: nil expansion. Montgomery Ward Company during the years 1939 to 1955 is the foremost example. The result was an irretrievable loss of its competitive position relative to arch-rival Sears.

In all these recountings of major mistakes, management intent was good; one or more key executives thought their judgment was correct. Of course, the future is uncertain, and one can be either recklessly optimistic or profoundly conservative.

THE DECISION OF NO-GROWTH

During the years from 1945 to 1952—the years following the curbs brought on by World War II—not a single new Ward store was opened. Actually

Table 8.1 Stores Operated by Ward, Sears, and Penney, 1938–1954

	1938	1946	1952	1954
Ward	600	632	605	568
Sears	496	610	684	718
Penney	1,539	1,601	1,632	1,614

Source: Moody's and Company annual report for respective years.

some 27 stores were closed, reducing the total number of Ward stores from 632 to 605; an additional 37 marginal stores were closed between 1952 and 1955. During all this time Sears was vigorously expanding, from 610 stores in 1946 to 684 by 1952. Table 8.1 shows the number of stores operated by Ward, Sears, and Penney during various years from 1938 to 1955.

Historically, Ward had opened its stores in small rural communities. This was in keeping with the farmer-consumer who was considered to be the market during the pre-World War II period. However, after World War II, most population growth was taking place in major metropolitan areas, particularly in their suburbs. Shopping centers were burgeoning and were inevitably taking business from downtown and from smaller business districts. But Ward repudiated expansion during this period of major change in shopping patterns, deliberately leaving the field to Sears, Penney, and other competitors.

Why? Why this obsession with stability and opposition to growth? Was it because the company had inadequate financial resources to support a vigorous growth program? Was it short in managerial resources? No! Ward was neither short of financial nor of managerial resources. The company was squirreling away millions of dollars during this time, so much so that one of the vice presidents made a widely quoted statement: "Ward's is one of the finest banks with a store front in the U.S. today."[1] Many able executives were also on the staff during the years immediately after World War II, although many were to leave in frustration. What then led to this durable decision for no-growth?

The answer was Sewell Avery, chairman of the board of Ward since 1932. He had an adamant belief that a depression was imminent after the cessation of hostilities of World War II. His basis for this was the depression that did occur after World War I. Avery foresaw that the nation would have difficulties trying to readjust to a peacetime economy, as industries halted production of war materials and reverted to peacetime production and as millions of returning servicemen tried to find employment. He predicted that

[1]As quoted in Business Week, September 27, 1952, p. 62.

"economic conditions are terrorizing beyond what we have known before." And he noted, "We (Ward) are starting nothing of any size; we are being cautious."[2]

If the expectations of Avery had been correct—if a severe depression had come within three or four years of the ending of the war—he would have been a hero; he might have achieved fame as the "shrewdest businessman in the U.S.," as *Business Week* magazine speculated.[3] The cash and liquid assets of Ward might have fostered expansion at bargain prices while everyone else was being forced to retrench. But with every passing year the soundness of the strategy of standing pat became more suspect.

Sewell Avery

Sewell Avery was born in Saginaw, Michigan, in 1874, the son of a wealthy Michigan lumberman. For many years of his life his was an admirable success story. He graduated from Michigan State University Law School in 1894 and started at the bottom in a small gypsum plant owned by his father. By the time he was 22 he was manager of the plant. Then in 1901 the small firm was absorbed by the U.S. Gypsum Company. Four years later Avery was president of U.S. Gypsum. *Time* magazine described him as a "suave and brilliant supersalesman,"[4] and he built U.S. Gypsum into one of the largest purveyors of building materials in the United States.

In the deep depression year of 1932, salesman Avery was called on by Ward's directors and creditors to rescue the foundering company, which had suffered an 8.7 million dollar deficit in 1931. Avery gathered around him sharp young executives. He added new luxury items to Ward's stock, and said, "We no longer depend on hicks and yokels. We sell more than overalls and manure-proof shoes."[5] He reentered the fashion-merchandise field. He improved the catalog. He closed 70 unprofitable stores.

And he was successful. In 12 years he had changed a $5.7 million loss (1932) into a $20,438,000 profit (1943). In 1932 the company lost 2.2 times as much money as Sears on a volume only 65 percent that of Sears; by 1939, Ward had 82 percent of Sears' business and 84 percent of Sears' profit.

Avery ruled Ward with an iron hand, with no regard for the feelings of employees or executives. He also earned a reputation as one of the nation's

[2]"Betting on a Depression . . . and What It Costs," *Business Week*, September 27, 1952, p. 61.

[3]Ibid., pp. 60–66.

[4]*Time*, May 8, 1944, p. 12.

[5]Ibid.

foremost Roosevelt-haters and labor-baiters. When he finally stepped down from active domination of the company in 1957, he was 83 years old.

BACKGROUND OF THE MONTGOMERY WARD COMPANY

In 1872, (Aaron) Montgomery Ward, former general-store manager, dry-goods salesman, and traveling salesman, opened in Chicago the first large business selling a wide variety of goods exclusively by mail.[6] Ward had worked among farmers for many years and knew of their dissatisfaction with the high cost of goods and the limited choices available from the inefficient general stores of the day. He also was familiar with an organization they had recently formed, the Grange, which advocated cooperative purchasing to save farmers money by eliminating the middleman.

Ward and his brother-in-law had amassed $2,400. With this they established their business in a twelve-by-fourteen-foot room in Chicago. They listed the articles for sale and explained how to order on a single sheet of paper. By 1874 the price sheet had become an eight-page booklet. The growth was phenomenal. Later in the same year the booklet became 72 pages; by 1884 a catalog of 240 pages listed nearly 10,000 items of merchandise.

At that time, Ward was the official supply house of the Grange, thus winning easy acceptance in the rural market. But even more important to the success was Ward's guarantee that goods could be returned to the company without transportation charges both ways if the customer was not satisfied. Montgomery Ward was not averse to using hoopla; as one promotional device he had barnstorming railroad cars displaying the firm's goods and offering entertainment of the minstrel variety. Customers were invited to visit the company's plant in Chicago, and during the World's Fair in Chicago some 285,000 did so.

Sears was not established until 1886, and then its chief business was selling watches by mail order. The company did not become the Sears, Roebuck and Company until 1893. However, by 1902 Sears had surpassed Ward in sales, although it was never able to far outdistance Ward until after World War II.

For virtually the first fifty years of operation, Ward was strictly a mail-order firm, as was Sears. Montgomery Ward had tried one venture of a "branch store" in Milwaukee, Wisconsin, in 1880, but it failed within two years. Finally in 1921 Ward began experimenting with "outlet stores"

---

[6]This section has been greatly condensed from Boris Emmet and John E. Jeuck, *Catalogs and Counters* (Chicago: University of Chicago Press, 1950).

located in basements of its mail-order plants; these were primarily used to dispose of overstocks and discontinued goods. After a depression in 1920–1921, two additional outlet stores were opened to dispose of the distress goods and these were not located in mail-order premises. The two stores were not identified with Ward, and higher prices were charged than through mail order. These stores, however, turned out to be complete failures, although the outlet stores in the mail-order plants were profitable.

By 1926, Ward had established "mail order agencies" in small towns as a stimulant for the mail-order business. Similar to present-day catalog order offices, these displayed samples of merchandise, but only tires could be purchased on the spot. During this time there was a real reluctance to open retail stores that might take away business from the mail-order operation. Finally an incident triggered the decision to go with retail stores; it illustrates how consumer demand can finally assert itself over obstacles placed by a firm:

> In the mail-order agency in Plymouth, Indiana, a would-be customer wanted to buy a certain saw which was on display and he refused to take "No" for an answer. Finally the agency manager in desperation allowed him to buy the saw. News of this transaction led to scores of persons clamoring to buy the other goods on display. Agency personnel gave in and sold everything; then promptly they reordered a full stock from the mail-order plant; just as promptly this was sold out.

> The extraordinary movement of goods to the Plymouth agency came to the attention of the president, and he was outraged when he discovered the agency was selling merchandise directly. But the evidence of the resulting profits of this course of action was overwhelming. Ward's top management soon became completely convinced. (Sears had opened retail stores a few years before and undoubtedly helped in convincing Ward's management of the wisdom of this move.)[7]

By the end of 1927, Sears had 27 stores in operation, three times the number of the previous year. Ward had moved even more rapidly and already had thirty-seven open by the end of that year, in addition to the outlet stores in each of its seven mail-order plants.

The rate with which stores were opened by both Ward and Sears during the next several years was amazing. Ward sought to get into "choice" towns before Sears did, even if some of the outlets were to prove to be mistakes. Two different location strategies were used by the mail-order giants: Ward favored going into towns with populations between 4000 and 75,000; Sears

[7]Ibid., pp. 342, 343.

entered much larger towns. By the end of 1929, Ward had opened 500 stores; sometimes as many as 25 were opened in one week. Sears reached a total of 324 stores in this time. Then the depression years of the early 1930s marked a period of consolidation by both Ward and Sears. Both firms eliminated marginal stores and new units were more carefully planned and researched. During the war, of course, expansion was thwarted. But when the war ended, Sears launched the greatest expansion drive since the late 1920s. Some $300 million was staked on the conviction that the postwar economy warranted immediate expansion, and in the first two years after the war, sales of Sears zoomed from one billion to almost two billion dollars. And Sewell Avery elected to sit tight and do nothing about expansion.

OTHER MISTAKES OF POST-WAR MONTGOMERY WARD

Of course, a major depression did not occur after World War II as Avery had expected. But aside from sacrificing growth and not entering the thriving big city and shopping-center markets. Avery made other mistakes. Not the least of these was the creation of an organization climate that led to the loss of key executives. Avery ran Ward with an iron hand and permitted no disagreements with his ideas. During his tenure, three presidents, more than 24 vice presidents, and numerous other high-level executives left. Among these were men who later became presidents of Lord & Taylor and W. T. Grant. The dictatorship of Avery was not conducive to retaining able executives who wanted freedom to make aggressive decisions.

In the process of standing pat and building up huge cash reserves, there was an overzealousness in paring expenses. Overhead in stores was minimized, and no expenditures for improvements were made. As an example of the pinchpenny philosophy existing at this time, in the publication of the $6 million catalog. Avery ordered that no professional models be used to show the clothes and accessories. Thereby $60,000 in modeling fees were saved, or one percent of the total cost of the catalog. But the quality of the catalog and the resulting lack of adequate display and dramatizing of clothing adversely affected mail-order sales.

A parsimony regarding payrolls led to a confrontation with an aroused union membership representing Ward's numerous facilities. The union members felt they were being treated unfairly, but they received no satisfaction on what they considered to be valid grievances. After months of negotiations, Avery declared that the union did not represent the majority of employees and that Ward would no longer recognize the union. The result was that the union petitioned the National War Labor Board for clarification and threatened to violate the no-strike clause.

Table 8.2   Sales/Inventory Ratio for Ward and Sears, 1942–1956

	Ward	Sears
1942	5.14	5.22
1948	4.18	5.65
1952	4.23	6.03
1956	3.47	6.44

Source: Moody's and Company annual reports for the respective years.

Avery refused government intervention in the labor-management conflict, and the union struck. Other unions honored the picket lines, and the federal government was placed in a quandary: if National War Labor Board recommendations were not complied with, this could lead to severe erosion of its effectiveness and result in an increase in labor unrest across the country. The time was 1944, and the nation was at its maximum war effort.

The federal government finally ordered a takeover of Ward by the Army in order to force compliance with NWLB recommendations. Avery challenged the authority of the President of the United States to seize the Chicago plant. In a celebrated action, Avery was removed bodily from his office by two Army men.

Along with the other "cost-savings" strategies of Avery in the years following the end of the war came an increasing reluctance to write off (or mark down) inventories as they became dated and unsalable. Table 8.2 shows the sales/inventory ratio* for Ward and for Sears during the years 1942 to 1956. As this ratio goes down, more money is tied up in merchandise relative to sales.

While this ratio had been declining for Ward, it was steadily improving for Sears and almost doubled that of Ward by 1956. A heavy investment in merchandise relative to sales generally reflects poor merchandise control in the sense that slow-selling goods are not weeded out fast enough and marginal items are stocked too heavily. Good merchandising policies and tight controls should eliminate these deficiencies. Obviously, from the statistics in Table 8.2, Ward was seriously lacking here compared to Sears. But then Sewell Avery was not really a merchant; his experience had been in sales, manufacturing, and general management.

*Editors note. While technically different (in that merchandise turnover is based on average stock throughout the year), we will consider the sales/inventory ratio (the sales/stock ratio as of the end of the year) as essentially the same as merchandise turnover.

Table 8.3 Sales and Income Statistics for Ward, Sears, and Penney, 1938–1954

Years	Ward		Sears		Penney	
	Sales (000)	Net Income (000)	Sales (000)	Net Income (000)	Sales (000)	Net Income (000)
1938	$ 414,091	$19,210	$ 537,242	$30,828	$ 257,971	$13,799
1942	632,709	22,353	915,058	29,934	490,356	18,058
1944	595,933	20,677	852,597	33,866	533,374	17,159
1946	654,779	22,932	1,045,359	35,835	676,570	35,495
1948	1,158,675	59,050	1,981,536	107,740	885,195	47,754
1950	1,084,436	47,788	2,168,928	108,207	949,712	44,931
1952	1,106,157	54,342	2,657,408	111,895	1,072,266	37,170
1954	999,123	41,195	2,981,925	117,882	1,107,157	43,617

Source: Moody's and Company annual reports for respective years.

CONSEQUENCES OF THE NO-GROWTH DECISION AND RELATED MISTAKES

Table 8.3 shows the sales and net income statistics for Ward versus those of the Sears and the J. C. Penney Company. Notice that sales and profits increased after the war until 1948, but began leveling off and declining for Ward after that. But compared with the growth of Sears during this period, the performance of Ward shows up poorly.

However, there were other costs of conservatism:

1. Market share eroded badly. For example, in mail-order business among the four major mail-order houses, Ward in 1945 did 41.7 percent while Sears had 50.7 percent of this total business; in 1951, Ward did 28.3 percent while Sears' share had risen to 66.1 percent.

2. Loss of profits that might have been earned with reasonable expansion. In 1939, just before World Ward II, Ward was closing in on Sears. By 1952 Sears did almost two and a half times the volume and over twice the net profits.

   Sears from 1946 through 1951 spent $305 million on 304 new or modernized stores, warehouses, and mail-order plants. Ward spent practically nothing for such during this time. Table 8.4 shows the current ratio (the ratio of current assets divided by current liabilities) during this period.

The current ratio is a measure of liquidity, and a ratio of 2.0 is acceptable by most creditors; that is, that current assets are twice as much as current liabilities. As you can see, Ward was well above this, and rose to

Table 8.4   Current Ratio of Ward and Sears, 1942–1956

	Ward	Sears
1942	4.49	3.57
1948	4.46	2.55
1952	5.43	3.13
1956	7.29	3.58

Source: Annual Reports for respective years.

the astronomical high of 7.29 by the end of Avery's tenture, reflecting idle assets that could be reinvested to the amount of $325 million in cash and securities. Sears, on the other hand, with its rapid expansion, was approaching the 2.0 minimally acceptable level of liquidity in 1948.

THE TURNABOUT

In 1955, Louis Wolfson attempted a raid on Ward to gain control, but was unsuccessful. John Barr, the legal counsel for Ward, led the fight against Wolfson. His successful defense led to his succeeding the aged Avery as chief executive.

Barr attempted to put Ward back on the growth trail, and he opened fifty-eight new stores between 1957 and 1961. But Barr was a lawyer and not an operating man. He could not resolve the problem of maintaining profits while vigorously opening new stores. As profits eroded he decided to cancel the new-store program and thereby eliminate the costs of new store openings.

Profits continued to diminish in 1960–1961. At that point Barr recognized his deficiencies and brought a strong operating man into the firm: Robert Brooker, who had been a major executive with Sears from 1944 to 1958 and who was the president of Whirlpool Corporation, a major appliance manufacturer.

Brooker was given a free hand in the reconstruction, and he promptly enticed a number of management people from Sears to work for him. Gradually the emphasis on small town locations was changed to big stores. With a $500 million expansion, he began opening new or renovated outlets in heavily populated urban areas. The *cluster concept* was utilized, with "clusters" of stores opened in such major urban areas as Chicago and Los Angeles. A major advantage of clusters is that such groupings of stores provide sales volume needed to sustain the high cost of advertising in major urban newspapers: the cost of the heavy advertising can be spread over a number of stores, thus permitting overall advertising expenditures to be increased without putting a severe strain on profits of any individual store.

The results of the store construction on Ward's operations are clearly evident. Between 1957 and 1965, 182 new stores were built. These accounted for 72 percent of 1965 sales, and 73 percent of pretax profits. Ward had also been slow in modernizing its catalog operations, and these contributed between 30 percent and 40 percent of sales. In the first years after Brooker had taken over, this part of the business had been in the red. The manually-operated mail order system was so backward that the volume of orders during Christmas of 1965 overwhelmed facilities and resulted in monumental delays and shipping errors. After this, the mail order part of the business was mechanized and computerized. Brooker noted in 1967, "We have lost none of our enthusiasm for the catalog business." And he pointed out that this type of selling was growing faster than conventional retailing.[8]

Brooker initiated merchandising policy changes as well as an expansion

---

INFORMATION SIDELIGHT

CONCENTRATION OF VENDORS

The supplier/retailer relationship functions best when each is important to the other. There are strong advantages in concentrating buying efforts with a few top-notch vendors:

1. The retailer becomes important to the supplier, and vice versa. The rapport and cooperation thus gained may become manifest in many ways, from priority with new merchandise and filling of orders, to prompt cooperative attention given to damaged merchandise. With a good relationship, a vendor may even help out a buyer who made a bad or ill-timed purchase, and arrange to take back the goods or have them transferred to another customer. The vendor may also accumulate special lots for sale events and other store promotions.

2. Costs can be lessened. Less search time is needed on the part of the buyer. Ordering and processing of goods are easier where fewer invoices and fewer shipments are involved. More continuity of stock records can be maintained. Salespeople can also be more knowledgeable about the performance and assortment of goods.

---

[8]"Somebody Loves Ward's," *Business Week*, April 1, 1967, p. 34.

and modernization program. He reduced the number of vendors that Ward did business with from 15,000 to 7200. Of these, 200 supplied half the goods flowing into Ward stores. Under Avery and Barr, Ward did not enforce a system of aging inventories and writing off older and slow-selling stock. This now became vigorously enforced, even though profitability of some stores was temporarily reduced by heavy markdowns. Before, Ward buyers were not allowed to make long-term contracts with manufacturers; they could only make one-time commitments. The effect of this was to deny manufacturers the assurances they needed of continued sales. Consequently Ward was often unable to get a sufficient supply of some goods and lowest prices and was not able to exercise demands for quality controls. Transportation charges were often higher because of the diversity of suppliers and the necessity of frantically seeking rush orders and fill-in merchandise.

Ward's fortunes at last began to experience a reversal as profits and sales rose. Share of the market also began to increase, and while this did not regain pre-war competitive levels with Sears, at least the disadvantage was lessened. Then in 1968, Ward merged with Container Corporation to form Marcor Corporation. Sales of the joint undertaking rose to over $4 billion in 1973, while net income was almost $100 million, with Ward contributing 55 percent of total earnings.

WHAT CAN BE LEARNED?

The no-growth philosophy of Ward points out a fundamental principle of American enterprise: a firm cannot stand still; it must grow if it is to stay viable. Customers, suppliers, executives, all are attracted to the firm that is growth-minded, because all stand to benefit from a firm's increasing growth and prosperity. While growth can be overemphasized to the extent that a firm has neither the finances nor the management resources to handle it, the opposite is just as dangerous. Moderation in expansion is to be desired.

A firm should be willing to shift strategies. It cannot remain wedded to a mistake, even for the sake of principles. The strategy of Avery after World War II might have been correct; however, after half a decade had passed without the expected economic collapse taking place, the time was overdue for reevaluation and refocusing of strategy. The competitive environment is dynamic; continual reassessment is needed if a firm is to be aggressive and successful.

The action of competitors cannot be disregarded. While Ward disdained expansion under the mistaken impression that its strategy would prove correct eventually, there was still a need to counter competitive actions; they should not be permitted to expand unchallenged, as Sears did for too many years. Eventually it becomes impossible to ever catch up.

Dictatorship in any organization is questionable at best. Everything then depends on the correctness of the judgment of the sole decision-maker. Far better is a more flexible approach, one that is alert to feedback about the marketplace and to the ideas put out by associates and subordinates. For retailing firms, sound merchandising principles should never be overlooked. The importance of merchandise turnover, of prompt mark-downs, of fresh and clean stocks, of being important to vendors—these cannot be spurned, and yet they sometimes are when the top executives have not come out of the ranks of merchandising (as Avery had not).

Eventually Ward pulled itself around and started anew an aggressive growth pattern. However, the lost years could never be regained. Poor judgment, which permitted no deviating opinions, cast a sorry spell over the company. A man who for much of his life had evinced outstanding success, led Ward down the wrong path and was too stubborn to admit it.

Update

In 1974, Mobil Corporation, its coffers bulging with oil profits, bought control of Marcor and Montgomery Ward for $1.5 billion. This move was widely criticized by the government and public interest groups, for it smacked of a disdain for what most perceived as the urgent national need for such profits to be invested in more petroleum and energy exploration and development.

In addition to the public criticism, however, Mobil's stockholders were not benefited either. The Montgomery Ward operation has remained substantially less profitable than the oil business, and also less profitable than most of the major competing retailers. For example, in 1978 Mobil's energy and chemicals business earned 14 percent on stockholders' equity. Ward earned only 9.3 percent, and the Container Corporation part of Marcor, because of extraordinary charges, earned only 2.4 percent. In 1976 and 1977, the two other years Mobil broke out the Ward earnings from the consolidated financial statements, Ward earned 8.1 percent and 9.5 percent respectively. This profitability of Ward compared poorly with 5-year average returns on equity for K mart of 18.2 percent, for Dayton Hudson of 17.8 percent, J.C. Penney of 13.0 percent, and Sears with 11.9 percent.[9] Some 20 years after the no-growth policy was disavowed, Montgomery Ward still had not regained the momentum it once had, and still could only be classed as an also-ran department store chain.[10]

[9]Statistics are from the various companies' annual reports and other public statements.

[10]For more detail about Mobil's questionable acquisition of Montgomery Ward, see "Mobil's Monkey." *Forbes*, June 11, 1979, pp. 41–42.

For Thought and Discussion

1. How would you go about evaluating vendors for possible weeding out? Be as specific as you can.
2. How does "aging" inventory contribute to profits?
3. What do you see as the relative merits of Ward's expansion into small towns during the late 1920s, rather than into larger cities, as Sears did? How valid would such a strategy have been in the 1940s and 1950s?
4. Why should a firm be "growth minded," rather than content with the status quo? Be as specific as you can.

Invitation to Role Play

Assume the role of vice president to Sewell Avery after World War II. What arguments would you give that some expansion efforts still should be made, even if his prediction of a major depression were eventually to come true? Be as persuasive as you can, and be prepared to counter the objections.

CHAPTER 9

J. C. Penney Company—
Unchanging Policies

At sunrise on a spring morning in 1902, a young man, Jim Penney, opened a tiny dry goods store in Kemmerer, a frontier town in the southwest corner of Wyoming. He called the store the Golden Rule, remembering his father's admonitions to deal with people according to the Biblical injunction: "Therefore all things whatsoever ye would that men should do to ye, do ye even so to them."[1] The opening day was advertised by handbills distributed throughout the town. Penney remained open that day until midnight, and his sales were $466.59. After that he opened at 7 a.m. on weekdays and 8 a.m. on Sundays, and remained open as long as there was a miner or sheepherder on the street. Sales for the first year were $28,898.11.[2]

Penney faced a tough competitor in Kemmerer. The town was dominated by a mining company, and a company-owned store had practically a local monopoly with most business done on credit or with the scrip issued by the mining company. Penney did not offer any credit, nor could he accept the scrip. What he did offer was values so much better that customers were willing to pay cash and carry home their purchases. He had no fancy fixtures, all the merchandise was piled on tables where customers could see and touch, and there was one price for all. Penney also had a return-goods

---

[1]Tom Mahoney and Leonard Sloane, *The Great Merchants* (New York: Harper and Row, 1966), p. 259.
[2]Ibid., p. 259.

policy; if customers were not satisfied, they could return the purchase and get their money back.

Jim Penney had not always been successful in his business dealings. He was born on a farm in Missouri in 1875 into the big family of a poor Baptist minister. Upon graduating from high school he worked as a clerk in a local dry goods store. His salary was \$2.27 a month. But poor health forced him to resign and move west. Not wanting to work for someone else, he scraped up enough money to open a butcher shop in Longmont, Colorado. However, he soon lost this along with all his savings. His first venture into entrepreneurship had failed. The second venture was not to fail; the little store in the small mining town in Wyoming became the seed of the J. C. Penney Company.

THE SUCCESSFUL GROWTH YEARS

Penney was not content to run just one store. As the store in Kemmerer prospered he thought of opening other stores. By 1905 he had two stores with total sales just under 100,000 dollars. In 1910, Penney changed his company's name from the Golden Rule to the J. C. Penney Company. By this time the chain had grown to 26 stores in six western states. He kept to the same strategy that had worked well in Kemmerer. He tried to give his customers honest values, which usually meant the lowest possible prices; he stayed with a cash-only policy, and he had no fancy fixtures or high overhead expenses. Thus he could offer low prices and still make money. Not the least of the success factors at this time was the environment Penney had chosen for his business. He confined his stores to small towns where the Penney managers could be well known, friendly, and respectable members of the community. The lack of strong competition that would have been encountered in larger cities helped the burgeoning growth, a growth from one store to almost 1500 in only 30 years.

Something else, another uniquely Penney policy, was also necessary for such a growth rate to be achieved. Where could Penney possibly find the trained, competent, and honest managers to run the hundreds of stores that were being opened? And almost as important, where could he find the financial resources to open so many stores in such a short period of time and stock them with sufficient merchandise?

Jim Penney both financed and created the managerial resources needed by taking in "partner associates." As each store manager was able to accumulate enough capital out of his store's earnings, he could buy a one-third partnership in a new store, *if* he had trained one of his employees to the point where he could go out and effectively manage such a new store. Here then we have the great incentive to provide the resources needed by

Table 9.1   Growth of J. C. Penney Company by Stores and Sales

Year	Number of Stores	Sales (Dollars)
1902	1	28,898
1905	2	97,653
1912	34	2,050,641
1919	197	28,783,965
1926	747	115,957,865
1933	1,466	178,773,965
1940	1,586	302,539,325

Source: Norman Beasley, *Main Street Merchant* (New York: McGraw–Hill, 1948), p. 222.

such a growing company: motivation by each store manager to find the best qualified employees and give them the best possible training. And profits would often be plowed back into the company to pay off partnership interests or to back new outlets.

By 1924 there were 570 stores and partners. Now in order to get the outside financial help needed to sustain further growth, the partnerships were formed into a corporation under which the stores became company owned. The days of managers getting one-third shares of stores were over. And the complexion of the company now underwent a major change.

Up to this time, store operations had been highly individualized, with each manager making his own decisions within rather general policies. Such looseness of organization now gave way to more centralized policies and activities, a trend that was to continue in the decades to come. Operations were made more uniform, with strict budgeting systems, improved operational methods, store arrangements, merchandise, and promotions planned by experts and followed by all stores. Central buyers had more authority over managers as to what goods and prices they would carry. And store managers were now evaluated against other store managers as to their performance; promotions to better stores or to the home office went to the better producers. Penney's was beginning to shape itself into a unified and efficient organization. Growth continued, despite the depression of the 1930s, as shown in Table 9.1.

EMERGING PROBLEMS

Despite the substantial growth of the Penney Company and the firm entrenchment it had achieved in middle America, by the 1950s some questions were beginning to be raised about the heretofore successful policies. Did they need to be changed? Were they archaic for today's

Table 9.2 Trend in Consumer Credit, 1940–1970 (billions)

	1940	1950	1955	1960	1965	1970
Installment: Consumer goods, other than automobiles	$1.8	$4.8	$7.6	$11.5	$18.5	$31.5
Noninstallment charge accounts	1.5	3.4	4.8	5.3	6.4	8.0
Ratio of total consumer credit to disposable personal income	10.9%	10.4%	14.1%	16.0%	19.0%	18.4%

Source: Compiled from the *Statistical Abstract of the U.S.*

society? Was the Penney Company vulnerable to competition as perhaps never before?

General merchandise firms were customarily compared with Sears. Sears was the benchmark, the model for efficient, progressive, large-scale enterprise. Montgomery Ward and Company found itself stacking up poorly against Sears due to a nonexpansion policy after World War II. And now the J. C. Penney Company, in looking at comparative sales statistics with Sears, found itself wanting.

Significant as Penney's achievement was in leading his company through difficult years of adolescence and rapid growth, the conservatism of his associates caused a long delay in the market adaptations needed for the two decades following World War II—credit, merchandise diversification, and catering to the urban market. Table 9.2 shows the growth of credit during this period, a period in which the Penney Company stuck resolutely with its cash-and-carry philosophy. Initially such a policy had been compatible with the needs of a population dissatisfied with the lethargic inefficiencies of many independent stores and their high prices. But four decades later a reevaluation was sorely needed.

Diversification of merchandise lines was also long delayed. Penney's remained only a dry goods and clothing operation until the 1960s. Appliances, furniture and carpeting, sporting goods, auto supplies—merchandise categories long carried by other general-merchandise chains such as Sears and Wards and by department stores—were ignored by Penney's.

Finally, most of the Penney stores were in the more sparsely settled smaller communities west of the Mississippi. The populous and growing East and burgeoning metropolitan areas were not Penney's domain.

A reassessment of policies was needed, indeed long overdue. While the viability of the firm was not yet in jeopardy, its stature as a competitive entity in the mainstream of American retailing was. At this point, in 1957, the

assistant to the president of Penney's, William M. Batten, wrote a memo to
the board of directors that had far-reaching consequences.

The Batten Memo

Probably one of the most influential, and widely publicized, memos in
modern corporate history was that penned by William Batten. He had
started with the company as an extra salesman twenty-six years before, and
had come a long way. He was ready to stake everything on what he saw was
a desperate need for change. He sent a memo to the board of directors
criticizing the conservatism of the company for not reacting to a changing
America.

In the 1950s, the growth of population was centering in the metropolitan
areas. Incomes per capita were rising, and consumer buying power was
being attracted toward "want" rather than "need" type of merchandise.
Fashion consequently was becoming more important, and Penney's was
extremely weak here. The memo bluntly stated that the world in which the
Penney Company had prospered was fast disappearing and that if Penney's
hoped to survive, it would have to change.

Batten suggested conducting a merchandising-character study to define
the kinds of stores that should be operated. He suggested the study should
concern three basic areas:

1. To assess Penney's immediate position in merchandising compared
   with chief competitors such as Sears and Wards.
2. To forecast market opportunities through examining changes in
   population and trends in shopping, work, and leisure.
3. To spell out desired changes in goods and services and voids in the
   marketplace that required filling.

Penney's had no formal market research or market intelligence* until
after Batten's memo. After two years, in 1959, the Merchandising Character
Study was completed. The conclusions were that Penney's was selling only
soft goods and limited home furnishings, and that most of the advertising
appeals were to women. It was decided that Penney's needed to pull in the
entire family in areas having the greatest population growth. As one vice
president commented in regard to the preponderance of apparel and home
furnishings:

Editors note. Some marketers consider marketing research as only one aspect of a
complete marketing intelligence system that provides information flow for decision-making. For
our purposes here we will use the term *marketing research* for all formal and systematic
marketing information-gathering.

We had no browsing areas for men while their wives shopped, like paint and hardware departments. We had nothing to attract the kids, like a toy department. We realized we needed to tend more toward the one-stop shopping idea.[3]

The year following his audacious memo, Batten was made president of Penney's with the mandate to implement the changes necessary. The question was whether it was now too late to catch up with its competitors, to regain the ground lost during the years of conservative and unchanging policies. The problems were at last defined and known to all. But could they be overcome, and quickly?

AT LAST, CHANGE

In September 1958, Penney's began testing the feasibility of offering credit. At first, only 24 stores were the object of this experiment. More than three years were required for Penney's to establish its credit operation chainwide. But at least the necessity of credit to keep up with changing times, and to do well with the big ticket items such as television and washing machines, was realized.

Coming late into the consumer credit field, however, afforded Penney's certain advantages. An almost completely computerized system was designed, in contrast to other retailers who had started with manual systems and then were forced to computerize at an enormous cost. In order to operate its credit system manually, 37 centers would be needed to serve all the stores. However, with the use of the advanced IBM computers, only 14 regional credit offices had to be set up. At the time of Penney's installation, Sears was the only other retailer who could allow customers to shop in any store across the country and receive one bill.

By 1962 all stores offered credit. By 1964 the results were notable: 28 percent of Penney's sales volume was done on credit. Revenues in 1964 amounted to $600 million from more than five million active accounts. By 1966, credit sales were responsible for 35 percent of all sales; by 1973 credit sales were over 38 percent of total sales. By 1967 Penney's had 12 million charge accounts, twice the number of Diners Club and American Express combined.

As intended, the establishment of credit led the way for Penney's to diversify its merchandise mix. It began to follow Sears into carrying hard goods (appliances, furniture, and the like) along with its soft goods. For many years Penney's had been the nation's largest seller of women's

---

[3]Alfred Law, "From Overalls to Fashion Wear," *Wall Street Journal*, October 22, 1964, p. 1.

INFORMATION SIDELIGHT

IMPORTANCE OF CREDIT

As an extreme example of the importance of credit in enhancing consumer demand and consequent purchasing, consider the Superior, Wisconsin, Penney store in 1959, one of the early stores experimenting with credit. Superior, an iron-ore shipping port at the far western end of Lake Superior, experienced wide fluctuations in business and income due to weather, strikes, and economic slowdowns. Sales at this Penney store had remained static for over three years. The first year that credit was offered, sales increased over 30 percent.

Admittedly, the Superior example is not a typical Penney store. The need for credit by people with irregular incomes is the greater. Now, in place of credit, Penney's had always offered the "layaway plan." Here a store held the selected goods for a customer until they were completely paid for—often by small weekly or biweekly payments—and only then released them to the customer. This plan was heavily pushed by Penney's for expensive items and for merchandise sold in advance of the season. But increasingly, customers did not want deferred gratification of their wants. Not if some other store was giving credit, thereby permitting them to have the immediate pleasure of a desired product.

---

hosiery, sheets and blankets, coats and dresses, work clothes, and men's underwear. Prior to 1960, soft goods averaged 95 percent of total sales. Admittedly, soft goods, to some extent, had shielded Penney's from the ups and downs in the economy, since soft goods normally are the last thing people cut down on during hard times; appliances and furniture, on the other hand, can usually be postponed or deferred until times look better. But such soft goods typically afford a low markup, and profitability rests on high turnover and sales volume. And there is a limit to how much soft goods the market can absorb, and certainly sales and profit potential is ultimately limited without diversification beyond soft goods.

First attempts at merchandise diversification came as Penney's moved into higher priced women's dresses, leather goods, and furniture. Merchandise assortment was widened by adding designer dresses and youth-minded sportswear for both men and women. By 1962 Penney's began to add hard goods, with the new merchandise appearing in new or enlarged stores, and to a lesser extent in other stores where space could be found. In 1963 Penney's opened its first full-line department store having such new departments for Penney's as appliances, televisions, sporting goods, paint, hard-

Table 9.3   Capital Expenditures of Sears and Penney's, 1968–1973

Year Ending January	Sears		Penney's	
	Capital Expenditures (000,000)	Percent of Sales	Capital Expenditures (000,000)	Percent of Sales
1968	$186	2.5	$111	4.0
1969	139	1.8	127	3.8
1970	211	2.4	139	3.7
1971	259	2.8	204	4.9
1972	339	3.1	185	3.8
1973	392	3.2	210	3.4

Source: Adapted from *Moody's Industrials*, and respective annual reports.

ware, tires, batteries, and auto accessories. The new stores subsequently allocated about 25 to 30 percent of total floor space to these new lines of hard goods.

By 1965, Penney's had 173 stores with radio-tv departments, 103 with major appliances, 67 with sporting goods, 58 carrying paint and hardware, and 42 centers handling tires, batteries, and auto accessories. Diversification had begun in earnest.

Penney's also sought to offer hard goods in stores that were too small to stock such goods. General Merchandise Company, a small but highly automated mail order company, was acquired in 1962. Catalog centers were then set up in many stores as a means of offering customers a much wider variety of goods. In 1971 catalog sales moved into the black, and Penney's at last had the means to compete on equal terms with the long established businesses of Sears and Ward.

Replacement of older, smaller soft-line stores averaging from 30,000 to 40,000 square feet with new full-line units was also proceeding in earnest. These new stores ranged in size from 43,000 to 220,000 square feet, averaging 165,000. Other diversifications into discount stores (Treasure Island stores), drug stores (Thrift Drug), and supermarkets proceeded. Overseas expansion was also occurring with a controlling interest in a major Belgian retailing firm, Sarma, S.A., obtained in 1968, while in 1971 Penney's entered the Italian market.

The conservative policies had been abandoned, and replaced with a vigorous growth orientation. But could the sales and profits that were lost ever be completely retrieved? Perhaps the more important question was: could the ground lost to Sears in the decade and a half of outmoded policies ever be regained?

Table 9.4   Relative Sales Volumes, Penney's and Sears, 1940–1974

| Year | Penney's (000) | Sears (000) | Market Share (Sales as a percent of total Penney's and Sears' sales) | |
			Penney's	Sears
1942	$ 490,295	$ 915,058	35	65
1944	535,363	851,535	38	62
1946	676,570	1,045,259	39	61
1948	885,195	1,981,536	32	68
1950	949,712	2,168,928	31	69
1952	1,079,257	2,932,338	28	72
1954	1,107,157	2,981,925	27	73
1956	1,290,867	3,306,826	28	72
1958	1,409,973	3,600,882	28	72
1960	1,437,489	4,036,153	26	74
1962	1,553,503	4,267,678	27	73
1964	1,834,318	5,115,767	26	74
1966	2,289,209	6,390,000	26	74
1968	2,745,998	7,330,090	27	73
1970	3,756,092	8,862,971	30	70
1972	4,812,239	10,006,146	32	68
1974	6,243,677	12,306,229	33	67

Source: Adapted from respective annual reports.

A MISTAKE RECTIFIED?

In the last decade and a half Penney's has acted aggressively; indeed it has at times almost met the expansion efforts of Sears, a firm more than twice as large. Table 9.3 shows the capital expenditures for Sears and Penney's during recent years, as well as the percentage of these expenditures to sales. You can see from this table the much greater percentage of sales commitment of Penney's to expansion. But has Penney's been able to make up the lost ground?

Table 9.4 shows the sales volume since 1940 of Penney's compared with Sears. It also shows the market share of Penney's relative to Sears, that is, the percent that Penney's sales are to total Sears and Penney's sales. Chart 9.1 shows the market share of Penney's more graphically, as well as the trends during the long period 1940 to 1974.

You can see from these that the sharp upward trend in market share (or sales relative to those of Sears) in the early and mid-1940s was reversed in the late 1940s. Penney's market share then eroded badly, reflecting the

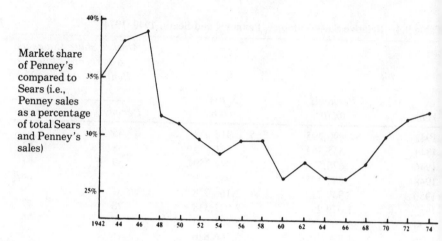

Chart 9.1. Market share of Penney's compared to Sears, 1940–1974.

outmoded policies of Penney's. Not until 1970 was Penney's able to improve its market share and begin a new favorable upward trend. Even though the actions in the 1960s improved the situation, the results are still far below the trend established earlier and the market share previously attained.

The recent growth efforts of Penney's can hardly be faulted or even improved upon. The fact remains, however, that unless major competitors also stumble, a substantial lead built up by one firm due to less aggressive or more error-prone efforts of another firm, is not likely to be caught. (The previous case describes the ultra-conservative efforts of Ward, also during about this same period of time and also involving Sears as the major competitor.)

HOW COME THE LAPSE OF 1945–1958?

It is one of the anomalies of human endeavor that men of great accomplishment and innovativeness can be both visionary and short-sighted, inspired and blinded. Henry Ford is perhaps the foremost example of such strengths and weaknesses: originating mass production of the automobile, but steadfastly refusing to budge from his original idea of a black Model T.

Jim Penney and his company fell into a similar myopia of resistance to changing times. The policies that worked so well in the early years of the Penney Company became outmoded. But still the temptation is to stick with the historically successful and proven. There is difficulty in breaking from accepted ways of doing things.

Partly accounting for the resistance to change of the Penney Company was the leadership. For the most part, top Penney executives fought their ways up through the ranks; the leadership was composed of Penney's associates who had been involved in the company's early growth. For example:

> Earl Sams worked first as James Penney's clerk in Kemmerer, then managed a store for him, and in 1917 became president of the company, serving from 1917 to 1946 whereupon he became board chairman.

> The successor of Sams, Albert Hughes, tutored Penney's sons in Latin, but deciding that retailing would be more exciting, started in the Penney store in Moberly, Missouri, and later managed stores in Utah and Georgia. He was named president in 1946 and served until he stepped aside for Batten (of the famous memo) in 1958.

> Even William Batten, the changemaker, was thoroughly imbued with the traditional Penney philosophy. He first worked for Penney in 1926 while attending high school, and joined the company full time in 1935 as shoe salesman.

> After Batten moved up to chairman in 1964, Ray Jordan became president, culminating a Penney career which began in the small town of Picher, Oklahoma, in 1930.

The Penney Company can boast of its firm policy of promotion from within, and proudly point out examples of this in the ranks of its top executives. But we might ponder whether such a policy can be carried too far. The absence of new blood can be a negative influence. While trainees may be inspired as to their opportunities and potential attainment, policies tend to become self-perpetuating and innovation stymied without the presence of fresh ideas and even disruptive influences of outsiders.

Marketing research was unknown in the Penney Company until the memo of William Batten in 1957 spurred a thorough study of the needs and opportunities of the environment that Penney's faced. Marketing research can provide a sensor of the market; it can keep a firm's executives apprised on how consumer needs and attitudes are changing, and how competition is adjusting. It is difficult to recognize and be responsive to the dynamics of the environment without it.

Even without a marketing research department, or similar department to provide market intelligence data about changing conditions, Penney executives should have been alerted to looming problems by the sharp drop in market share compared with Sears (as shown in Chart 9.1). For ten years market share had been shrinking before Batten issued his memo calling for a research study. One wonders what top Penney executives must have thought during these years as they saw their market position relative to Sears relentlessly eroding away. Or did they ever make such a market share analysis? After all, sales were rising during this period—by no means as much as those of Sears—but still there were sales gains. Did this assuage any worries about emerging problems?

Another factor played a role in the myopia of the Penney Company. Penney stores were mostly located in small rural communities, and generally west of the Mississippi. In many such towns the Penney manager was the highest salaried person in town, and had stature and respect, as did the store he ran. But competition in such rural small towns was certainly less severe than in bigger cities. Perhaps there was a fear of direct competition with big city retailers, such as the major department stores. Was Penney's sophisticated enough to beard such competitors, and on their home ground? Was this perhaps a worry of top Penney executives during this time?

Of course, today Penney's is in most of the major metropolitan markets. But this is a relatively new policy, as new as the adoption of credit, of marketing research, and of merchandise diversification. The reluctance to leave small towns may have thwarted the major direction of Penney's growth for a number of crucial years.

WHAT CAN BE LEARNED?

Most of the marketing mistakes described in this book are due to a lack of responsive marketing. Changing customer preferences and attitudes are undetected, and adjustments to these are not taken or else long delayed. Now, how does a firm practice responsive marketing? A willingness to act, a disavowal or abandonment of familiar modes of operation, are often necessary. But first, the changing environment must be recognized and evaluated. These changes need to be detected, and marketing research can help here. But marketing research alone is no guarantee of responsiveness. It may be used primarily in routine assignments, or its findings may not be accepted and acted upon—or the data may not accurately sensor the marketplace. Even with marketing research, decisions may be left to intuition and expediency, or they may not take place at all, despite changing conditions.

The Penney's example suggests the need for fresh blood in an organization. Total reliance on inbreeding and promotion from within tends to foster a narrow and parochial perspective. The traditional way of doing things often prevails in such an environment. (The fact that Batten, in moving up through the ranks, was able to point his finger at the flaws and emerging dangers in such an eminent tradition reflects all the more on his strengths. But he was the exception.) We are not suggesting here that the opposite course of action—heavy commitment to filling important executive positions with outsiders—is to be advocated. Such plays havoc with morale of trainees and lower-level executives. Rather, a middle ground usually is more desirable—filling many executive positions from within the organization, promoting this idea so as to encourage both the achievement of present executives and the recruiting of trainees, and at the same time bringing strong outsiders into the organization where their strengths and particular experiences can be most valuable. Moderation then may be more desirable than major reliance either on promotion from within or from without.

The lack of innovativeness of the Penney Company in the 1940s and 1950s reflects a need in many organizations to foster innovative thinking among employees and executives. Top management support and encouragement of this usually is required. More than this, a receptivity to change and a willingness to change are important, since, if ideas are never acted upon, the creative instincts of an organization are soon atrophied.

Fostering innovation can take many forms. One way is to expose personnel to fresh thinking, either through some mix of sharp new people, or through seminars and institutes where there is exposure to people from other organizations and experiences. Stimulating creativity can also come from quickly recognizing and rewarding creative individuals.

Update

As Penney's moved into the 1980s, it had 552 full-line department stores, 1130 smaller units devoted to soft goods (apparel and piece goods), a $1.54 billion catalog business, 361 Thrift drug stores, an insurance business generating $42 million, and a Brussels-based chain of 76 food and general merchandise stores under the Sarma label. It had phased out 37 discount units under the Treasury name at the end of 1980. In 1977 it had disposed of several other operations that were not performing satisfactorily profitwise, including its Italian retail stores and the supermarket operations.

By 1981, emphasis was being given to expanding the full-line department stores, and upgrading the fashion image of the company.[4] The success of efforts to expand beyond the original soft-line commitment of the company could be seen in the full-line stores where by 1981, one-third of total sales were accounted for by hard-line departments, such as furniture, appliances, and sporting goods.

Sales and profits for 1980 for the five largest nonfood retailers were:

[4]See "J. C. Penney's Fashion Gamble," *Business Week*, January 16, 1978, pp. 66–74.

	Sales	*Profits*
Sears	$25,124,000,000	$566,000,000
K mart	14,204,000,000	260,500,000
Penney	11,353,000,000	233,000,000
Woolworth	7,218,000,000	160,900,000
Federated	6,301,000,000	277,700,000

As can be seen, Penney's had lost some ground to Sears, with its sales as a percent of total Sears and Penney's sales being 30.6 percent, whereas in 1974 this ratio was 33 percent (see Table 9.4), and in 1978 it had reached 36.8 percent. During the decade of the 1970s, K mart had been the big success story.

For Thought and Discussion

1. Can you think of other less drastic incentives for store managers to develop trainees than that practiced by the Penney Company in its early years of growth?
2. How might a good marketing research department have alerted Penney top management to the need for credit and merchandise diversification? Could such alerting have been accomplished without formal research?
3. Do you think the growth of the Penney Company in the last decade-and-a-half could have been accomplished any quicker? If so, how?

Invitation to Role Play

1. Place yourself in the position of Batten in 1957. Would you have taken the risk of sending a highly critical memo to the board of directors? What do you think would be the consequences of such a memo in some firms?
2. Assume the role of chief assistant to Batten after he has taken over the presidency in 1958. You have been assigned the responsibility of setting up the diversification into appliances, furniture, sporting goods, hardware, and other hard line departments never before carried by Penney's. Be as specific as you can be as to how you would go about doing this.

PART Three

DANGERS OF RASH GROWTH

10

World Football League— The Tainted Promise

"The National Football League has no strong rival," said the World Football League's founding father and first commissioner, Gary L. Davidson. "It has grown arrogant and complacent. The doors are open to a rival. There are plenty of quality players available. A number of NFL players are discontent. The war is on!"[1]

Conceptually, the idea seemed unassailable: another pro football league, only more colorful, more aggressive, more responsive to the fans and the players than the conservative National Football League. All that would be needed for success was the organizational and promotional ability to secure the support of wealthy franchisees and then carry out the idea. And securing financial support ought not to be particularly difficult since income tax laws regarding tax shelters were tailor-made to woo wealthy investors, as we shall see later. A bit of experience in developing new sports leagues would be an extra bonus, of course. And the man was available to provide all of these needed qualities: Gary Davidson.

HISTORY OF PRO FOOTBALL UP TO 1973

Over the years football had gained popularity so as to rival baseball as America's national pastime, this despite a much shorter season and many

---

[1]As quoted by Wells Twombly, "Super Flop I," *New York Times Magazine*, January 12, 1975, p. 10.

fewer games played. Football first became popular at the college level and in the early decades of this century many schools developed long-lasting rivalries. Emerging from the success of football at the collegiate level, the National Football League was established in 1924, with six teams. But success was slow in coming and spectators were sparse. From time to time new professional football leagues were formed, but they folded quickly, although some of the teams from these ill-fated leagues were added to the established NFL.

Eventually the National Football League matured and gained in popularity. By 1959 it comprised the following teams:

Eastern Conference	Western Conference
New York	Baltimore
Cleveland	Chicago Bears
Philadelphia	Green Bay
Pittsburgh	San Francisco
Washington	Detroit
Chicago Cardinals	Los Angeles

In 1960, a major rival, the American Football League, was formed. It was to provide competition, not only for fan support but also for players and coaches. At the time of its establishment, the AFL had the following teams:

Eastern Division	Western Division
Houston	Los Angeles[a]
New York	Dallas
Buffalo	Oakland
Boston	Denver

[a] The Los Angeles franchise was soon moved to San Diego after incurring severe financial losses.

The AFL had the support of several influential and wealthy backers who helped "insure" its success; for example, men like Barron Hilton and Lamar Hunt. The story is told of the newsman who remarked to Hunt's father, H. L. Hunt, that Lamar could lose a million dollars a year on his Dallas Texans (now the Kansas City Chiefs). The senior Hunt is supposed to have replied after a thoughtful pause, "That means he has a hundred and twenty years to make it profitable."[2]

[2]C.G., Burck, "Why Those WFL Owners Expect to Score Profits," *Fortune*, September 1974, p. 147.

Table 10.1   Comparison of Paid Attendance, Regular Season, AFL–NFL 1960–1969

	AFL	NFL
1960	926,156 (56 games)	3,128,296 (78 games)
1961	1,002,657 (56 games)	3,986,159 (98 games)
1962	1,147,302 (56 games)	4,003,421 (98 games)
1963	1,208,697 (56 games)	4,163,643 (98 games)
1964	1,447,875 (56 games)	4,563,049 (98 games)
1965	1,782,384 (56 games)	4,634,021 (98 games)
1966	2,160,369 (63 games)	5,337,044 (105 games)
1967	2,295,697 (63 games)	5,938,924 (112 games)
1968	2,635,004 (70 games)	5,882,313 (112 games)
1969	2,843,373 (70 games)	6,096,127 (112 games)

Source: Robert L. Treat, *The Encyclopedia of Football* (New York: A. S. Bournes, 1977), p. 685.

However, the new league lagged far behind the NFL in attendance in the early years. Table 10.1 gives a comparison of the attendance figures and number of games played for 1960–1969. For most of the 1960s the two leagues fought with each other for the top collegiate talent and also for recognition as the top league. Finally, in 1967, the two leagues met in a championship game, billed as the Super Bowl. Financial reward was the prime motivator for such a contest (61,946 spectators viewed the first Super Bowl), although the senior league undoubtedly thought the inferiority of the upstart AFL would be clearly proven. And it seemed to be: in 1967 it was Green Bay 35, Kansas City 10; in 1968, Green Bay 33, Oakland 14. The result of these Super Bowls was to help establish the credibility of the new league, even though it seemed below par to the senior NFL. This was to change dramatically and completely with the 1969 Super Bowl, when the AFL team, the New York Jets, with Joe Namath at the helm, won the Super Bowl 16 to 7 over Baltimore, in a tremendous upset. Now no one could say the AFL was inferior to the NFL.

During the 1960s, new teams had been added to each league and there was also some relocation of franchises to other cities. Then, in 1970, the AFL merged into the NFL, with the NFL now being divided into the National Conference and the American Conference. This merger of the two rival leagues at last ended the suicidal financial battle between the two leagues in recruiting talent.

The popularity of professional football continued to mushroom. At the end of 1970 the NFL, under its two new conferences, had a total attendance of 9,533,333, up from barely 4 million for the two leagues only ten years before. By the end of 1973, the NFL had expanded its two conferences to a

Table 10.2   Paid Attendance, Regular Season, NFL, 1970–1975

1970	9,533,333	(182 games)
1971	10,076,035	(182 games)
1972	10,445,827	(182 games)
1973	10,730,933	(182 games)
1974	10,236,332	(182 games)
1975	10,213,193	(182 games)

Source: Encyclopedia of Football, p. 685.

total of 26 teams, with a total attendance of 10,730,933. See Table 10.2 for attendance and number of games figures for 1970 through 1975.

The NFL had become a great growth industry, with football's gross revenues zooming by 210 percent—aided substantially by increased income from television—during the ten-year period ending in 1973. The Gross National Product during this time increased by only 88 percent. Between 90 and 100 million people—roughly half the population of the United States— were watching the Super Bowl telecast.

ESTABLISHING THE WORLD FOOTBALL LEAGUE

The burgeoning success of professional football was not lost on 38-year-old Gary Davidson. He was a typical Southern California "golden boy"— dimple-chinned, blond, tanned, addicted to exercise. He had passed his bar exam in 1961 and joined a law firm specializing in the legal work involved in launching new businesses and dissolving sick ones. He soon came to realize the potential rewards to be made by the principals and promoters of such activities. (Within a decade, Davidson would be described by some of his former business colleagues as nothing more than "a slick rip-off artist," although he stoutly maintained that he was a major contributor to the American culture.[3]) As he saw it, he provided an important service to wealthy men who needed a means of nourishing their vanity—to be achieved by owning a professional sports team.

Besides being an idea man with the ability to sway others to his proposed ventures, Davidson had the experience of founding not one but two new leagues in other sports, both in the face of well-established and successful rival leagues: the World Hockey Association and the American Basketball Association. The fact that neither league had yet attained profitability was disregarded: each at least had achieved some measure of respectability, and there was always future promise.

Davidson had no undue difficulty in lining up franchisees for the new

[3]Twombly, p. 10.

ootball venture. A WFL franchise could be had for $650,000 in 1974 (the lecision was made in the summer of 1974 to put a $4.2 million price tag on ιny new franchises issued in 1975), far less than the $16 million it took to get ιn expansion team in the NFL. And with all teams starting from scratch in he WFL, there was at least an even chance of a franchise coming up with ι league champion. In contrast, for $16 million for a new NFL expansion ·lub, the owner could be virtually assured of being dead last for a long time.

The tax shelter consequences of an athletic franchise could be very ιttractive to a wealthy investor, since a depreciation allowance would permit ι considerable amount of personal income from other sources to be written)ff and not subject to income tax. Then, assuming that the new league was ·ven moderately successful, the potential for significant appreciation of the ηvestment—which would be taxable at lower capital gains rates—made this ιn especially attractive proposition. Furthermore, there was the example of he National Football League to spur enthusiasm: the Philadelphia Eagles vere bought in 1969 for $16 million and sold in 1973 for $21 million, thus ·esulting in $5 million in capital gains subject to the lowest income taxes— ιot bad for a four-year commitment. Then, the "greater fool's philosophy" vas also rampant: typically an owner says, "I may have been a fool to buy ·his, but there's a bigger fool who'll buy from me."[4]

Marketing Strategies

Davidson introduced some new promotional strategies to the game of ·ootball. The league was organized into twelve teams, with a proposed ·wenty-game season to start July 1974, weeks before the NFL commenced play. The new teams had such catchy and original names as the Chicago Fire, Philadelphia Bell, Southern California Sun, and Portland Storm. Changes in the rules of football designed to give it more action and entertainment were:

The ball will be kicked off from the thirty-yard line to ensure more runbacks.

The goalpost will be moved back to the rear of the end zone.

Missed field goals will be returned to the line of scrimmage except when attempted inside the twenty-yard line.

A two-point conversion attempt (passing or running) will be optional.

Receivers will need just one foot in bounds for a completion.

[4]For more details on the tax savings consequences of investing in athletic teams, see Burck, p. 144.

There will be a fifth quarter, split into two seven-and-a-half minute segments, t break ties.

Fair catches will not be permitted on punts.

An offensive back will be permitted to go into motion toward the line o scrimmage before the ball is snapped.

The hash marks will be moved in toward the center of the field.

An incompleted pass on fourth down will return the ball to the line o scrimmage. This replaces the rule that states that a fourth-down incomplete pas inside the twenty-yard line shall be returned to the twenty.

(Some of these rules changes were soon to be adopted by the NFL either ir whole or with modifications.) A multicolored football was to be used ir contrast to the traditional drab brown. The season was to culminate with a championship World Bowl game between the top divisional leaders, whicl would determine the WFL equivalent to the NFL Super Bowl championshi team.

Obtaining Players

The new league, no matter how attractive the marketing strategy might be could hardly operate without a cadre of able players. The most attractive source for such was obviously the ranks of the existing NFL teams. Draftin; graduating collegians—in competition with the NFL—was more of a long term supply source. The other recourse was to obtain pro castoffs—those unable to make it with an NFL team—and while this was hardly compatible with quality, it became a necessity if 12 teams were to be fielded.

Davidson and his organization recognized the obvious need to woo NFL players—especially stars—over to the WFL camp. Consequently, ir bid up salaries. It also undermined the cartel arrangements the NFL as well as most other professional leagues steadfastly maintained. Under the reserve clause or the slightly different option system, teams had been able to trade players at will, and even prevent them from playing anywhere else in a majo league. But the WFL made itself a highly attractive alternative for NFL players willing to gamble on the league's future, since a player could fulfil his contract and then pick up and go to any team that wanted his services.

In its efforts to wrest major player talent from the NFL, a coup was achieved in the spring of 1974: three top-flight players of the Miami Dolphins, Warfield, Kiick, and Csonka, were signed for $3.5 million to begin playing for the WFL in 1975. This gained major credibility for the new league and led the way for other NFL stars to make the switch. On April 2, Ken

Stabler, conference-leading quarterback of the NFL Oakland Raiders, signed a multi-year contract to play with the WFL Birmingham Americans, starting in 1975. One week later, Randy Johnson, number two quarterback of the New York Giants, and Calvin Hill, the Dallas Cowboys' 1000-yard rusher, signed multi-year contracts to play with the WFL Hawaiians in 1975. Other stars defecting for the 1975 season included Dallas Cowboy quarterback Craig Morton; Claude Humphrey, Atlanta Falcon defensive end; Tom Mack, Los Angeles Ram guard; John Brockington, Green Bay Packer running back; and Daryl Lamonica, veteran quarterback teammate of Stabler's.

Admittedly, however, the big names who were signed were not to join the WFL until 1975, since they were already under contract for the NFL 1974 season. The WFL was not as successful in signing collegiate players, with the exception of the Southern California team that did sign a number of UCLA and University of Southern California graduating seniors.

The effect of the new and aggressive competition for player talent was predictable. NFL salaries rose as much as 60 to 80 percent as a result of the Warfield, Kiick, and Csonka deal, and as frightened NFL owners acted to prevent the wholesale erosion of their talent. One player agent gleefully noted: "All it takes is one WFL owner to say, 'I don't care what it costs; I'm going to buy a winning team,' and that will blow the roof off, as far as money is concerned."[5]

Obtaining Places to Play

As the new league approached its July opening-game schedule, the future continued to look bright. The biggest problem for some teams was finding suitable stadiums, although it was generally conceded that older, temporary stadiums could be used until new ones were built. The New York Stars finally had to settle for Downing Stadium on Randall's Island—". . . its turf was scarred, press box facilities were strictly high school level, the old stands were a splintered eyesore, the lighting system was totally inadequate for Wednesday-night football, and the locker rooms were built long before the age of present-day professional football squads."[6]

Two of the original franchises had to be moved before opening day. The Toronto Northmen were forced to vacate Toronto when the Canadian Parliament considered them too much of a threat to the sovereignty of the Canadian Football League in general, and the Toronto Argonauts in particu-

[5]Herb Gluck, *While the Gettin's Good—Inside the World Football League* (New York: Bobbs–Merrill Company, 1975) p. 42.
    [6]Ibid., p. 91.

lar. The Washington Ambassadors also had to be moved, because the NFL Redskins had a tight lock on Washington's Robert F. Kennedy Stadium they ended up in Orlando, Florida, with the use of the Tangerine Bowl under the name Florida Blazers.

Now the 12 teams of the WFL were centered either in new uncharted cities for professional football, or in cities where rival NFL teams had persistently been a disappointment to their fans, as for example Houston which had won a total of only two games the previous two seasons. Similar chronic NFL losers deemed vulnerable were the Chicago Bears and the Philadelphia Eagles.

Davidson entertained future plans for expansion within five years to such cities as Tokyo, Madrid, London, Munich, Paris, Dusseldorf, Rome Mexico City, and Stockholm. "There is absolutely no way this league can fail," he confidently proclaimed.[7]

Gaining TV Exposure

The new league needed a television contract to help establish its credibility and to provide some additional revenues beyond gate receipts. While at this time a contract as lucrative as those of the NFL teams could hardly be expected—each NFL team was paid about $500,000 a year—still the importance of TV exposure could not be minimized and might indeed be vital to the new league. And Davidson came through, despite the already saturated TV network sports programming, with a TV contract that would net each team about $100,000 for the year: "But this year's not for the money; it's for the exposure."[8]

Five of the six weekly WFL games were to be broadcast on Wednesday nights in the hometowns of the teams that were on the road. The sixth, the so-called "game of the week," was to be televised nationally on Thursday nights (football widows could well weep, with the starting of a full schedule of football programming in July). In these early days of the new league's operation, the ratings suggested that die-hard fans were hungry enough for their sport in July to disrupt customary summer evening activities once or twice a week.

THE FIRST SEASON—AN ADVENTURE
IN ILL-FATED MISCALCULATIONS

The beginning of the season augured well. The league's first nationally televised game, on a hot July evening in Jacksonville, Florida's Gator Bowl,

[7]Twombly, p. 10.
[8]Burck, p. 197.

drew 60,000 spectators and captured a satisfactory 16 percent share of the national TV audience. The game itself was exciting, with the home team Jacksonville Sharks beating the New York Stars on a blocked punt late in the fourth quarter.

In the July 11 *Jacksonville Journal,* an Associated Press story read:

> The World Football League was a box office success in its debut last night, with over 200,000 fans in attendance in five cities. Philadelphia announced 55,534 fans paid their way into John F. Kennedy Stadium, tops in the league, and only the Florida Blazers played before an announced crowd of fewer than 30,000.[9]

But the situation quickly deteriorated. In August both the Philadelphia Bell team and the Jacksonville Sharks admitted that paid attendance figures for their first two home games had been greatly exaggerated. For example, Philadelphia had reported the sale of 121,000 tickets when actually only 20,000 were sold. Before IRS investigators, a Philadelphia Bell executive ruefully excused the release of the phony figures because "if the truth got out we would've been a joke."[10]

Attendance woes were now looming menacingly, with actual figures well below the estimated breakeven point needed of around 35,000 average paid attendance per game. In late August, 12,000 fans came to see the New York Stars maul the Houston Texans. In the rematch in Houston's vast Astrodome, 7,000 Texans were in attendance. On Labor Day on the Stars' home field, 6,000 fans watched. The following week, less than 3,500 customers watched the Stars against the Florida Blazers in the rain.

Things got no better for the league as September matured. On September 18, the debt-ridden Houston franchise was transferred to Shreveport, Louisiana. On September 21, the quarterback of the Detroit Wheels sent a distress message to Davidson: "The situation here is desperate. We haven't been paid in weeks. We've been calling off practice sessions because we can't afford the laundry service."[11] On September 24, the WFL took over the deeply-in-debt Jacksonville franchise. Gary Davidson gathered $65,000 in escrow funds to partially satisfy Jacksonville players who had gone without paychecks for five weeks and were threatening to strike.

The situation was not to improve, not now with the NFL in its full schedule. As the gloomy season progressed, newspapers began to give less coverage to WFL activities (except when there was something negative to report). One consequence of the Chicago newspapers' silence about an

---

[9]Gluck, p. 136–7.
[10]Ibid., p. 154.
[11]Ibid., p. 171.

upcoming game between the Chicago Fire and the New York Stars was tha
fans were not informed about a rescheduling of the game, with 5000 trooping
out to Soldier Field one evening too soon.

In October, the owner of the Chicago club threatened to take his team
out of the league unless a new commissioner was installed and the league
offices shifted from Davidson's Newport Beach, California, locale to New
York City. Gary Davidson readily resigned as commissioner.

The final standings of the teams for the 1974 season are shown in Table
10.3. The average attendance per game for the twelve teams was 21,000, well
below the breakeven point. Almost all the teams broke the record for the
most money lost in a single season. The previous record, $1.3 million, was
rung up in 1960 by the Los Angeles Chargers of the then newly-formed
American Football League, before the franchise was shifted to San Diego
where they were later to become the successful San Diego Chargers.

With such losses, all the teams were in serious financial trouble. Some
of the financial woes bordered on the ludicrous. For example, the New York
Stars in midseason moved to Charlotte, North Carolina, and became the
Charlotte Hornets. Less than three weeks after this move, lawmen arrived

Table 10.3   World Football League Final Standings, 1974

Western Division		
	W	L
Southern California	13	7
Hawaii	9	11
Portland	7	12
Shreveport	7	12

Central Division		
	W	L
Memphis	17	3
Birmingham	15	5
Chicago[a]	7	12
Detroit[a]	1	13

Eastern Division		
	W	L
Florida	14	6
Charlotte	10	10
Philadelphia	8	11
Jacksonville[a]	4	10

[a] Teams disbanded before close of season.

to attach their uniforms for nonpayment of bills owed in New York. The same fate was to befall the Birmingham Americans, who won the first (and only) World Bowl at the conclusion of the season before 32,000 spectators (still below breakeven), only to have their uniforms confiscated by a creditor after the game.

The players found themselves in pitiable circumstances, as some went for weeks without pay. Some found themselves charity cases, being fed and clothed by sympathetic fans; players in Hawaii were left stranded without funds thousands of miles from home; players in Orlando were turned away from banks and stores while trying to cash personal checks. The coach of the Florida Blazers himself had to supply the clubhouse with toilet paper during the tail end of the season.

In the meantime, the football players who said they were jumping to the WFL in 1975 were trying to back off from such ill-conceived ideas. Ken Stabler, for example, had signed to play for Birmingham, for more money of course, but also because this was close to his home. However, the Birmingham club failed to pay him the agreed $30,000 on a specified date before the Oakland Raiders ended their season. Before reconsidering the contract he wanted a guarantee the Birmingham Americans would still be playing in his home state the next year, but could gain no such assurance.

The only true winner was Gary Davidson. For 1974 he had a $100,000 guaranteed salary and also was paid 10 percent of the receipts from the television contracts.

THE SECOND SEASON—1975

After the fiscal disaster of 1974, many people expected the WFL to fold permanently at the end of its title game. However, Chris Hemmeter, a 35-year-old millionaire from Hawaii, devised a new plan for a revitalized attempt by the WFL in 1975. His credentials seemed most reassuring. In 1967, when he was only 28, he had made his first million in the restaurant business. Now he was chairman of the executive committee of the Bank of Honolulu. Hemmeter realized the problems of the previous year and felt that better organization and management was needed in order to promote a new image for the league, one where debts were paid on time. His plan involved the following:

   1. Gate receipts and television income were to be broken down
      proportionately for the following:
      42%—Players' and coaches' salaries
      10%—Stadium rental
      10½%—League assessments
      37½%—Operating expenses and profit account

Table 10.4   WFL Standings, 1975[a]

	Western Division	
	W	*L*
Southern California	7	5
San Antonio	7	6
Shreveport	5	7
Hawaii	5	7
Portland	4	7
Chicago[b]	1	4

	Eastern Division	
	W	*L*
Birmingham	9	3
Memphis	7	4
Jacksonville	6	5
Charlotte	6	5
Philadelphia	4	7

[a] League disbanded Oct. 22, 1975. The schedule originally called for 20 games.
[b] Team disbanded Sept. 2, 1975.

2. New owners were required to help pay past WFL debts as well as maintain a large working capital.
3. Travel expenses were to be prepaid before the start of the season.
4. Gate sharing with visiting teams was to be reintroduced so as to provide a more equitable balance.

Hemmeter calculated that with less frills and overhead expenses, the breakeven point for a team would be 17,000 paid attendance per game. In referring to his plan, Hemmeter optimistically stated: "The plan is mathematically infallible."[12]

San Antonio was added for 1975, while Detroit and Florida were dropped. However, all clubs but Memphis and Philadelphia were under new management. The lineup of teams for 1975, and their win-loss record, is shown in Table 10.4.

For the 1975 season the league hoped to benefit from a number of name NFL players who were now free to join the new league. In addition, Hemmeter hoped to sign Joe Namath for the 1975 season, but this fell through. The lack of credibility gained from the previous season still appeared to hamper operations. The final straw, however, was the inability

[12]As quoted in J. Marshall, "Once and Future League," *Sports Illustrated*, April 21, 1975, p. 29.

INFORMATION SIDELIGHT

THE BREAKEVEN POINT

A breakeven analysis is a vital tool in making go/no-go decisions about new ventures. This can be shown graphically as follows:

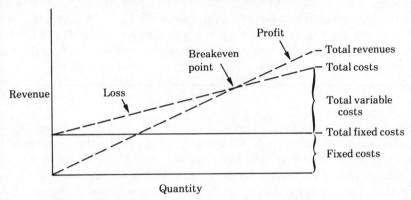

Below the breakeven point, the venture suffers losses (as WFL did); above it, the venture becomes profitable.

Hypothetical Example for a WFL Team

For this example, let us assume that salaries, uniforms and supplies, stadium rent, promotional expenses, transportation and meals, league assessments, interest expenses, and miscellaneous operating expenses are estimated for the first year to be $4.6 million. These are fixed costs or overhead the team would incur regardless of attendance. Let us further assume that at an average ticket price of $7, some 60 cents would be variable costs, leaving $6.40 to cover the overhead and any profit. The attendance needed then to break even is:

$$\frac{\text{Total Fixed costs}}{\text{Contribution to overhead}} = \frac{\$4,600,000}{\$6.40} = \frac{718,750 \text{ for a 20-}}{\text{game season, or about}} \\ 35,940 \text{ per game}$$

An attendance of 21,000 then would be far below such a breakeven point.

These expenses can be estimated quite closely. What cannot be determined as surely are the attendance figures. Now, of course, an organization can do certain things to affect the breakeven point. Obviously, the breakeven point will be lower if the overhead can be reduced, say from $4.6 million to $4.2 million; some expenses and frills might

---

be eliminated. Higher ticket prices would also result in a lower breakeven (but would probably affect attendance adversely). Promotional expenses can be either increased or decreased and would affect the breakeven point and would probably also have an impact on attendance. So there are a number of variables that can be controlled, although the range of discretion for an expensive operation such as a professional football team is not very great. The most practical way of reaching and surpassing the breakeven point so as to make a profit is to increase attendance. And this the WFL was not able to do. With hindsight, this should have been a "no-go" decision.

---

of the league to obtain a national TV contract. The revenue became so sparse that some teams could not even afford to pay the cheerleaders $10 a game; other teams hired ambulance drivers as trainers for the team. The league succumbed to a quiet death just past the halfway mark of the season. The great experiment was over. At the end, Hemmeter had this to say: "We failed in marketing . . . maybe pro sports is a little too swinging for me . . . most of us are bankers and we lacked charisma."[13]

What happened to the players of the doomed league? The NFL at first would not accept them, but pressure from court action by a number of players reversed the ruling, and some began filtering back to either their former teams or to others that needed their specialty. For the time being, Csonka, Kiick, and Warfield remained with Memphis, which, along with Birmingham, attempted to join the NFL as complete teams for 1976, but were unsuccessful.

WHY THE FAILURE?

The rosy promise of the WFL so quickly faded. How could this be? While the motives and abilities of Gary Davidson can be criticized, this was no con job. Even though he emerged with his financial future secure, he can hardly have revelled in the attack by the press on his reputation; his wife had filed for divorce, and his creation was collectively over $20 million in debt—while he himself had been rather ignominiously pressured into resigning as commissioner. But bad business judgment was certainly present in quantity.

---

[13]W. O. Johnson, "Day the Money Ran Out," *Sports Illustrated*, December 1, 1975, p. 85

The direct causes of the failure are easily identifiable.

1. Fan support was lacking, and average attendance fell considerably short of the breakeven point.
2. Television coverage was lacking, especially in the second year of the WFL.
3. At least for the crucial first year, the league lacked big-name talent, even though some had been signed for the 1975 season. The caliber of play, therefore, had to be conceded as inferior to the NFL.
4. The owners were unwilling or unable to contribute additional capital to continue their teams and the league.

While these were the surface causes, we must probe deeper to ascertain the factors or contributors to them. These deeper, fundamental mistakes were in marketing.

If we calculate the percentage year-to-year increase in paid attendance for AFL–NFL football, we see that since 1966 attendance had been, for the most part, increasing at a decreasing rate. (See Table 10.5 for the percentage figures, based on the total attendance data given in Tables 10.1 and 10.2. Especially since 1970, the percentage increase in attendance had steadily fallen, until in the recession year of 1974, when the WFL commenced operation, attendance actually decreased, the first such decrease in pro football since 1951. At the same time, more and more games were being

Table 10.5   Percentage Increase in Paid Attendance Pro Football, 1960–1973 (Exclusive of Post-Season Games)

Year	Percent Increase Over Previous Year
1961	23.05%
1962	3.25
1963	4.30
1964	11.89
1965	6.75
1966	16.85
1967	9.83
1968	3.43
1969	4.96
1970	6.64
1971	5.69
1972	3.67
1973	2.72
1974	(4.61) decrease
1975	(.23) decrease

played, rising from 154 combined AFL-NFL games in 1965, to 182 by 1968. This strongly suggests that saturation was occurring with pro football, with virtually every major city having one or more teams, with the season becoming longer and longer, and with more and more TV coverage.

At the time of the establishment of the WFL in 1973, there were 26 professional football teams in the NFL, covering all geographical areas of this country. The founders of the WFL considered their opportunity and potential market as similar to those at the formation of the AFL in 1960. But at that time there were only 12 professional football teams, and the popularity of pro football was just beginning to emerge. The environment was much different in 1973, but this went undetected.

The WFL made two flawed premises in regard to locating their franchises. First, teams were established in small cities, such as Charlotte North Carolina, and Shreveport, Louisiana, without considering whether there was enough population to support a major football franchise. The other faulty premise was that major cities that had losing NFL teams were ripe candidates for a new league entry.

In addition to indications of a saturation of attendance, TV saturation of sporting events was becoming more and more evident by 1974, especially when the seasons for the different sports overlapped, as they increasingly did. Table 10.6 shows the sporting events on TV for New York City during one week in October of 1974. This was fairly typical of prime TV markets and it did not include ABC's Wide World of Sports or CBS's Sports Spectacular, diversified Saturday and Sunday afternoon shows that provided still more sports exposure. Friday traditionally is a blank spot in professional sports broadcasting, partly because most high school athletic events are scheduled for Friday evening. This heavy TV lineup of established sports necessarily would put a substantial obstacle in the path of an upstart unproven, and (in the absence of name players) presumed inferior newcomer professional league. While the early start of the WFL season (in July assured some initial TV exposure, this was quickly lost when the regular NFL season commenced.

The product was inferior. Like it or not, the WFL in 1974 fielded teams composed of second- and third-rate players. This is a natural consequence for any expansion team, and much more so for an entire expansion league. For something as specialized and demanding as big-time pro sports, the pool of available talent is limited. There are only so many adequate and/or superior athletes. The introduction of a whole new league created a serious imbalance in the supply/demand situation for good football talent. The consequence could not be surprising, given a limited financial pool: inferior players—even mere bodies—had to be relied upon for many positions.

The best players are tied to their own teams with contracts. Eventually

Table 10.6 Example of Sporting Events on TV[a] Week of October 14 to 20, 1974, New York City

Monday	Football
Tuesday	Baseball
Wednesday	Baseball
	Hockey
Thursday	Football
	Baseball
	Hockey
Friday	—
Saturday	Football
	Football
	Baseball
	Basketball
	Horseracing
Sunday	Football
	Football
	Football
	Football
	Baseball

[a] Not included is ABC's Wide World of Sports or CBS's Sports Spectacular, which are diversified Saturday and Sunday afternoon shows.

if the newcomer can dangle enough money and can wait long enough, some of the big names—along with other less well-known, but capable players—will shift allegiance. In the case of the NFL, a surprising number of big names were induced to come over, but not for the 1974 season. Had the WFL remained strong and viable into 1975, it undoubtedly would have fielded a much better product. The lack of sufficient money—especially the reluctance of the owners to sink more money into their enterprises—led to a serious all-around image of inferiority, not only of players, but also of facilities. A poor product placed in an environment of declining potential, and trying to match strongly entrenched competition, hardly had a fighting chance.

Finally, the loss of credibility coming from the widespread exposure of greatly padded attendance figures undoubtedly cast a negative pall over the entire league that was lasting, particularly with the influential sports writers, as well as with any prospective financial backers. As the season progressed, the sorry publicity of missed pay-rolls, franchise shifting and folding, and confiscated equipment and uniforms because of nonpayment of debts further destroyed any credibility and created an image—which was to carry on into the short-lived 1975 season—of a loser from the start. Furthermore, the negative press murdered the possibility of TV advertising, and with it the likelihood of TV coverage for 1975.

WHAT CAN BE LEARNED?

While the World Football League involved a different kind of product from what we normally deal with in marketing, the strategy and tools needed differ little from those used in marketing a tangible product. Similar mistakes can be made, whether we are dealing with entertainment services or a tangible product. The battle seldom goes to the reckless or careless, or to an effort based on tenuously supported optimism. And this is all the more true when our marketer is a newcomer going up against strongly entrenched competition.

In the situation of a firm or organization attempting to gain market entry against a strong existing competitor, the utmost care must be given to carefully assessing the potential, the weaknesses, if any, of the competitor, as well as what unique strengths the newcomer might have or any distinct and relatively untapped parts of the market that a strategy might be developed for. The task of achieving a profitable niche for a new and unknown organization—especially one whose resources are limited vis-à-vis the established competition—must not be taken lightly: this usually presents the strongest challenge that marketers can encounter, and success is often elusive.

The WFL based most of its efforts on the smooth talk and optimistic statements of an acknowledged promoter. The enticement of a tax shelter for rich investors as well as the macho thrill of owning an athletic team led to investors accepting the idea with only a scanty assessment of the potential and of the risks of heavy financial failure. Confidence and, admittedly, some innovative ideas (in making pro football more entertaining) are not substitutes for careful analysis and planning.

What can we generalize as a constructive learning experience from the WFL debacle?

First, some solid notion of market potential must be established. Is there room for an interloper? In the case of the WFL, the evidence suggests that there was not. Saturation with both attendance and TV coverage was becoming strongly evident, as shown in Tables 10.5 and 10.6.

Second, assuming that there is some untapped potential, how can the new venture offer sufficient unique strengths to gain market entry? The major WFL thrust was to smaller cities and to those supposedly disillusioned with poorly performing NFL teams. Unfortunately, the potential in such untapped small cities was apparently insufficient to achieve breakeven, while the poorly performing NFL cities were hardly patsies for a newcomer that could hardly assure them of a higher quality of performance. The market segment sought should be sufficiently large to be profitable, but it should also be vulnerable to a new marketer or marketing strategy.

Third, if an organization is to achieve market penetration against an entrenched competitor, it needs sufficient resources to tolerate several years of losses and heavy promotional and developmental expenses. It also needs sufficient resources in terms of product and/or raw material quality. In the case of the WFL, such resources were severely lacking, at least for 1974, so that the acceptance of the product package by customers was practically doomed from the start.

Fourth, public relations that have to do with the public image of an organization or firm must be scrupulously protected, especially during the vulnerable formative period. There must be no insinuation of spurious dealings or lessening of product quality. Yet, the WFL fell prey to this caveat almost from the beginning.

Finally, the strategy of an interloper must offer customers something unique, something sufficiently desirable that some will switch, or at least test. The WFL had an innovative approach to making pro football more entertaining. Unfortunately, its ideas were easily copied. The NFL, in fact, the next year adopted some of the playing ideas proposed by the WFL. Consequently, the sole competitive advantage of the WFL in offering a more exciting brand of football was quickly nullified by rule changes by the NFL.

The result was that WFL found itself with a static or even declining market potential, inferior resources in the way of player talent and stadium and other facilities, and even no unique differentiation that might have made it attractive to a sufficiently large body of customers.

The mistakes of the WFL have implications beyond professional football.

For Thought and Discussion

1. Would marketing research have helped with the assessing of the market potential for the WFL? How? How would you have designed effective marketing research to help the go/no-go decision?
2. Do you think the WFL gave up too soon?
3. Would more aggressive promotional efforts have been effective? Why or why not?
4. Do you think Joe Namath would have made the difference?
5. Would adequate financial resources have made the WFL viable?

Invitation to Role Play

1. Assume the role of Chris Hemmeter. It is the second season, after the disaster of 1974. What marketing strategy would you have used to give the WFL a better chance of achieving viability? Be as specific as you can.
2. Assume the role of marketing director for a particular franchise of the WFL in 1974. You have carefully calculated that the breakeven point in attendance is about 35,000 per home game, and your team is averaging only 20,000. Develop a promotional program to significantly increase attendance for the remaining five home games. (Assume that your city has a population of 300,000 and 200,000 more people live within fifty miles.)

11

Burger Chef—Why Not Another McDonald's?

In 1967, General Foods Corporation acquired Burger Chef Systems, a fast-food franchising operation of some 700 units, for $16 million. In less than four years, General Foods amassed a pre-tax loss of $83 million in this venture. During this same time, 1967 to 1971, McDonald's net income rose from $7,072,000 to $27,248,000, for a 285 percent increase. While some marginal fast-food franchisors collapsed during this period when there appeared to be a saturation of hamburger, chicken, and other restaurants, General Foods was no marginal firm. It was the nation's largest manufacturer of convenience foods, with sales approaching $3 billion. It was an astute and aggressive marketer and the country's third-largest national advertiser (behind only Procter & Gamble and American Home Products), spending over $150 million a year. It had had an unbroken string of annual increases in sales dating back to 1935. During this time the last decline in net earnings was in 1962. With such backing for an already established and growing franchise chain, how could disaster strike, and in just a few years?

FRANCHISING

Franchising is a contractual arrangement in which the franchisor extends to independent franchisees the right to conduct a certain kind of business according to a particular format. While the franchising arrangement may involve a product, a common type of franchise today involves a service rather than a product, with the major contribution of the franchisor being a carefully developed, promoted, and controlled operation, both through external signing and commonality of physical plant to internal standards and procedures, such as provided by McDonald's, Howard Johnson, Kentucky Fried Chicken, and Burger Chef.

Franchising dates back to at least 1898, when General Motors established its first independent dealer to sell and service automobiles. By 1910, franchising was the principal method of marketing automobiles and petroleum products. By 1920 it was being used by food, drug, variety, hardware, and automotive-parts firms. The major growth of franchising began after World War II. Soft ice cream outlets typify this growth: in 1945 there were 100 soft ice cream stands in the United States; by 1960 there were almost 18,000.

Franchise sales of goods and services by 1978 were about $275 billion, almost 30 percent of all retail sales. In 1978 there were almost half a million franchise establishments in the United States, and these employed over four million workers.[1]

Advantages of Franchising

A firm has two major advantages in expanding through franchised outlets rather than with company-owned units. First, expansion can be very rapid since the franchisees are putting up some or most of the money—almost the only limitations to growth are the need to screen applicants, to find suitable sites for new outlets, and to develop the managerial controls necessary to assure consistency of performance. The other major advantage is that more conscientious people normally can be obtained to operate the outlets, since franchisees are entrepreneurs with a personal stake, rather than hired managers.

A potential franchise or licensee finds the major advantage over other means of self-employment lies in the lower risk of business failure or, to say it positively, a greater chance of success. By going with an established franchisor, our entrepreneur will have a business that has a proven consumer acceptance and perhaps wide recognition. The franchisee can also benefit from well-developed managerial and promotional techniques and from the group buying power that is afforded.

---

[1]U.S. Department of Commerce, *Franchising in the Economy*, 1977–1979 (Washington, D.C.: Superintendent of Documents, U.S. Government Printing Office, 1979), pp. vi, 1.

Fast-Food Restaurant Franchising

Franchised fast-food restaurants have made a major impact on the food service industry since the second World War. Employment in fast-food franchising by the 1970s accounted for almost 30 percent of total franchising employment, and over 30 percent of all persons employed in eating and drinking places in the United States.[2] Illustrative of the successful growth of this industry, let us briefly look at two of the stars: Kentucky Fried Chicken and McDonald's.

Colonel Harland Sanders and Kentucky Fried Chicken. In 1955, Sanders was operating a moderately successful Southern fried chicken restaurant on a main highway in Kentucky on the north-south route from Detroit to Miami. But a new highway was built which bypassed his business by seven miles, and he was forced to close. And he was 65 years old and all he had left was a sixth-grade education and $105, his first social security check.

On a hunch, he took five frozen frying chickens and a special cooker, along with some flour and spices, and began calling on restaurants in Indiana and Ohio. His method was to cook chickens at high temperatures for less than eight minutes. After three years he finally made some headway. He gave franchises away; he leased cookers or converted stoves for high temperature; he supplied at cost paper, napkins, and buckets with his image and the Kentucky Fried Chicken name—and he received 5 cents for each chicken sold by these restaurants.

Customers liked the product. In eight years he had granted more than 500 franchises and his revenues were over $2.3 million. He was his own sales force and he never had more than eighteen employees. In 1962, then 72 years of age, he expanded the business to include take-home sales. In 1964 he sold the entire business, including patents, to a group for $2 million, retaining for himself the lifetime job of goodwill ambassador. The new management concentrated on take-home sales. By 1968, sales were over $250 million and there were more than 1500 outlets.

Ray Kroc and McDonald's. At age 51, in 1954, Ray Kroc was the sole distributor for a Chicago firm making a multi-mixer for milk shakes (i.e., a mixer for six milk shakes at a time). He became excited when he received his largest order: eight multi-mixers from one store in San Bernardino, California, operated by Maurice and Dick McDonald. He flew out to California to see for himself this "super" restaurant, and found a clean, efficiently run, high-volume drive-in restaurant with a limited menu based around the

[2]Ibid., p. 11.

hamburger. Kroc immediately thought that if there were only 100 other such restaurants he'd be rich (8 multi-mixers × 100 restaurants = 800 multi-mixers sold). He persuaded the McDonalds to let him franchise their outlet throughout the country, with one-half of one percent of the gross receipts going to them. Kroc opened the first franchise in Des Plaines, Illinois, in 1955. Five years later there were 228 restaurants. In 1961 Kroc bought out the McDonald brothers for $2.7 million. By 1966, McDonald's units were generating sales of $266 million; by 1971, $784 million; and by 1975, $2.5 billion.

THE GENERAL FOODS COMPANY

General Foods can trace its beginnings back to C. W. Post Cereals in 1895. It was incorporated in 1922 as the Postum Cereal Company, manufacturers of Post cereals and Postum beverage. Then, in 1925, the firm began consolidating with certain other companies, among them the Jell-O Company and the Maxwell House Coffee Company. In 1929 the Postum Cereal Company changed its name to General Foods.

The company continued to grow and diversify, not only through internal development of many new products, but also by acquisition and mergers with other firms. By 1965 its sales were $1.5 billion, a 60 percent gain over 1956; during that same period, net earnings more than doubled to $177 million. Well-known brands of this major processor and marketer of packaged food products included: Maxwell House, Yuban, and Sanka coffees; Jell-O desserts; Bird's Eye frozen foods; Post cereals; Swans Down cake mixes; Baker's chocolate; Minute Rice; Kool-Aid soft drink mixes; Gaines pet foods; Tang breakfast drink; and Log Cabin syrup.

During the 1960s, however, some indicators of performance began showing deterioration. While sales revenues increased steadily, net profits did not keep pace with sales. As a result, profit margins on sales began declining from the high of 6.5 percent in 1963. Furthermore, returns on stockholders' equity also began declining from the 17.5 percent of 1963. Figure 11.1 shows these trends graphically. Still, in 1966 when a new man, C. W. "Tex" Cook, came in as chairman and chief executive, and Arthur E. Larkin became president and chief operating officer, GF stood at the forefront of the packaged foods industry with net profits at 6 percent of sales being among the industry's highest. Furthermore, of six major food categories, GF led in all but cereals, with no competitor even close in instant coffee, desserts, and dog food.

More tangible problems emerged in 1968 when the Federal Trade Commission forced GF to divest of its S.O.S. soap-pad business, which it had acquired in 1957. Chairman Cook bitterly took umbrage at this decision:

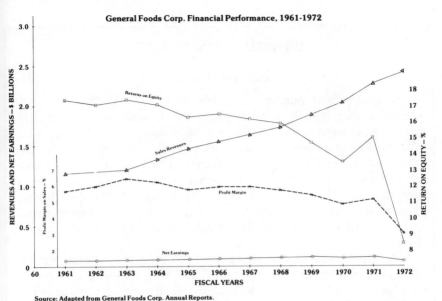

Source: Adapted from General Foods Corp. Annual Reports.

Figure 11.1. General Foods Corp. financial performance, 1961–1972. (Source: Adapted from General Foods Corp. annual reports.

They laid down some pretty severe strictures regarding what we could and could not do for "X" number of years. For instance, they made it very clear that we were precluded from touching anything of consequence that went through the supermarket on a national basis. Similarly, they would frown on something that depended very heavily on consumer advertising. So that we were almost directed away from the kinds of things where our experience and expertise had, over the years, given us most of our benefits.[3]

To add to the problems connected with antitrust action, three of GF's biggest divisions began running into trouble. The Bird's Eye Division lost ground to Green Giant Company, which had developed ready-to-cook vegetables in plastic bags that could be dropped directly into boiling water, thereby offering consumers a very attractive convenience. Furthermore, supermarkets were increasingly bringing out their own private branded products, which they could sell below the prices of General Foods' national brands, and consumer acceptance of these was further cutting into GF's market share and profit margins.

[3]As quoted in "The Rebuilding Job at General Foods," *Business Week,* August 25, 1973, p. 50.

INFORMATION SIDELIGHT

PRIVATE BRANDS

Wholesalers and retailers often use their own brands—commonly referred to as private brands—in place of or in addition to the branded goods of manufacturers. Private brands usually are offered at lower selling prices than nationally advertised brands, yet they typically give dealers more per-unit profit since they can be bought on more favorable terms, partly reflecting promotional savings involved. Some firms, such as Sears, Penney's, and A&P, stock mostly their own brands. Thereby they have better control over repeat business, since satisfied customers can repurchase the brand only through the particular store or chain.

With private brands directly competing with manufacturers' brands, sometimes at a better price, you may ask: Why do manufacturers sell some of their output to a retailer under a private brand? A major reason is that manufacturers thereby may minimize idle plant capacity. The manufacturers can always rationalize that if he refuses business with private label seekers, someone else will not, and the competition with private brands will not be eliminated. Other manufacturers welcome private brand business because they lack the resources and know-how to enter the marketplace effectively with their own brands.

The Maxwell House Division, which had been generating more than a third of General Foods' sales revenues, began finding sales leveling off. To a considerable extent this reflected changing consumer tastes, particularly those of young adults, whose consumption of coffee was not matching that of their parents.

Probably for the same reason—a change in consumer tastes—the dry cereal market growth slowed markedly. Added to this, competitor General Mills was exerting a massive promotional push with the result that General Foods Post Division (Post Toasties, Grape Nuts, 40% Bran Flakes, etc.) was displaced from second place behind Kellogg.

Faced with governmental constraints, a tangible loss of profit momentum, and an eroding competitive stance, GF began seeking diversification in directions that would at least have some compatibility with the company expertise: food-related activities. During the mid-1960s, fast-food restaurants—McDonald's and many others—had been experiencing burgeoning growth rates. In fact food sold away from home was growing at twice the rate of food sold in stores for home consumption.[4]

In late 1967, the acquisition for somewhat over $16 million of Burger Chef Systems, an Indianapolis-based chain of 700 (mostly franchised) fast-food hamburger restaurants, seemed altogether reasonable and expeditious. Six Rix roast-beef sandwich restaurants were also acquired at that time. The logic seemed inescapable. General Foods had great expertise in food processing, 1968 was a boom year, and companies like McDonald's were growing at rates in excess of 25 percent a year. Burger Chef was already operating in thirty-nine states and was selling a million hamburgers per day. Needless to say, expectations for the fast-food business were high.

BURGER CHEF UNDER GENERAL FOODS

In an effort to capitalize on the opportunities of the times, a vigorous expansion program was undertaken for Burger Chef. By March 1969, not much more than a year after the acquisition, there were 900 outlets operating across the country. That same month, Burger Chef moved into Canada with the opening of an outlet in Toronto.

By December 1969, there were 1022 outlets in the United States, and 29 in Canada. Exactly one year later, the totals were more than 1200 outlets in the United States and 36 in Canada, representing an increase of over 70 percent in three years. Some 84 percent of the outlets were franchised, with 16 percent operated by Burger Chef. Advertising expenditures averaged $2.5 million a year.

A complication for GF in its fast-food acquisitions was the loss of key executives from these operations. The founder of Burger Chef left to pursue other interests shortly after the acquisition. Another key executive had a heart attack. Other departures for various reasons resulted in an almost complete management turnover during the first two years. But this seemed to pose no severe problems, as GF supplied the new management for its acquisition from its own ranks.

The bad news, when it came, was sudden and shocking. In January 1972, General Foods announced a write-down amounting to $83 million pre-tax dollars, nearly $1 a share after taxes. GF informed its stockholders that it was cutting back, pruning rather drastically, after its ambitious expansion into fast food. It was closing all seventy of its Rix hot roast beef restaurants. Of some 1200 Burger Chef hamburger stands, it announced that it had already closed 100 and was writing off many more. The faster GF tried to expand its fast-food operation, the bigger the problems became.

[4] "We've Turned a Corner," *Forbes,* March 15, 1969, p. 46.

Forbes magazine questioned how so big a company could go so wrong in so seemingly simple a business as frying hamburgers and slicing roast beef. In an interview with *Forbes* reporters, President Larkin explained: "We couldn't get enough people to come into our stores. The kids didn't want roast beef and later the adults didn't want it either. Roast beef was just a fad." Regarding the Burger Chef operation, Larkin admitted the problem was simply management: "The key man got a heart attack. We sent one of our own men and he just did not know his way around this kind of operation."[5]

The heavy loss was a shocker. The original investment in Burger Chef had been $16 million. GF discovered, however, that long-term lease commitments are debts too, especially if an outlet goes bad. Then, the expansion of the two chains, neither one on sound footing, was like throwing good money after bad, so that the $16 million investment escalated into an $83 million loss.

Struggle for Survival

For 19 straight years, General Foods had managed to achieve gains in per-share earnings. But the hamburger and roast beef disaster broke the trend in 1972. Although, the viability of the multi-billion dollar company was not in danger, and the company still made profits overall, despite the fast-food drain. Still, the heavy losses suffered with Burger Chef hurt the image of the company, especially with its major food chain customers. This image further suffered when GF cut back on some customer services in order to absorb the fast-food losses.

Arthur Larkin, who presumably had been the heir apparent for the chairman's position, took an "early retirement," As part of a company-wide efficiency drive, salaried personnel were cut by 10 percent, and GF took a hard look at its total marketing operation.

While some other aspects of the operation were also causing problems, the biggest rebuilding job continued to be the Burger Chef chain. The total number of units was pruned to about 1000, and more attention was given to clustering these in major markets to obtain a more efficient sharing of advertising expenditures. More thorough screening and training of franchise owners and managers was instituted. A new building design, new logo, more emphasis on product quality, a more varied menu, and even a new plastic wrapper to keep hamburgers warm longer, were belatedly introduced. Yet, it seemed likely the fast-food division would be years away from making a major contribution to GF's earnings. Table 11.1 shows how Burger Chef

[5]"The Bigger They Are . . . ." *Forbes,* February 15, 1972, p. 21.

	1974		1973		1972		1971	
	A	B	A	B	A	B	A	B
1. McDonald's	1,940,000	19.8	1,507,000	17.7	1,032,000	15.2	784,000	13.4
2. Kentucky Fried Chicken	1,150,000	11.7	1,000,000	11.8	840,000	12.4	900,000	15.4
3. International Dairy Queen	590,000	6.0	530,000	6.0	510,000	7.5	424,000	7.3
4. Burger King	466,500	4.8	388,600	4.0	270,700	4.0	226,000	3.9
5. Burger Chef	275,000	2.8	225,000	2.6	200,000	2.9	225,000	3.9
6. A & W International	265,000	2.7	264,000	3.1	241,000	3.5		
7. Hardee's	259,000	2.6	206,000	2.4	136,000	2.0	107,000	1.8
8. Denny's	252,964	2.6	204,016	2.4	163,411	2.4	132,332	2.3
9. Jack-in-the-Box	244,000	2.6	170,000	2.1	132,000	1.9		
10. Pizza Hut	242,000	2.5	160,000	2.0	115,000	1.7	77,680	1.3
11. Bonanza	193,000	1.9	140,700	1.7	92,846	1.4	64,000	1.1
12. Sambo's	190,000	1.9	138,000	1.7	92,152	1.4	61,582	1.1
13. Gino's	170,521	1.7	170,521	2.1	128,044	1.9	95,300	1.6
14. Dunkin Donuts	169,474	1.7	141,757	1.7	126,693	1.8	99,593	1.8
15. Ponderosa	155,000	1.6	96,552	1.1	96,552	1.4	64,065	1.1
16. Church's Fried Chicken	126,000	1.3	101,600	1.3	79,354	1.2	51,200	0.9
17. Shoney's	120,401	1.2	101,349	1.2				
18. Arby's International	120,175	1.2	100,000	1.2				
19. Jerrico	98,870	1.0	61,678	0.7				
20. Frisch's Big Boy	91,000	0.9	88,000	1.0	79,000	1.2	73,000	1.2
21. Morrison's	90,800	0.9	66,000	0.8	52,250	0.8		
22. Friendly Ice Cream	90,000	0.9	71,775	0.8	61,249	0.9	49,379	0.8
23. Shakey's	87,000	0.9	74,500	0.9	63,650	0.9	73,000	1.2
24. Mr. Steak	85,000	0.9	81,700	1.0	64,000	0.9	49,800	0.9
25. Sizzler	85,500	0.9	62,200	0.6	43,443	0.7		

Key: "A" represents Total Sales, given in $1,000's (000).
"B" represents Market Share, given as a percentage (%).
Sources: Advertising Age, June 3, 1974, p. 52; May 14, 1973, p. 93; and June 30, 1975, p. 49.

fared in these years against its major fast-food competitors. Notice that while sales increased slightly each year, in no way did they match the increases of the major competitors, so that market share slipped every year.

POST MORTEM

Evaluation of Strategy after General Foods Acquisition

Such a perfect acquisition it seemed in 1968. How could such a compatible union go wrong? In retrospect, a fast-food operation was vastly different from the marketing of packaged food sold in supermarkets, despite their both dealing with food. There were major differences in promotional efforts needed, in competition, in facilities required, and most important, in management controls needed. Unfortunately, GF did not realize this until much of the damage was done.

No single event can be selected as the cause of the Burger Chef debacle; rather, it was a combination of circumstances. These, however, were by no means hidden; they were obvious and should have been identified and corrected by an astute management.

At the time of the acquisition, Burger Chef suffered from a lack of distinction and identity. McDonald's had its golden arches, gaudy though they might be, but they readily identified an outlet; Kentucky Fried Chicken was easily recognized; so were most of the other successful fast-food establishments. But what did Burger Chef have: a red and yellow sign, of no particular distinction, and not even universally used, and certainly inconspicuous among the multitude of other signs proliferating along commercial strips. The outlets themselves tended to be cheaply constructed gas station-quality buildings, some with walk-up windows, but few with sit-down accommodations. Furthermore, there was little uniformity in design among the mostly franchised operations.

Burger Chef faced a considerable disadvantage in that its 700 outlets at the time of acquisition were thinly dispersed and spread over 39 states. As a result, a major metropolitan area might have only a handful of restaurants, in contrast to McDonald's and some of the other major franchisors. Consequently, supervision was difficult and costly and the benefits of concentrated promotional efforts, which could have been shared among a number of outlets at no prohibitive cost for any, had to be curbed, leaving the competitive advantage to those firms with more concentration of outlets. The better policy, then, would have been a slower geographical expansion, doing so on a market-by-market basis.

The quality of food and the limited assortment available also contributed to the poor performance. At the time when competitors were adding fish sandwiches, double and triple-decker hamburgers, onion rings, and fruit pies to their food assortment, Burger Chef was standing pat. And the food quality varied with franchisee and area, and was a major problem.

Company spokesmen admitted their selection of franchisees, and their training of them, was questionable at best. Persons who expressed an interest in a Burger Chef franchise, and who had satisfactory character references and financial standing and some experience in running a filling station or whatever, were approved. While these new franchise holders would then be sent to a training school for a brief period, there was no on-the-job training to familiarize them with hiring people, to teach them how to be hospitable, how to handle the problems of a teen-age gathering place, and so on.

A further flaw became apparent in the Burger Chef operation. Emphasis was on expanding—expanding in number of outlets just as rapidly as possible. In the process, existing outlets and their problems were ignored. As a result, location mistakes, problems of controlling quality of product and service, and others were not corrected for the new units being established. The expansion was coming on top of an unstable and even wobbly base.

An economic recession in 1969–1971 should have discouraged pell-mell expansion, or at least caused some introspection and review of the overall marketing strategy for this division. During this time, some of the marginal fast-food franchisors bit the dust. But the stronger ones survived with little ill effects. With the formidable resources of General Foods, Burger Chef should have strengthened its market share, focusing on upgrading and improving the outlets it had, instead of enlarging its mediocrity. As President Larkin said: "We moved too far, too fast, under the pressure of the times."[6]

Comparison of Burger Chef with McDonald's

The deficiencies of the Burger Chef operation are more apparent when we compare it with the most successful in the industry, McDonald's. What was the key to the overwhelming McDonald's success?

This statement is widely quoted: "McDonald's success is based on the fact that it changed the smelly, roadside hamburger stand into a clean, efficient family restaurant."[7] Kroc offered the public a clean, family atmosphere where service was quick and cheerful. Cleanliness of outlets, including the toilets, and friendliness of salespeople became major competitive advantages. Efficient speed, friendly service, and assured cleanliness

[6]Marylin Bender, "At General Foods, Did Success Breed Failure?" *The New York Times*, June 11, 1972, p. III–18.

[7]"McDonald's Keeps Them Cooking," *Financial World*, August 28, 1974, p. 45.

were not maintained without great pains. At Hamburger University, a special McDonald's training school for managers and owners, heavy emphasis was given customer service. A 350-page operating manual required adherence to strict standards, not only in preparation of food but also in care and maintenance of the facilities. For example, the manual called for door windows to be washed twice daily. Similar tight standards concerned service, food, and cooking procedures. There was even an employee dress code, with men required to keep their hair cropped to military length and their shoes highly polished. Women must wear dark, low shoes, hair nets, and only very light makeup. All employees wore prescribed uniforms.

The cooking was completely standardized. A pound of meat must have less than 19 percent fat. Buns must measure 3½ inches wide, no more than ¼ oz. of onions was permitted per hamburger, and so on. The holding time for each of the cooked products was set by corporate headquarters: for example, french fries, 7 minutes; burgers, 10 minutes; coffee, 30 minutes—after this time the products must be thrown out. Company auditors closely scrutinized this part of the operation to assure that all food served was of the same quality.

Consistency in adhering to the high standards was another notable mark of McDonald's. Close supervision of store operations by strong regional offices was maintained in order to prevent a weakness in one restaurant from having a detrimental effect on other stores in the system.

Franchises were granted store by store, and operators permitted to expand only if they satisfactorily met the stiff standards. This contrasted with most other franchisors, who granted area franchises to large investors who promised to put up a given number of outlets in a specified period. Although the rate of growth was rapid, there were few problems with substandard conditions at either company-owned or franchised outlets.

McDonald's rigorously analyzed potential sites to insure each unit of the maximum chance for success, and failures due to poor locations were few. The distinctive buildings and the arches, of course, made a McDonald's unit visible and conspicuous from a distance.

McDonald's was one of the biggest users of mass media advertising of any retailer, budgeting over $50 million each year. Who is not familiar with the jingle "You Deserve a Break Today"? How successful has this mass advertising been? In a survey of school children in the early 1970s, 96 percent identified Ronald McDonald, ranking him second only to Santa Claus.[8]

Judiciously, and only after considerable testing, McDonald's began

---

[8]"The Burger that Conquered the Country," *Time*, September 17, 1973, pp. 84–92.

broadening its product line. In 1975 a new breakfast menu resulted in 5 to 10 percent sales increases for those outlets serving it.[9] Other kinds of sandwiches—for example, a quarter pounder with lettuce and tomato—were tested, as was also the possibility of adding chicken to the menu, a move estimated to increase sales 15 percent, but also requiring about $14,000 worth of additional equipment per store.[10]

In all these areas of operation, Burger Chef showed up poorly compared to McDonald's. It lacked image, consistency, a diversifying product line, and promotional expenditures—only $2.5 million annually during the growth years, versus $50 million for McDonald's—to bring it recognition, distinctiveness, and customer appeal. In addition, it lacked a well-planned and organized selection procedure for franchisees and also a training program to assure that desirable operational procedures would result. Finally, Burger Chef controls and auditing in no way compared with the thoroughness and strictness practiced by McDonald's.

Comparison of Burger Chef with the Losers

Burger Chef was not quite a loser. While it was trimmed in size, it did not go out of business (although we can speculate that GF might have been better off selling the division rather than continuing the drain on financial and managerial resources). A useful perspective can be gained by comparing it against the real losers in the industry, especially those franchise firms that faded in the late 1960s and early 1970s.

Some franchisors failed because of difficulty in obtaining qualified franchisees or licensees. McDonald's believed that a key factor for success was for a licensee initially to work full time in the business. The unsuccessful franchisors failed to attract or insist on licensees who met prescribed qualifications. They tended to be interested primarily in getting the initial franchise fee. Business was viewed as a quick buck scheme, to be milked dry with the franchisor then exiting.

Poor site selection plagued some franchise operations. In eagerness to secure footholds in major markets, they failed to research for satisfactory locations. Too fast an expansion led to indiscriminate site selection sometimes influenced by opportunistic realtors. Another factor inducing poor locations was lack of capital to purchase the more desirable sites.

When business and the economy in general is going well, a lack of effective management controls is not always readily apparent. However,

---

[9]"Broader Menus for Fast Foods," *Business Week,* July 14, 1975, p. 118.
[10]"For Ray Kroc, Life Began at 50, or Was It 60?" *Forbes,* January 15, 1973, pp. 24–30.

when the economy experiences a downturn and, more important, when competition intensifies, lack of effective controls can be fatal to these businesses.

In order to gain quick public attention and recognition, many fast-food franchisors in the 1960s used the name of either an entertainer or professional sports figure to lure potential licensees. For example, Minnie Pearl's Chicken, Here's Johnny Restaurant (Johnny Carson), Al Hirt Sandwich Saloon, Broadway Joe's (Joe Namath), Jerry Lucas Beef 'n Shake, and Mickey Mantle's Country Cookin' Restaurant. What soon became apparent, however, was that while the public might pay to see the entertainer or sports figure perform, they would not necessarily be willing to frequent a fast-food outlet simply because of the famous name—unless the food and service warranted their patronage, and most of these did not. Two successful exceptions have been Gino's, primarily located on the East Coast, and owned by Gino Capelletti, former All-Pro defensive end for the Baltimore Colts, and Roy Rogers Restaurants, sponsored by the former cowboy star. But both offer good food and amenities.

Deceptive advertising was sometimes used to vastly inflate profit claims, thus better to attract investors. Sometimes the profit claims were based on questionable accounting procedures. For example, Minnie Pearl's Chicken. In May 1968, there were 405 franchises and stock was first issued at $20 a share. By December of that year, there were over 1200 franchises and the stock reached a high of $68. Success appeared phenomenal. By the end of 1969, 1600 franchises had been sold, although only 263 stores were in operation. By 1970, there were only 183 stores operating out of 1840 franchises sold, and success was turning to failure. What happened? It became apparent that profits had been vastly inflated by counting the sale of franchises as current income, instead of conservatively taking this into income only in increments from year to year. The stock that had reached $68 in 1968 plummeted to 50 cents in 1970.[11]

Burger Chef exhibited none of these irregularities of deceptive advertising and profits, and opportunistic speculation. It was a solidly backed operation, geared to playing a major role in the fast-food industry. Yet, its flawed operational procedures nullified its strengths. It had the ball and fumbled it.

[11]Reported in "Fried Chicken that Went into Politics," *Business Week,* September 19, 1970, p. 37; and Richard Elliott, Jr., "Home to Roost: Excesses of the Fast Food Franchisers are Catching Up with Some," *Barrons,* September 22, 1969, p. 5.

WHAT CAN BE LEARNED?

Franchising presents some significant differences from the other business operations examined in this book. The major distinction is the very rapid growth possible through franchising—far more rapid than a firm can achieve on its own, even if it has substantial resources. Since somebody else is putting up most or all of the capital for an outlet, the major impediment to expansion is finding and wooing sufficient investor-licensees, and also finding sufficient attractive sites for units to be placed. As we have just seen, both of these requirements can be carelessly done in the quest for wild expansion or, as with McDonald's, can be carefully adhered to for controlled expansion.

A further distinction of franchising is that a few poor operations can be detrimental to the other outlets, since all are operating under the same format and logo. While this is not dissimilar to any chain operation—in that a few bad stores can hurt the image of the rest of the chain—a franchise system is composed of independent entrepreneurs who will tend to be less controllable than the hired managers of a chain operation.

Illusion of Rapid Growth

The great growth possible through a franchise system can be its downfall. Since growth in number of units can occur so easily and quickly, there is the temptation to be a slave to it, to rush headlong into opening ever more units to meet the clamoring demand of prospective licensees. Such emphasis on growth often means that existing operations will be largely ignored. As a consequence, they will be undercontrolled, with emerging problems not receiving adequate attention. Screening people and locations tends to become superficial. Eventually the bubble bursts and the firm is forced to recognize that many outlets are marginal at best and will have to be drastically pruned, if indeed the total operation can even survive. This was the scenario with Burger Chef as well as others that failed. While an aggressive and ambitious firm seeks growth, this must be prudent and controlled—even if a slower growth rate must be tolerated in order to achieve adequate assimilation.

Necessity for Tight Controls

Any firm needs to maintain tight controls over far-flung outlets if it is to be sufficiently informed of emerging problems and opportunities and if it is to maximize the resources of the firm and maintain a desired image and standard of performance. In a franchise operation this is all the more essential, as we have noted before, because we are dealing with independent entrepreneurs rather than hired managers, and because a few inferior units can adversely affect the others. Controls should mean not only prescribing standards—remember the 350-page operating manual of McDonald's—but also monitoring to assure that the standards are maintained. Regional and/or home office executives should make frequent, unscheduled calls on stores, probably with a checklist in hand, and grade their performance according to the prescribed standards. All aspects of the operation should be checked, ranging from the grease content of french fries to the soap supply in restrooms. Where performance of a particular outlet deviates significantly from that prescribed, remedial action will have to be taken, from warnings to even taking a franchise away in the event of continuing deficiencies.

Other controls are needed for screening and selecting franchisees and for training them. Specifications should also be established for site selection and building standards. Only in this way can uniformity of operation at a desired quality level be achieved and maintained.

Need for a Distinctive Image

Any firm needs to develop a distinctive image, one that differs from competitors, and is unique and identifiable. This is especially important in a highly competitive environment. Burger Chef failed badly here, in the midst of competitors who were highly effective in developing such distinctions. To this day, Burger Chef has not achieved a distinctive image.

Admittedly, uniqueness is not always easy to achieve, especially where many competitiors have already adopted more obvious possibilities. But the search should go on. Uniqueness can come from a distinctive design or logo, or roof, or building style; it can come from a different menu, somewhat different services, a different promotional approach; it can even be achieved by appealing to a different customer segment.

Imitation Should Not Be Disdained

A willingness to imitate may seem a contradiction to the previous section, the need for a distinctive image. But not so. We are talking here about adopting proven successful business practices, not imitating a sign or a building style, or even a menu without any changes.

Burger Chef had the supremely successful example, McDonald's, to learn from. McDonald's management and operational procedures were not unknown; indeed, they were highly publicized. It required no genius to recognize the merits in what McDonald's was doing, and put these into effect in another operation. But Burger Chef failed to do this; other franchisors—

for example, even Burger King, a Pillsbury Company acquisition—also either failed to fully imitate the successful strategy, or did so only belatedly, as Burger King finally began to do in the late 1970's.[12]

When a firm has developed a proven and successful format, why should other firms hesitate to imitate it? They can still maintain their own distinctive images, but ones fully structured on successful management and control practices. While imitation may be viewed as not creative, it represents sound and astute learning. Creativity can be reserved for other aspects of the operation.

For Thought and Discussion

1. Playing the devil's advocate (one who takes the opposing viewpoint for argument's sake), criticize the acquisition of Burger Chef by General Foods as thoroughly as you can.
2. In an exercise in creativity, perhaps brainstorming,[13] offer suggestions for a distinctive image or format for Burger Chef.
3. Would you advocate changing the name of Burger Chef? Why or why not?
4. How do you account for the reluctance of competitors to imitate successful examples of other firms in their industry?
5. Do you think the FTC was justified in curbing General Foods' expansion in 1968? Discuss both sides of this action—i.e., from the viewpoints of the FTC and GF.

Invitation to Role Play

Assume the role of the GF executive responsible for Burger Chef after the acquisition. Be as specific as you can in formulating a marketing strategy for the growth of this venture.

[12]As reported in "The Man Who McDonaldized Burger King," *Business Week,* October 8, 1979, pp. 132–136.

[13]Brainstorming is a technique to stimulate group creativity. A group of persons (5 to 8 persons seems to be the best sized group) are brought together for the sole purpose of producing ideas, with this best achieved when: criticism is ruled out; free-wheeling is welcomed; quantity of ideas is wanted, with no emphasis on quality at this point; participants are encouraged to build on and/or modify the ideas of others.

CHAPTER 12

W. T. Grant Company— Ill-Conceived Expansion

In June of 1975 James Kendrick, 62-year-old chief executive of W. T. Grant Company, had his back to the wall. He was in charge of a retail giant of almost 1200 stores having sales of nearly $2 billion. But the company was in financial jeopardy, on the verge of bankruptcy. Grant owed $600 million in short-term loans and $100 million in long-term debt to 143 banks. Furthermore, it had just encountered a staggering $175 million loss for 1974. And the losses were continuing: in the first quarter of 1975, Grant's loss was $54 million. Dividends, which had proudly been paid for 69 years, were suspended. On June 2, 1975, Grant was to pay $57 million to retire its debt to 116 of the banks. Failure to do so might well induce some of the creditors to push Grant into bankruptcy.

PRELUDE

The blame for this situation was not Kendrick's. The previous management had been deposed in a director's revolt in August of 1974. Kendrick was a long-time Grant employee who had been running a subsidiary, Zelle's, Ltd., in Canada. Seven years before, he had been a candidate for president of Grant; at the time he was Grant's first sales vice president. But he was passed over then and exiled to Canada because he questioned certain policies of Edward Staley, Chairman of the Board. Now Staley and the other top executives had been ousted and for the company's greatest trial Kendrick had at last been tapped.

Staley's influence came from his closeness with founder William T. Grant. Staley was Grant's brother-in-law, and as the aged Grant became less active, he turned increasingly to Staley to run the Company. Staley was president from 1952 to 1959, but he remained in active control under various titles for over twenty years, until 1974. He supported Richard C. Mayer, the president of Grant from 1968 to 1974, who led Grant into an expansion course that was both heady and disastrous.

When Richard Mayer became Grant's president in 1968, he was culminating a 21-year career. He had set up the company's credit operation so successfully that it contributed 25 percent of sales in 1972. Mayer was interested in vigorous expansion. Shortly after he assumed the presidency, the company broke out of a three-year earnings rut and joined the ranks of one billion dollar-plus retail firms. Encouraged by this progress, Mayer set a goal of \$2 billion in sales by 1972. While this figure was never achieved in his reign, Grant embarked on one of the most ambitious expansion programs ever plotted by a retailer.

These are the principals of this case, except for one other, the founder of the W. T. Grant Company, whose influence came through his support of Staley.

HISTORY

"Looking back to the earliest days that I can remember, it seems to me that I always wanted a store," wrote William T. Grant. He sold shoes in his home town of Malden, Massachusetts and headed the shoe department of a Boston department store when he was only 19. In 1906, taking his life savings of \$1000, he opened his first store in Lynn, Massachusetts. This was successful, a second store was opened within two years, and the firm continued a steady growth.

While his stores were similar to the five-and-tens of Woolworth and Kresge, William Grant saw an opportunity for prices above those of the five-and-tens and below the more expensive department stores. So his first stores carried the 25-cent price theme. As the company expanded through the years, it was thought of primarily as a variety store. Then, in the late 1960s, Grant's went heavily into high-ticket durables such as TV sets, furniture, and appliances.

At age 48, Grant retired from active management of the company, but continued as chairman of the board until his ninetieth birthday in 1966. On his fiftieth anniversary with the company in 1956, Grant reiterated his childhood conviction about the thrill of retailing: "I know of no other business which could give a man so much action, so much challenge, so much satisfaction and so rich a reward for good service to the community than this wonderful business of ours. I have enjoyed every minute of it."[1]

THE GO-GO EXPANSION YEARS

As 1972 drew to a close, Richard Mayer, president of Grant, looked back with some satisfaction at the company's growth in the previous ten years, and he ordered the record of this growth to be distributed to the financial community, company employees, interested vendors, and stockholders. The statistics were indeed impressive. Some of the more important ones are as follows:

	1962	1972	Percentage Increase in Ten Years
Total number of stores	1,032	1,208	17
Total sales	$686,263,000	$1,644,747,000	140
Credit sales	$ 97,478,000	$ 406,763,000	317
Net earnings	$ 9,004,000	$ 37,787,000	320
Net worth	$141,381,000	$ 334,339,000	137
Percent earned on net worth	6.4	11.3	
Dividends paid on common stock	$ 6,997,000	$ 20,807,000	197

Mayer was particularly proud of the statistics on store growth since he had assumed the presidency in 1968:

	1963–1967	1968	1969	1970	1971	1972
New stores opened	202	41	52	65	83	92
Stores enlarged	55	11	3	8	5	5
Stores closed	148	35	49	44	31	52
Store space in thousands of square feet:						
Opened during period	10,933	3,205	3,950	5,360	7,254	7,070
Closed during period	(2,962)	(759)	(1,277)	(1,058)	(693)	1,198)
At end of period	28,736	31,182	33,855	38,157	44,718	50,618

Source: W. T. Grant Company, *Facts and Highlights, Ten Fiscal Years Ended January 31, 1973*, p. 5.

[1]Adapted from a publication of the W. T. Grant Company commemorating the decease of William T. Grant.

Table 12.1   Retailing's Biggest Builders, 1971 and 1972

Space Rank		Company	1971 Added Space (sq. ft.)	1972 Added Space (sq. ft.)
1971	1972			
3	1	Kresge	6,532,500	9,602,000
1	2	Penney	7,634,000	7,630,000
2	3	Grant	7,283,000	7,280,000
5	4	Woolworth	5,000,000	5,860,000
4	5	Sears	5,450,000	5,150,000
11	6	Safeway	2,000,000	2,825,000
12	7	Kroger	1,877,000	2,717,000
10	8	A & P	2,136,000	2,678,000
13	9	City Products	1,378,000	2,493,000
6	10	Montgomery Ward	2,770,000	2,253,000

Source: Adapted from *Chain Store Age*, November 1972, p. 22.

Given these comparative statistics, Grant looked like a winner, a true growth company, attractive both to investor and creditor.

However, one aspect of the operational performance nagged Mayer a bit and was gaining some attention from the investment community. Earnings were in a three-year decline from a high of $41,809,000 in 1969, despite sales having risen by over $500 million in those three years. However, he had a ready explanation for this. He figured three to five years were necessary for a new store to "mature" before customer acceptance build a store's sales and profits to an acceptable level. Mayer was quick to assure his critics that he expected a couple of years of flat earnings as multiple openings caused start-up expenses to balloon at the same time that recently opened stores were still in the maturing period.

Certain other statistics should have given him some concern. Long-term debt had risen from $35 million to $126 million in the ten-year period, an increase of 377 percent. Furthermore, as we will examine later, the stock to sales ratio had risen sharply. Finally, sales per square foot between 1968 and 1972 dropped from $35.13 to $32.50. More important, Grant's sales per square foot remained less than half those of its major competitors. Yet during this period the company had closed six million of its least productive square feet, mostly in marginal stores. This suggested that the new stores were not showing a very strong sales picture.

Table 12.1 compares the expansion efforts of Grant with the other major retailers during 1971 and 1972, as measured by square feet of space added each year.

As can be seen, Grant ranked a close second to Penney in 1971, and was third in 1972 behind Penney and Kresge. The expansion policies of Grant are

more noteworthy when we consider how much larger Penney and Kresge are
than Grant:

	Sales	
	1971	*1972*
Penney	$4,812,000,000	$5,530,000,000
Kresge	3,140,000,000	3,875,000,000
Grant	1,375,000,000	1,645,000,000

Furthermore, Grant was far exceeding the expansion efforts of Sears, the
largest retailer, with sales about ten times greater than Grant's.

The new stores Grant opened were more than twice the size of the
average store of 1964, and some 75 percent were housed in suburban
shopping centers. (The smaller stores that were being phased out were often
located in deteriorating downtown locations.) Average sales per store had
risen to about $1 million compared to $646,000 in 1964, reflecting the larger
units.

Grant's expansion was highlighted by their "superstores," stores of
180,000 square feet, although the size of other new stores ranged down to
60,000 square feet. Two separate location strategies were in operation. The
big stores, 120,000 to 180,000 square feet, were being placed in medium-size
enclosed malls, with a Sears, Ward, or even a major discounter as a
co-anchor. At the same time the smaller stores that were being built in
neighborhood and convenience centers were aimed at dominating a small
market, where there was no nearby competition from major general mer-
chandisers.

The larger stores were necessitated by a vigorous effort to expand and
upgrade the product lines. Emphasis was turning toward big-ticket items
such as television sets, major appliances, power tools, automobile accessories, sporting goods, and camera equipment. The superstores even carried
garden equipment, furniture and auto servicing. By 1971 the product line
was made up of about 25 percent family fashions, 50 percent hardgoods, and
25 percent small wares and services. This was a distinct change from the
variety chain that once had 50 percent of its product line in family fashions,
and very little in hardgoods. The average store now stocked over 21,000
items in all price ranges. About 70 percent of the merchandise carried the
Grant private label; this permitted Grant to offer somewhat lower prices than
if nationally advertised brands were handled.

As expansion was proceeding all-out, a program was designed to cut
down the development time for the new stores from 90 days to 60 days. No
longer was the developer's architect required to submit working drawings to

the chain for final approval, provided the architect would certify that they conformed to Grant's specifications. Under the old method, plans were submitted to Grant and usually many changes had to be made before final approval. Eliminating this review procedure resulted in widely fluctuating costs. But with an objective of pell-mell expansion, shortcuts had to be taken.

APPROACHING DISASTER, 1973 AND 1974

Mayer's expansion plans continued unabated for most of 1973. Table 12.2 shows how Grant compared with other major retailers in 1973 construction.

Grant's operations were deep in the red for the first nine months of 1973. But since the last quarter of the year is the most crucial one for retail operations because of the peak November/December Christmas business, management waited until December to make any further decisions regarding the expansion program. In December, Grant had gains of 3.7 percent, the smallest of any major retailer. The expansion program had been a disaster. Management was now becoming aware that more stores do not necessarily mean profitable sales, if they have low productivity. While remaining chief executive, Richard Mayer gave up the presidency to operations man Harry Pierson. The expansion program was over.

For the full year of 1973 sales rose to $1.8 billion. But profits dropped 78 percent, to $8,429,000, the lowest profits since 1962, when sales were only $575 million. And 1973 was a year when Sears, Penney, Kresge, and Woolworth all showed record earnings. Grant's return on equity, once a good 15 percent, dropped to under 5 percent. More ominous, however, was

Table 12.2 Retailing's Biggest Builders, 1973

Rank	Company	1973 Added Space (sq. ft.)
1	Kresge	10,000,000
2	Grant	6,300,000
3	Woolworth	4,782,000
4	Sears	4,014,000
5	Penney	4,000,000
6	Kroger	3,239,000
7	A & P	3,050,400
8	Safeway	2,832,000
9	City Products	2,780,000
10	Montgomery Ward	2,765,000

Source: *Chain Store Age*, November 1973, p. E22.

Table 12.3   Sales and Long-Term Debt, 1970–1974

	Sales (000)	Long-Term Debt (000)
1970	$1,214,666	$ 35,000
1971	1,259,117	131,526
1972	1,378,251	128,000
1973	1,648,500	126,000
1974	1,849,802	222,834

Source: Company Records.

the rise in debt: long-term debt increased to $222 million, while short-term debt was up to $450 million. Table 12.3 shows the increase in long-term debt from 1970.

At this point Grant's troubles were only beginning. The next year, 1974, found sales falling to $1.7 billion. And this was accompanied by a gargantuan loss of $175 million. Dividends were suspended for the first time in the 69-year history. And James Kendrick was brought in to engage in an eleventh-hour effort to save the nation's seventeenth largest retailer from extinction.

To cut costs, Kendrick planned to close 126 stores in 1975, trim the payroll from 82,500 to 69,000, and pare the company's credit unit, which accounted for 62 percent of the 1974 losses. Also contributing to the staggering results was a loss of $24 million for store closing costs, heavy interest charges, and massive markdowns of slow-moving goods.

JUNE 1975

Finally Kendrick was sweating out the June 2, 1975, payment of $57 million required to retire the company's debt to 116 of the 143 banks that had provided the financing for the ill-fated expansion. Failure to pay these smaller creditors might well force bankruptcy. The bigger banks with more at stake in their loans to the company (for example, Chase Manhattan and First National City Banks of New York City each had $82 million loaned to Grant, and they were more willing to try to rescue the faltering firm and recoup their investments) would not be so inclined to sink the company in an effort to get a faster settlement. While the financial and investment community waited, the news finally hit the press and the market tape that Grant had somehow managed to come up with the $57 million. Kendrick now had a little breathing room.

Causes of the Dilemma

Ill-conceived and too-vigorous expansion certainly must take the blame for many of the Grant problems. Kendrick said: "The expansion program placed a great strain on the physical and human capability of the company to cope with the program. These were all large stores we were opening, and the expansion of our management organization just did not match the expansion of our stores."[2] A former operations executive noted: "Our training program couldn't keep up with the explosion of stores, and it didn't take long for the mediocrity to begin to show."[3]

Another underlying factor also played a major role in the Grant dilemma. While too rapid expansion causes assimilation problems, other firms have expanded rapidly in the past, such as the Penney Company and most of the other major chains in the 1920s; Kresge and their K-mart stores have vigorously expanded for over a decade, and have been the epitome of success. But Grant's expansion was hindered by a lack of a definable and distinctive image.

What was the image and how did consumers see the store?—as a variety chain? A discounter? A general-merchandise chain? This was the question, and the dilemma. What should Grant be? Or more realistically, what should it strive to be? The company assumed some sort of mid-position between a discounter and a general-merchandise firm—neither fowl nor ass. As merchandise lines were expanded and prices upgraded, Grant veered strongly away from the variety-store image, yet in some ways still retained it. For example, certain typical variety-store departments, such as candy, were still kept near the front of stores. On the other hand, Grant did not try to keep up with K-mart in being a discounter, although it was price competitive enough to be called promotional. Mayer coined the phrase "one-stop family shopping stores," suggesting a general-merchandiser such as Sears and Penney. However, Grant lacked the punch of either of these and was unable to offer the service or the established brands that Sears or Penney could. For example, Grant's major brand, Bradford, was practically unknown, and many people were reluctant to buy appliances and similar goods where quality and service were questionable. Given time, Grant could have established acceptance of its own brand, but problems were emerging too fast under its expansion policies.

The vigorous expansion, which led to inefficiencies and mediocre performance, added to an uncertain and murky image, and resulted in

---

[2]As reported in "How W. T. Grant Lost $175 Million Last Year," *Business Week,* February 24, 1975, p. 75.
[3]Ibid.

inventory problems as some merchandise from the broadened product line—especially appliances—did not sell. Store buyers, in their eagerness to stock huge stores, often bought larger quantities than could be moved as seasons, styles, and tastes changed. But there was a reluctance to mark down and clear out this inventory. One merchandising executive recalled "mounds of goods that just sat year to year collecting dust; they had so much stuff just sitting there that they couldn't free up the dollars to do a good seasonal merchandising job."[4]

Many of the new stores were not living up to expectations and with certain merchandise categories stagnant, Grant began a heavy credit promotion in an effort to move this merchandise. But too much leniency in granting credit led to disastrous uncollectable accounts and credit write-offs.

The mix of stores added to Grant's difficulties. The new stores were never really standardized. They came in sizes from 54,000 square feet to 180,000, with different interiors and exteriors and different merchandise assortments. Some stores were free-standing, without other stores nearby; others were in malls; still others in strip centers. Whereas K-mart stores were standardized, such was not the case with Grant.

Now the flaws in Grant's planning were perpetuating. Since so many Grant stores had low sales productivity, developers often refused to give them choice locations. Consequently, many of the new stores were in poor sites. On top of these problems, Grant filed a suit in February 1975, against three former employees charged with taking "hundreds of thousands of dollars in bribes in connection with store leases," which relegated Grant to many poor store locations. Lawsuits were pressed against the former real estate vice president, the southern real estate manager, and the midwest real estate manager alleging kickbacks and bribery: "some store sites and rental terms may not have been in our best interest and may have contributed to some of our problems."[5]

CLIMAX, 1975

The $57 million payment toward the debt reduction was made, even though the investment community had been holding its breath. Slender breathing room had been gained, but could Kendrick bring the company back to viability? There is something sad at contemplating the demise of an undertaking more than half a century old that owed its success to the dreams, hard work, and creative vision of a founder and his successors, and then to suddenly give this all up and succumb amid only five years or so of misguided management.

[4]Ibid., pp. 75, 76.
[5]Ibid., p. 76.

INFORMATION SIDELIGHT

IMPORTANCE OF MAINTAINING STAPLE GOODS

Staple items sell day-by-day in steady, if unspectacular, amounts. In many departments, such as stationery, notions, hosiery, housewares, hardware, sporting goods, candy, toilet goods, and domestics and linens, staples account for most of the total sales. But because such goods sell steadily and without fanfare, there is the temptation to pay little attention to them. Special purchases, new items, interesting styles—these tend to get the attention and enthusiasm.

But a serious error is made in minimizing the importance of staple goods. Out-of-stocks here not only affect the potential sale that would have been made, but since many staple items do not have ready substitutes, customers are forced to go to competitors to satisfy such needs. Sending a customer away may have these undesirable consequences:

The store may lose customer good will, because of the extra shopping effort required.

A customer may perceive the store as inefficient and poorly merchandised, and decide to shift business permanently.

A customer may decide to satisfy other buying needs in the competing store where the staple item is available.

Kendrick sought to undo the damages and move ahead. He proposed going after the same mass market as K-mart and Woolco, to be competitive in price. He would de-emphasize the big-ticket items, and strengthen infants' and children's wear, white goods, and curtains and draperies. He planned to spend six million dollars on television spots in 35 major markets. Mayer had been a credit man, little versed in merchandising and operations. Now Kendrick proposed to stress basic merchandising, such as keeping stocks fresh and clean and taking prompt markdowns. "We failed to stock staples, which in turn led to an overabundance of slow-selling items," Kendrick pointed out. He also recognized that Grant's merchandising program may have been too promotional-minded, and that not enough reliance was placed on national brands.[6]

In the next few years, Kendrick hoped to get down to a core group of 900 stores, and stabilize sales volume at about $1.5 billion. He intended to

---

[6]"It's Get Tough Time at W. T. Grant," *Business Week*, October 19, 1974, p. 46.

increase the use of brand-name goods and increase the dollar volume per square foot. Complicating the problem of streamlining, however, were the many long-term leases running anywhere from ten to twenty years for some stores due to be closed because of poor locations. Unless these could be subleased, their expense drain would continue for some time.

As a further merchandising tool, Grant planned to accept BankAmericard and Master Charge sales, thereby playing down its own dismal credit operation. While recognizing the expenses involved in these bank cards, the company hoped to attract more customers.

Despite the efforts of Kendrick and the sharp reversal of previous policies, the picture steadily worsened during 1975. For the six months ended July 31, 1975, the chain lost $111.3 million, further straining financial resources. Landlords were asked to roll their store rents back 25 percent; some complied. Loan agreements were renegotiated with 27 banks headed by Morgan Guaranty, in which $300 million of the $640 million owed to the banks was subordinated (that is, given lower priority for repayment) to bills owing suppliers, and, in general, the loan provisions were moderated. Subordinating the bank loans was vital, since Grant had some $500 million worth of goods on order, but many suppliers were holding up deliveries for fear they would not be paid.

Grant was losing money faster than anticipated and was forced to announce that it was operating with a "negative net worth"; that is, that its debts exceeded its assets. This was the beginning of the end. On October 2, 1975, Grant entered bankruptcy proceedings, filing a petition under Chapter 11 of the federal Bankruptcy Act. W. T. Grant Co. thus became the second biggest U.S. company ever to enter bankruptcy proceedings (the biggest was Penn Central Transportation Co. in 1970), and the largest retailer ever to do so.

Under Chapter 11, a company continues to operate, but has court protection against creditors' lawsuits while working out a plan for paying its debts. Some shareholders, in a separate action, filed to have the proceedings converted to Chapter 10. This is a more drastic move in which control of the company passes to a court-appointed trustee whose interests are more with the creditors and who will try for a complete financial reorganization and, if necessary, may liquidate some or all of the company's assets to raise money to pay creditors.

In the fall of 1975, the company squeaked past the threat of complete liquidation, retrenching with hundreds of store closings, including most of those west of the Mississippi. If there was to be any chance for survival and eventual payment of creditors, strong Christmas sales were needed. However, with suppliers fearful of providing goods because of the bankruptcy proceedings, the chance of the company being adequately stocked for Christmas, 1975 business was jeopardized. Thus, a major constraint on a faltering firm trying to maintain sufficient viability to work itself out of a constricting mess, that of difficulty in acquiring needed goods from suppliers for day-to-day business, remained a real concern and bleakly colored the future of Grant.

WHAT CAN BE LEARNED?

Even if Grant, with its huge debt and destroyed profits, could survive and eventually become profitable, its excesses would undoubtedly curb growth for years to come. A retrenchment and assimilation of the better parts of the operation would be the only hope if the immediate crisis could be weathered.

The mistakes, for the most part, reflect a disavowal of rather traditional retailing principles. Ignored was a basic principle that growth should not be more rapid than organizational efforts to cope with expansion through training of managers and personnel, location research and analysis, judicious merchandising, and prudent financial considerations.

To be successful, a retailer needs to develop a distinctive image, as we noted in Chapter 2. The Grant Company had not really done this when the vigorous expansion effort was begun. It was like a voyager without a map, with no unified direction. Consequently, the stores varied greatly in size and location. Prices and quality were sometimes competitive and sometimes not. The guiding force of a unified image needed for coordination of expansion was not there.

Basic merchandising principles were violated in the rush toward expansion of square feet of selling space. Markdowns were not taken when needed, so merchandise was no longer fresh, clean, and attractive. Staple or basic merchandise should have been carefully maintained to avoid "out of stocks." New merchandise lines should have been carefully tested and planned, rather than being abruptly put in stock.

Finally, sensors of deteriorating situations should have been watched and corrective action taken quickly. The burgeoning debt, lessening merchandise turnover, the sorry sales/square foot ratio—all these should have alerted management that something was seriously amiss.

For example, the creeping problem of inventories becoming too heavy and out-of-line should have been detected and prompt action taken. The worsening position from 1969 on can be seen from the following table:

	Total Sales (000)	Year-end Inventory of Merchandise (000)	Inventory Percent of Sales
1969	$1,210,918	$222,128	18.3
1970	1,254,131	260,492	20.8
1971	1,374,812	298,676	21.7
1972	1,644,747	399,533	24.3

In the six years before 1969, the stock-to-sales ratio had never been higher than 19.0 percent. When it reached 20.8 percent in 1970, and certainly when it reached 21.7 percent in 1971, corrective action should have been taken. (The argument that expanding merchandise lines and going into higher priced items such as appliances and furniture justified the higher stock-to-sales ratio was hardly valid, since such diversification should have resulted in proportionately higher sales and should not have been at the expense of a worsening stock-to-sales ratio.)

Perhaps the major point to be learned from the experience of Grant is the fallacy of a growth-at-any-cost philosophy. In an effort to make W. T. Grant Company a major factor in the general-merchandise market—and perhaps the siren call was to repeat Kresge's K-mart success—stores were opened without regard either for sound location selection or for an adequately trained organization. Adding millions of square feet of selling space each year was bound to increase sales. But at what cost? A growth-at-any-cost philosophy usually has severe consequences for profits; in an extreme case, as with Grant, the very viability of the company can be jeopardized.

Update

W. T. Grant Company, as we all know, did not make it. On February 9, 1976, six banks and one vendor on the creditors' committee that had been formed after Grant went into Chapter 11 bankruptcy proceedings voted for liquidation (four other creditors on the committee voted against the liquidation). On February 11, the federal Bankruptcy Court in New York ordered the liquidation to begin. Some 1073 retail stores were closed, and 80,000 persons put out of work. Furthermore, Grant's banks had to write off approximately $234 million in bad loans, and its suppliers some $110 million in unpaid bills.

Kendrick was not present at the burial. With Grant so heavily in their debt, the banks began to play a bigger role in managing the company by late 1975. They wanted a new top executive to replace Kendrick and they invested $2.5 million to guarantee the salary and pension to Robert

Anderson, former vice president of Sears. Anderson became chairman and chief executive in October 1975, as Grant filed for Chapter 11. He and the committee of creditors were empowered to direct the company. The task was to shrink Grant to manageable size by closing losing stores, reducing number of employees, getting inventory flowing, settling liens, and reducing losses. To reassure vendors who were fearful of shipping merchandise, the banks again agreed to subordinate their claims to those of suppliers. But all was to no avail. The behemoth, racked with losses, staggering debts, confused inventory and accounting records, and a scandalous lack of controls, ignominiously produced the biggest retailing mistake of all time.[7]

For Thought and Discussion

1. What image do you think Grant should have aimed for? How should Grant have gone about developing such an image?
2. How would you counter the argument that an increasing stock/sales ratio is necessary in order to diversify the merchandise mix and provide stock for new stores?
3. How do you think it might have been possible for Grant to expand as vigorously as they did and to do so successfully?

Invitation to Role Play

1. Place yourself in the role of Richard Mayer as he assumes the presidency in 1968. What growth strategy would you have pursued? Be as specific as you can.
2. You are a staff assistant to James Kendrick. He has just assumed leadership of the company. You have been asked by him to develop plans for a course of action to keep the company viable. Be as specific as you can, and be prepared to defend your recommendations.

[7]For more details of the final steps leading up to the liquidation decision, see "Investigating the Collapse of W. T. Grant," *Business Week,* July 19, 1976, pp. 60–62; and "Notes of Grant Creditors' Panel Filed, Show Firm's Effort to Avoid Bankruptcy," *Wall Street Journal,* June 21, 1976, p. 5.

Four

ERRORS IN
MARKETING
STRATEGY

13

The Edsel—Marketing Planning and Research Gone Awry

Perhaps the classic marketing mistake of the modern business era, the one most widely publicized and commented upon, is the Edsel. Interestingly enough, the same firm, the Ford Motor Company, also was responsible for another monumental marketing blunder, this one before the era of modern business with its emphasis on marketing.

AN EARLIER BLUNDER

Henry Ford introduced the Model T in 1909. It sold initially for $850 and was available only in one color, black. The Model T quickly became a way of life. Ford conducted mass production on a scale never before seen, introducing and perfecting the moving assembly line so that the work moved to the worker. Ford sold half the new cars made in this country up to 1926 and had more than double the output of his nearest competitor, General Motors. Prices by 1926 had fallen to as low as $263. For seventeen years the Model T had neither model changes nor significant improvements, except for a lowering selling price as more production economies were realized.

But by the mid-1920s, millions of Americans wanted something fancier, and General Motors brought out Chevrolet, featuring color, comfort, styling, safety, modernity, and—most of all—a showy appearance. And the Model T was doomed.

In desperation, Henry Ford had the Model T painted attractive colors, fenders were rounded, the body lengthened and lowered, the windshield slanted. But still sales declined. Finally in May 1927, Ford stopped production altogether for nearly a year while 60,000 workers in Detroit were laid off, and a new car, the Model A, slowly took shape, with a changeover estimated to have cost Ford $100 million. While the Model A was successful, the lead lost to General Motors was never to be regained.[1]

In the 1920s a failure in market assessment was devastating. To some extent the failure of the Edsel was also due to bad market assessment, but this time not for want of trying.

THE EDSEL

The Edsel, Ford's entry into the medium-price field, was introduced for the 1958 model year in early September of 1957. This gave it a jump on competitors who traditionally introduce new models in October and November of the previous year. Ernest Breech, the board chairman of the Ford Motor Company, set the 1958 goal for the Edsel Division at 3.3 to 3.5 percent of the total auto market. In a six-million-car year, this would be about 200,000 cars. However, the company executives considered this a very conservative estimate and expected to do much better. Ten years of planning, preparation, and research had gone into the Edsel. The need for such a car in the Ford product line appeared conclusive. Approximately $50 million was spent for advertising and promotion in the pre-introduction and introduction of the car. And in the late summer of 1957 the success of the massive venture seemed assured. The company did not expect to recover the $250 million of development costs until the third year, but the car was expected to be operationally profitable in 1958.

Rationale

The rationale for the Edsel seemed inescapable. For some years there had been a growing trend toward medium-price cars. Such cars as Pontiac, Oldsmobile, Buick, Dodge, DeSoto, and Mercury were accounting for one-third of all car sales by the middle 1950s, whereas they had formerly contributed only one-fifth.

Economic projections confirmed this shift in emphasis from low-priced cars and suggested a continuing demand for higher-priced models in the decade of the 1960s. Disposable personal income (expressed in 1956 dollars)

---

[1]Adapted from Jonathan Hughes, *The Vital Few* (Boston: Houghton Mifflin, 1966), pp. 274–358.

had increased from about $138 billion in 1939 to $287 billion in 1956, with forecasts of $400 billion by 1965. Furthermore, the percent of this income spent for automobiles had increased from around 3.5 percent in 1939 to 5.5 or 6.0 percent in the middle 1950s. Clearly, the economic climate seemed to favor a medium-price car such as the Edsel.

The Ford Motor Company had been weakest in this very sector where all economic forecasts indicated was the greatest opportunity. General Motors had three makes, Pontiac, Oldsmobile, and Buick, in the medium-price class; Chrysler had Dodge and DeSoto appealing to this market; but Ford had only Mercury to compete for this business, and Mercury accounted for a puny 20 percent of the company's business.

Studies had revealed that every year one out of five people who bought a new car traded up to a medium-price model from a low-price car. As Chevrolet owners traded up, 87 percent stayed with General Motors and one of its three makes of medium-priced cars. As Plymouth owners traded up, 47 percent bought a Dodge or DeSoto. But as Ford owners traded up, only 26 percent stayed with the Ford Motor Company and the Mercury, its one entry in this price line. Ford executives were describing this phenomenon as "one of the greatest philanthropies of modern business," the fact that Ford uptraders contributed almost as much to GM's medium-price penetration as Chevrolet had been able to generate for GM.[2]

So the entry of the Edsel seemed necessary, if not overdue.

Research Efforts

Marketing research studies on the Edsel automobile covered a period of almost ten years. Some studies dealt with owner likes and dislikes, other studies with market and sales analyses. Earlier research had determined that cars have definite personalities to the general public, and a person buys a car best thought to exemplify his or her own personality. Consequently, "imagery" studies were considered important to find the best "personality" for the car and to find the best name. The personality sought was one that would make the greatest number of people want the car. Ford researchers thought they had a major advantage over the manufacturers of medium-priced cars because they did not have to change an existing personality; rather, they could create what they wanted from scratch.

Columbia University was engaged to interview 800 recent car buyers in Peoria, Illinois, and another 800 in San Bernardino, California (considered to

[2]Henry G. Baker, "Sales and Marketing Planning of the Edsel," in *Marketing's Role in Scientific Management*, Proceedings of the 39th National Conference of the American Marketing Association, June 1957, pp. 128–9.

be rather typical cities), as to what images they had of the various makes. Thereby a personality portrait of each make was developed. For example, the image of a Ford was that of a fast, masculine car of no particular social pretension. On the other hand, Chevrolet's image was of a car for an older, wiser, slower person. Mercury had the image of a hot-rod, best suited to a young racing driver, this despite its higher price tag.

The conclusions were that the personality of the new car (called the "E-car" initially, before the Edsel name had been selected) should be one that would be regarded as the smart car for the younger executive or professional family on its way up. Advertising and promotion, accordingly, would stress this theme. And the appointments of the car would offer status to the owner.

The name for the E-car should also fit the car's image and personality. Accordingly, some 2000 different names were gathered and several research firms sent interviewers with the list to canvass sidewalk crowds in New York City, Chicago, Willow Run and Ann Arbor, Michigan. The interviewers asked what free associations each name brought to mind; they also asked what words were considered the opposite of each name since opposite associations might also be important. But the results were inconclusive.

Edsel, the name of Henry Ford's only son, had been suggested for the E-car. However, the three Ford brothers in active management of the company, Henry II, Benson, and William Clay, were lukewarm to this idea of their father's name spinning "on a million hubcaps." And the free associations with the name Edsel were on the negative side, being "pretzel," "diesel," and "hard sell."

At last ten names were sent to the executive committee. None of the ten aroused any enthusiasm, and the name Edsel was finally selected, although not one of the recommended names. Four of the ten names submitted were selected for the different series of Edsel: Corsair, Citation, Pacer, and Ranger.

Search for a Distinctive Style

Styling of the Edsel began in 1954. Stylists were asked to be both distinctive and discreet, in itself a rather tall order. The stylists studied existing cars and even scanned the tops of cars from the roof of a ten-story building to determine any distinguishing characteristics that might be used for the Edsel. The consumer research could provide some information as to image and personality desired, but furnished little guidance for the actual features and shape of the car. Groups of stylists considered various "themes" and boiled down hundreds of sketches to two dozen to show top management.

INFORMATION SIDELIGHT

MOTIVATION RESEARCH

Motivation research was in vogue in the early 1950s and was heavily used in the marketing research efforts for Edsel. Motivation research concentrates on emotional or "hidden" stimuli to consumer action. It is often used to determine the "why" of behavior, for example, why consumers buy one brand instead of another. It often is designated as qualitative research, since it is not concerned with developing quantitative data such as would be obtained from carefully selected samples of the population being studied. Motivation research may be defined as:

> a set of tools, borrowed from the fields of psychology and sociology, to uncover and evaluate the motives or drives that are back of human behavior in the consumer market.[3]

Depth interviews are frequently used. These are probing interviews that can be given to individuals or to small groups. In their more sophisticated form, they are best conducted by trained psychologists, and frequently take an hour or more. Projective techniques, such as word associations, sentence completion, story completion, pictorial techniques or the Thematic Apperception Test, are frequently used.

In general today, with the former popularity of motivation research more soberly viewed, we can conclude that while it sometimes can be a useful tool in uncovering ideas and hypotheses worthy of further testing, it leaves a lot to be desired when used by itself as an aid to decision-making. The findings coming from motivation research, even if they are completely valid, still have to be translated into practical marketing decisions. And motivation researchers do not always agree in their conclusions; this is confounding and casts doubts on the validity of motivation research. It is best used to supplement other research efforts, not as a substitute.

Clay and plaster mock-ups were prepared so that three-dimensional high lights and flair could be observed. The final concept was satisfying to all 800 stylists.

---

[3]From a talk, "Rationality and Irrationality in Motivational Research," by L. Edward Scriven, given to the Washington, D.C., chapter of the AMA, June 23, 1955. Reprinted in Robert Ferber and Hugh G. Wales, eds., *Motivation and Market Behavior* (Homewood, Ill.: Irwin, 1958), p. 65.

The result was a unique vertical front grill—a horse-collar shape, set vertically in the center of a conventionally low, wide front end—push-button transmission, and luxury appointments. The vertical grille of the Edsel was compared by some executives to the classic cars of the 1930s, the LaSalle and Pierce Arrow. Push buttons were stressed as the epitome of engineering advancement and convenience. The hood and trunk lid were push button; the parking brake lever was push button; the transmission was push button. Edsel salesmen could demonstrate the ease of operation by depressing the transmission buttons with a toothpick.

The Edsel was not a small car. The two largest series, the Corsair and the Citation, were two inches longer than the biggest Oldsmobile. It was a powerful car, one of the most powerful made, with a 345 horsepower engine. The high performance possible from such horsepower was thought to be a key element in the sporty, youthful image that was to be projected.

A Separate Division for Edsel

Instead of distributing the new Edsel through established Ford, Mercury, and Lincoln dealers, a separate dealer organization was decided upon to be controlled by a separate headquarters division. These new dealers were carefully selected from over 4600 inquiries for dealer franchises in every part of the United States. Most of the 1200 dealers chosen were to handle only Edsel, with dual dealerships restricted to small towns. Consequently, there were now five separate divisions for the Ford Motor Company: Ford, Mercury, Lincoln, Continental and Edsel.

While establishing Edsel as a separate division added to the fixed costs of operation, this was thought to be desirable in the long run. An independent division could stand alone as a profit center, and this should encourage more aggressive performance than if Edsel were merely a second entry in some other division.

The dealer appointments were made after intensive market research to learn where to place each dealer in the nation's 60 major metropolitan areas. Population shifts and trends were carefully considered, and the planned dealer points were matched with the 4600 inquiries for franchises. The Edsel was to have the best located dealer body in the automobile industry. Applicants for dealerships were carefully screened, of course. Guides used in selection included: reputation, adequate finances, adequate facilities, demonstrated management ability, the ability to attract and direct good people, sales ability, proper attitude toward ethical and competitive matters, and type of person to give proper consideration to customers in sales and service.[4] The average dealer had at least $100,000 committed to his agency. Edsel Division was prepared to supply skilled assistance to dealers so that each could operate as effectively and profitably as possible and also provide good service to customers.

Promotional Efforts

July 22, 1957, was the kickoff for the first consumer advertising. It was a two-page spread in *Life* magazine in plain black and white, and showed a car whooshing down a country highway at such high speed it was a blur. The copy read: "Lately some mysterious automobiles have been seen on the roads." It went on to say that the blur was an Edsel and was on its way. Other "pre-announcement" ads showed only photographs of covered cars. Not until late August were pictures of the actual cars released.

The company looked beyond their regular advertising agencies to find a separate one for the Edsel. Foote, Cone and Belding was selected, this being one of the two in the top ten who did not have any other automobile clients. The campaign designed was a quiet, self-assured one that avoided as much as possible the use of the adjective "new," since this was seen as commonplace and not distinctive enough. The advertising was intended to be calm, not to overshadow the car.

The General Sales and Marketing Manager, J. C. Doyle, insisted on keeping Edsel's appearance one of the best kept secrets of the auto industry. Never before had an auto manufacturer gone to so much trouble to keep the appearance hidden. Advertising commercials were filmed behind closed doors, the cars were shipped with covers, and no press people were given any photographs of the car before its introduction. The intent was to build up an overwhelming public interest in the Edsel, causing its arrival to be anticipated and the car itself to be the object of great curiosity.

Some $50 million was allocated for the introductory period. Traditional automobile advertising media were used. Newspaper advertising was allocated 40 percent of all expenditures; magazines were budgeted at 20 percent (trade publication started on April 29 with a two-color spread in *Automotive News* as part of a dealer recruitment campaign); TV and radio were budgeted at 20 percent; outdoor billboards were given 10 percent of the budget, with a final 10 percent for miscellaneous media.

The advertising agency and the marketing executives at Edsel recognized that they faced a challenge in most effectively promoting the car. Because of the determined need for secrecy, traditional advertising research had to be eliminated. For example, copy tests could not be made without

---

[4]Baker, p. 143.

disclosing the features of the car. Furthermore, the introduction of the car and the promotion to accompany it had to be done at one time all over the country; there was no possibility of testing various alternatives and approaches.

THE RESULTS

Introduction Day was September 4, 1957, and 1200 Edsel dealers eagerly opened their doors. And most found potential customers streaming in, out of curiosity if nothing else. On the first day more than 6500 orders were taken. This was considered reasonably satisfying. But there were isolated signs of resistance. One dealer selling Edsels in one showroom and Buicks in an adjacent showroom reported that some prospects walked into the Edsel showroom, looked at the Edsel, and placed orders for Buicks on the spot.

In the next few days, sales dropped sharply. For the first ten days of October there were only 2751 sales, an average of just over 300 cars a day. In order to sell the 200,000 cars per year (the minimum expectation), between 600 and 700 would need to be sold each day.

On Sunday night, October 13th, the Ford Motor Company put on a mammoth television spectacular for Edsel. The show cost $400,000 and starred Bing Crosby and Frank Sinatra, two of the hottest names in show business at that time. Even this failed to cause any sharp spurt in sales. Things were not going well.

For all of 1958 only 34,481 Edsels were sold and registered with motor-vehicle bureaus, less than one-fifth the target sales. The picture looked a little brighter in November 1958 with the introduction of the second-year models. These Edsels were shorter, lighter, less powerful, and had a price range from $500 to $800 less than their predecessors.

Eventually the Edsel Division was merged into a Lincoln-Mercury-Edsel Division. In mid-October 1959, a third series of annual models of Edsels was brought out. These aroused no particular excitement either, and on November 19, 1959, production was discontinued. The Edsel was dead.

Between 1957 and 1960, 109,466 Edsels were sold. Ford was able to recover $150 million of its investment by using Edsel plants and tools in other Ford divisions, leaving a nonrecoverable loss of more than $100 million on the original investment plus an estimated $100 million in operating losses.

WHAT WENT WRONG?

So carefully planned. Such a major commitment of manpower and financial resources, supported by decades of experience in producing and marketing automobiles. How could this have happened? Where were the mistakes? Could they have been prevented? As with most problems there is no one simple answer. The marketplace is complex. Many things contributed to the demise of the Edsel: among them, poor judgment by people who should have known better (except that they were so confident because of the abundance of planning) and economic conditions outside the company's control. We will examine some of the factors that have been blamed for Edsel's failure. None of these alone would have been sufficient to destroy the Edsel; in combination, the car didn't have a chance.

Exogenous Factors

One article, in discussing the failure of the Edsel, said, "In addition to mistakes, real and alleged, the Edsel encountered incredibly bad luck. Unfortunately it was introduced at the beginning of the 1958 recession. Few cars sold well in 1958; few middle-price cars sold, even fewer Edsels."[5] A dealer in San Francisco summed it up this way: "The medium-price market is extremely healthy in good times, but it is also the first market to be hurt when we tighten our belts during depression . . . when they dreamed up the Edsel, medium-priced cars were a big market, but by the time the baby was born, that market had gone 'helter-skelter'."[6]

The stock market collapsed in 1957, marking the beginning of the recession of 1958. By early August of 1957, sales of medium-priced cars of all makes were declining. Dealers were ending their season with the second-largest number of unsold new cars in history up to that time. Table 13.1 shows total U.S. car sales from 1948 (as the country was beginning production after World War II) until 1960. You can see from this table that 1958 sales were the lowest since 1948.

Table 13.2 shows the production of the major makes of medium-price cars from 1955 to 1960. Note the drastic drop-off of all makes of cars in 1958, but the trend had been downward since 1955.

The trend was changing from bigger cars to economy cars. American Motors had been pushing the compact Rambler, and in the year the Edsel came on the market, sales of small foreign cars more than doubled. This change in consumer preferences was not alone a product of the 1958 recession, which would indicate that it would not reverse once the economy improved. Sales of small foreign cars continued to be very strong in the following years, reflecting public disillusionment with big cars and a desire

[5]William H. Reynolds, "The Edsel Ten Years Later," *Business Horizons*, Fall 1967, p. 44.

[6]"Edsel Gets a Frantic Push," *Business Week*, December 7, 1957, p. 35.

Table 13.1   U.S. Motor Vehicle Sales, 1948–1960

Year	Units Sold
1948	3,909,270
1949	5,119,466
1950	6,665,863
1951	5,338,436
1952	4,320,794
1953	6,116,948
1954	5,558,897
1955	7,920,186
1956	5,816,109
1957	6,113,344
1958	4,257,812
1959	5,591,243
1960	6,674,796

Source: *1973 Ward's Automotive Yearbook* (Detroit: Ward's Communications), p. 86.

for more economy and less showy transportation. Table 13.3 shows the phenomenal increase in import car sales during this period, a trend that should have alerted the Edsel planners.

Other exogenous factors were also coming into play at the time of Edsel's introduction. The National Safety Council had become increasingly concerned with the "horsepower race" and the way speed and power were translating into highway accidents. In 1957, the Automobile Manufacturing Association, in deference to the criticisms of the National Safety Council, signed an agreement against advertising power and performance. But the Edsel had been designed with these very two features uppermost: a big engine with 345 horsepower to support a high performance, powerful car on

Table 13.2   U.S. Medium-Price Car Production, 1955–1959 (units)

	1955	1956	1957	1958	1959
Mercury	434,911	246,629	274,820	128,428	156,765
Edsel			54,607	26,563	29,677
Pontiac	581,860	332,268	343,298	219,823	388,856
Oldsmobile	643,460	432,903	390,091	310,795	366,305
Buick	781,296	535,364	407,283	257,124	232,579
Dodge	313,038	205,727	292,386	114,206	192,798
DeSoto	129,767	104,090	117,747	36,556	41,423

Source: *1973 Ward's*, pp. 112, 113.

Table 13.3   U.S. Sales of Import Cars, 1948–1960

Year	Units Sold
1948	28,047
1949	7,543
1950	21,287
1951	23,701
1952	33,312
1953	29,505
1954	34,555
1955	57,115
1956	107,675
1957	259,343
1958	430,808
1959	668,070
1960	444,474

Source: *Automobile Facts and Figures, 1961 Edition* (Detroit: Automobile Manufacturers Association), p. 5, compiled from U.S. Department of Commerce statistics.

the highways. Designed to handle well at high speeds, its speed, horsepower, and high performance equipment could not even be advertised.

Consumer Reports was not overly thrilled about the Edsel. Its 800,000 subscribers found this as the first sentence in the magazine's evaluation of the Edsel: "The Edsel has no important basic advantage over the other brands." Negative articles and books regarding the "power merchants" of Detroit were also appearing about this time. John Keats published his *Insolent Chariots,* and the poet Robert Lowell condemned our "tailfin culture."[7]

Marketing Research

The failure of the Edsel cannot be attributed to a lack of marketing research. Indeed, considerable expenditures were devoted to this. However, these efforts can be faulted in three respects.

First, the motivation research efforts directed to establishing a desirable image for the new car were not all that helpful. While they were of some value in determining how consumers viewed the owners of Chevrolets, Fords, Mercurys, and other brands and led the Edsel executives into selecting the particular image for their car, in reality there was an inability to

[7]As reported in John Brooks, *The Fate of the Edsel and Other Business Adventures* (New York: Harper and Row, 1967), p. 57.

translate this desired image into tangible product features. For example, while upwardly mobile young executives and professionals seemed a desirable segment of consumers for Edsel to appeal to, was this best done through heavy horsepower and high speed performance features, or might other characteristics have been more attractive to these consumers? (Many of these consumers were shifting their sentiments to the European compacts about this time, repudiating the "horsepower race" and the chrome-bedecked theme of bigness.)

Second, much of the research was conducted several years before the introduction of the Edsel in 1957. While demand for medium-priced cars seemed strong at that time, the assumption that such attitudes would be static and unchanging was unwise. A strong shift in consumer preferences was undetected—and should have been noticed. The increasing demand for imported cars should have warranted further investigation and even a reexamination of plans in light of changing market conditions.

The last area where the marketing research efforts can be criticized is in the name itself, Edsel. Here the blame lies not so much with the marketing research, which never recommended the name in the first place, as with a Ford management that disregarded marketing research conclusions and opted for the name, regardless.

Now much has been written about the negative impact of the name. Most of this may be unjustified. Many successful cars on the market today do not have what we would call winning names. For example, Buick, Oldsmobile, Chrysler, even Ford itself are hardly exciting names. A better name could have been chosen—and was a few years later with the Mustang, and also the Maverick—but it is doubtful that the Edsel's demise can justifiably be laid to the name.

The Product

Changing consumer preferences for smaller cars came about the time of the introduction of the Edsel. Disillusionment was setting in regarding large size, powerful cars. However, other characteristics of the car also hurt. The styling, especially the vertical grille, aroused both positive and negative impressions. Some liked its distinctiveness, seeing it as a restrained classic look without extremes. But the horse-collar shaped grille turned other people off.

The biggest product error had to do with quality control. There was a failure to adhere to quality standards; cars were released that should not have been. Production was rushed to get the Edsel to market on schedule and also to get as many Edsels as possible on the road so that people could see the car. But many bugs had not been cleared up. The array of models increased the production difficulties, with eighteen models in the four series of Ranger, Pacer, Corsair, and Citation.

As a result, the first Edsels had brakes that failed, leaked oil, were besieged with rattles, and sometimes the dealers could not even start them. Before these problems could be cleared up, the car had gained the reputation of being a lemon, and this was a tough image to overcome. The car quickly became the butt of jokes.

The Separate Edsel Organization

Another mistake that can be singled out, in retrospect, was the decision to go with a separate division and separate dealerships for Edsel. While this separation was supposed to lead to greater dealer motivation and consequently stronger selling push than where such efforts are diluted among several makes of cars, the cost factors of such separation were disregarded. Having a separate division was expensive and raised breakeven points very high due to the additional personnel and facilities needed. Furthermore, Ford did not have ample management personnel to staff all its divisions adequately.

Despite the care used in selecting the new Edsel dealers, some of these were underfinanced, and many were underskilled in running automobile dealerships compared to the existing dealers selling the regular Ford products. Other Edsel dealers were "dropouts" or the less successful dealers of other car makers.

An additional source of difficulty for the viability of the Edsel dealers was they had nothing else to offer but Edsel sales and service. Dealers usually rely on the shop and maintenance sections of their businesses to cover some expenses. Edsel dealers not only did not have any other cars besides the Edsel to work on, but the work on the Edsel was usually a result of factory deficiencies so the dealers could not charge for this work. The dealers quickly faced financial difficulties with sales not up to expectations and service business yielding little revenue.

Promotional Efforts

Contrary to what could be reasonably expected, the heavy promotional efforts before the Edsel was finally unveiled may have produced a negative effect. The general public had been built up to expect the Edsel to be a major step forward, a significant innovation. And many were disillusioned. They saw instead a new styled luxury Ford, uselessly overpowered, gadget and chrome bedecked, but nothing really so very different; this car was not worth the build-up.

Another problem was that the Edsel came out too early in the new-car model year—in early September—and had to suffer the consequences of competing with 1957 cars that were going through clearance sales. Not only did people shy away from the price of the Edsel, but in many instances they did not know if it was a 1957 or 1958 model. *Business Week* reported dealer complaints: "We've been selling against the clean-up of 1957 models. We were too far ahead of the 1958 market. Our big job is getting the original lookers back in the showrooms."[8]

While some dealers had complained about over-advertising too early, now they were complaining of lack of promotion and advertising in October and November when the other cars were being introduced. At the time when the Edsel was competing against other new models, advertising was cut back as the Edsel executives saw little point in trying to steal attention normally focused on new models.

Finally, one of the more interesting explanations for the failure of the Edsel was:

> oral symbolism . . . responsible for the failure of the Edsel. The physical appearance was displeasing from a psychological and emotional point of view because the front grille looked like a huge open mouth. . . . Men do not want to associate oral qualities with their cars, for it does not fit their self-image of being strong and virile.[9]

For Thought and Discussion

1. How would you have designed marketing research to have provided more useful information for the Edsel marketing decisions?
2. Should the Edsel have been test marketed? Why or why not?
3. How would you respond to the comment that the failure of the Edsel despite extensive planning (starting ten years before the product finally was introduced) means that planning too far in advance is futile?
4. List as many pros and cons as possible for having Edsel as a separate division (with separate dealers) rather than as part of an existing division (and dealer organization) such as Lincoln-Mercury. On balance, which direction does the weight of pros and cons seem to point?
5. How could the Edsel have been a more innovative entry into the medium-price market? What features might have made it successful?

[8]"Edsel Gets a Frantic Push," p. 35.
[9]Gene Rosenblum, *Is Your VW a Sex Symbol?* (New York: Hawthorn, 1972), p. 39.

Invitation to Role Play

Assume the role of the Ford executive responsible for the Edsel operation. What strategy would you have used both in the introductory period and in the subsequent several years to enable it to attain both viability and success? Be as specific and complete as you can and be prepared to defend your proposals against other alternatives. Be sure your recommendations are reasonable and practical.

14

Du Pont's Corfam— Technological Breakthrough Spurned

Researchers and executives of E. I. du Pont de Nemours and Company were excited in the spring of 1963 with possibly another nylon on their hands, ready to be marketed.

A new material called Corfam had been developed, designed to replace leather for shoe uppers, with some happy advantages over leather. In order to determine the market acceptance of this new material, some 15,000 pairs of shoes made from it had been consumer tested under typical wearing conditions; a sample of consumers were given these shoes to wear and were then questioned as to their satisfaction with them. Interestingly, many were unaware that they were not wearing leather shoes. Since the researchers had found that the new material did not stretch or conform to the foot as leather did, they were particularly concerned about what these consumers had thought of the comfort. About 8 percent did admit that the Corfam shoes were uncomfortable. However, this compared with 3 percent who complained about the comfort of leather shoes, and a sizable 24 percent who found fault with the comfort of another leather substitute, vinyl-coated plastic shoes. The researchers at Du Pont accordingly breathed a sign of relief. The comfort concerns of Corfam were deemed to be not serious.

Further reason for enthusiasm came from long-range marketing studies that had concluded that by 1982 there would be a major shortage of leather, and that 30 percent of shoes would have to be made from an alternative material by that time. Since most leather substitutes, primarily the vinyl-coated fabrics, had a serious flaw of impermeability (inability to "breathe"), the opportunity for Corfam seemed clear.

Corfam was the result of twenty-five years of research. Bill Rossi, editor of the trade journal, *Boot and Shoe Recorder*, said, "No product has been more thoroughly market tested prior to coming to market than Corfam."[1] And 30 of the 36 shoe manufacturers approached by Du Pont representatives prior to Corfam's introduction indicated they wanted Corfam.

THE PROMISE

In October, 1963, Corfam was officially unveiled at the Chicago National Shoe Fair. The first national consumer advertising appeared in newspapers of 20 target market cities on January 26, 1964.

Corfam as a leather substitute offered certain advantages over real leather, which the advertising was able to stress. It breathed and flexed easily, yet did not lose its shape. It weighed only one-third as much as leather and could be advertised as more comfortable. It was highly resistant to abrasion and water repellent. Unlike leather, it did not have to be polished; merely wiping with a damp cloth renewed the shine.

The uniformity of Corfam as a synthetic material offered definite advantages to shoe manufacturers over natural leather. While it cost somewhat more ($1.05 to $1.35 per square foot at the time, versus 50 cents to $1.00 per square foot for leather), these costs could be particularly offset by other savings. For example, there was less waste and the material could be used more efficiently than leather pieces, which are often uneven and oddly shaped. Being of uniform thickness meant that the material could be machine cut, thus doing away with the expensive hand cutting of leather.

Du Pont was unstinting in its introductory promotional efforts. On February 23, 1964, the Du Pont Show of the Week on NBC TV featured Corfam. The company went on to spend $2 million advertising Corfam that year.

Du Pont's marketing strategy centered on getting Corfam accepted as high fashion, high quality. *Sports Illustrated, The New Yorker, Harpers Bazaar, Vogue,* and *Esquire* were the media selected to convey this image. Tight control was maintained over distributors, and Du Pont sold direct only to manufacturers of high priced men's and women's shoes. With a promising future forecast for Corfam, there was little difficulty in attracting such manufacturers.

Retail distribution was limited to selected prestige retailers who were required to heavily promote Corfam shoes. In return the retailers benefited

[1]"Another Nylon?" *Forbes*, October 15, 1964.

from the extensive national advertising campaign. Du Pont also sent merchandising representatives to these retail outlets to help with displays and in the training of salespeople to sell Corfam shoes. This training emphasis concerned more perfect fitting of customers. This was of vital importance to Corfam-made shoes since the material did not stretch as leather did; the person fitted incorrectly would always find those shoes uncomfortable.

With a high style image and massive promotional efforts, and initial manufacturer and dealer enthusiasm, it appeared that Corfam was on its way. In August 1964, Du Pont opened a new plant in Old Hickory, Tennessee, solely for the purpose of manufacturing Corfam material. Then in 1966 the synthetic shoe market received a strong shot in the arm. Due to booming leather exports in 1965, the United States was experiencing a leather shortage and higher leather prices. Demand for Corfam outstripped the ability of Du Pont's production to meet it. Corfam and nylon continued to be talked about in the same breath by Du Pont researchers and executives.

BACKGROUND

The growth of Du Pont occurred in two stages. Prior to 1930 the company grew by acquisitions that moved it into a number of different markets. After that, growth was primarily by internal innovation; technological research was used to find highly saleable new products protected by patents that would give Du Pont an entrenchment in new markets to enjoy a return on investment far superior to that of less creative companies. With such a policy, Du Pont increased its sales from $649 million in 1946 to $3 billion in 1965. About $4 billion were invested in plant and equipment, and more than $3 billion were paid in dividends to shareholders during this period without incurring long-term debt.

Such products as neoprene, the first synthetic rubber, and nylon, the first and still most important of all its synthetic fibers, were innovations coming from Du Pont's research. While the cost of such research—over $100 million per year—was high, with much of it offering no immediate payoff or even leading to a commercially acceptable product, the few outstanding successes were certainly sufficient justification for such research efforts.

In the late 1930s, Du Pont's first fundamental research on porous polymeric film took place. Nothing was done to exploit this work until the fifties, when the fabrics and finishes department began to look seriously at the market for shoe uppers. A special poromeric—a two-layered material made up of a web-base and a porous coating on top—was developed for this purpose and named Corfam.

In appraising the market potential of Corfam, a relatively new mathematical modeling technique known as venture analysis was used. Inputs for the model came from historical data of the shoe and leather industry, experimental data on costs of the pilot plant operating capability, market testing for serviceability and perceived value on the part of distributors and consumers, and the judgments of experts in the shoe and chemical industries. The mathematical model predicted that a strong demand would result from a quality product unlike anything the public had ever known. Furthermore, the model predicted there would be an inadequate supply of leather for up to 20 years ahead. Provided that the assumptions put into the model were reasonably correct, the future appeared bright.

In order to solve cracking, softening, and hardening problems, Du Pont tested Corfam shoes within the company. Under close Du Pont supervision, top shoe manufacturers were contracted to produce small lots of shoes. These were then distributed to Du Pont employees for the purpose of spotting any flaws in the material. After correcting problems resulting from wear (cracking, softening, and hardening), more than 15,000 pairs were given consumer use-testing. Corfam was now ready for the market.

PROBLEMS

The leather industry, of course, could be expected to try to counter the incursions of Corfam. After all, it was a direct substitute for leather. The trade association of the industry, Leather Industries of America (LIA), increased its advertising twofold after Corfam hit the market. Such slogans were used as, "Naturally you prefer leather; that's why they're trying to imitate it." The connotation was clear: the leather industry wanted to portray Corfam as a cheap substitute. LIA went as far as adding this little message at the end of every advertisement: "Important! Make sure you get what you pay for."

During 1965 the Old Hickory plant struggled with the process, and the technical procedures resulted in the product being changed in order to improve it. Sales reached ten million square feet. But start-up difficulties, because of the complexity of the process, were resulting in low yields and high costs. Still, the quality control program was adhered to rigidly, and substandard material was destroyed rather than sold. Toward the end of the year, production problems began to ease.

In 1966 some twenty million square feet were produced, and there was considerable optimism as losses decreased substantially from those of 1965. Production costs were being decreased and market demand remained high.

However, the market began demanding more attractive finishes in greater variety, so the cost of finishing increased significantly over forecasts.

Furthermore, the leather market was experiencing fluctuating prices, so shoe manufacturers were alternately hot and cold toward substitute materials.

Corfam was also being plagued by several other problems regarding consumer acceptability of the material. The comfort question was being raised more often than earlier surveys had indicated. Despite the insistence of Du Pont technicians that Corfam was more porous than leather and breathed easier, many wearers complained that the shoes felt hot. And because this material would not acquire a permanent stretch as leather did, wearers complained of the tight fit despite prolonged wear. Du Pont suggested as a solution that consumers purchase a slightly larger size. But this idea met the irrational psychological fact that few people wanted to admit having bigger feet.

Other influences were also at work. An increasing number of shoes were being imported to the United States. European shoes, especially women's, became popular due to their elegant materials and workmanship and their high style. Because of lower material and production costs, these foreign-made leather shoes were priced below those made of Corfam.

Vinyl-coated fabrics were also finding spectacular growth as shoe upper materials. These plastic materials, widely used for automotive and office upholstery because of a leather-like appearance, had sales of about 30 million pairs per year prior to the introduction of Corfam. Producers of vinyl-coated fabrics could offer a wide variety of colors, embossments, and other finishes at about half the retail price of Corfam. By the beginning of 1967 such shoes were selling at the rate of more than 100 million pairs a year and still increasing. In 1967, Georgia-Bonded Fibers, General Tire and Rubber Company, B.F. Goodrich, Union Carbide, Armstrong Cork, Celanese, and 3M all entered the synthetic market to provide Corfam with additional competition.

Despite initial success of Corfam in the United States, efforts to market Corfam in Europe were not successful. At first production was so limited that the strong U.S. demand necessitated limiting sales to domestic consumption. At last, in December 1967, Du Pont announced a concerted effort to tap the European market. However, in Europe high-priced shoes made up a much lower percentage of the total market. And Du Pont was not able to persuade foreign shoe manufacturers to offer Corfam shoes in any but the highest price lines, thus greatly limiting volume potential. By the time Corfam was ready for the European market, two competitive materials, clarino and ortix, were already available in lower-priced shoe lines. Furthermore, Corfam, in going overseas, had to absorb various tariffs (22.2 percent for example, in the United Kingdom).[2] European consumers steadfastly showed preference for softer materials and not for the firmness characteristic of Corfam.

STILL, PROMISE

Throughout 1966 and 1967, efforts were made to increase production efficiency, enlarge the capability of the original plant, and generate sufficient production economies to reduce prices. Leather prices began firming, and while no big price reductions were made for Corfam, orders began accelerating. But the plant, in trying to keep up with demand, experienced production difficulties and fell behind the planned production level until late in 1967. About 24 million square feet were shipped in 1967, and at the end of the year the backlog of unshipped business totaled over 10 million square feet. However, excessive expenses involved in adapting the plant to higher production levels resulted in losses that exceeded those of 1966.

For 1968 the outlook appeared brighter. Demand continued strong, and production problems had been solved so that the backlog of orders could be handled without serious delay. Operating costs were improving also, raising expectations that the corner had been turned. Sales reached 35 million square feet in 1968, and prices were dropped to an average of a little under 80 cents per square foot. While the operation was still not realizing profits; losses had fallen significantly.

However, instead of an indication of better things to come, 1968 turned out to be the year of highest production and sales, and demand thereafter faltered. Several adverse factors were becoming apparent. First, the leather industry had responded to the Corfam threat to their business and was producing and heavily promoting very soft, glove-like leather particularly appropriate for the casual dress becoming popular at the time. Leather prices were softening, and the price disadvantage of Corfam was becoming greater. Imports continued to increase, and vinyl shoes were gaining larger market shares. The result was that Corfam's sales declined almost 25 percent in 1969.

In October 1970, Du Pont introduced Corfam II as a lower cost porometric, as well as one having certain improved characteristics. Expectations were that the more competitive prices, which could now be offered, would rejuvenate demand for Corfam. But such was not to be.

The synthetic market had ceased to grow. In addition, Japan had entered the market with a good quality, inexpensive material to provide still more competition for American manufacturers. Still worse, vinyls were

---

[2]"Du Pont Stubs Its Toe," *Dun's Review*, June 1967, p. 61.

becoming available at one-third to one-fifth less than synthetics, and vinyls were considered high style, making them the ideal choice of many customers.

ABANDONMENT

After seven years of heavy losses estimated to range from $80 million to $100 million, on April 14, 1971, President Charles B. McCoy announced to shareholders that Du Pont was abandoning Corfam. A key problem with Corfam had been its inflexible production process that could respond to neither leather price cuts nor to style changes. With sales not living up to expectations, indeed with the sales trend sharply downward and with foreign imports pinching the U.S. market, this decision was made.

The company ceased Corfam production and order-taking in June of 1971. Du Pont sold its remaining Corfam supplies for $6 million to a Boston leather brokerage firm, George Newman & Company, and later sold its technology and production equipment for the Old Hickory, Tennessee, plant to Polimex-Sekop, a Polish government-owned manufacturing operation. This sale included selling rights under Du Pont patents throughout the world, excluding North America and Japan. Polimex-Sekop expected to continue production of Corfam for Polish consumption. Most of the people involved with the poromeric venture, totaling about 1,000 at the peak, were reassigned within Du Pont.

WHAT WENT WRONG?

The predictions of the venture analysis model described earlier at the preintroductory stage of Corfam can be compared with the actual situation that existed in 1968, five years after Corfam was introduced. The comparisons of actual with predicted results showed that:

The volume of material sold was approximately that originally predicted (35 versus 37 million square feet).

The average price obtained for the material was approximately as predicted.

Costs of making the impregnated fibrous web and of coating it were approximately as predicted.

A more expensive woven interlayer had to be used in some of the production, which added between 10 and 15 percent to total mill cost.

Costs of finishing due to the variety of effects needed (to meet fashion needs) added 15 percent to 25 percent to mill cost.

Technical expenses were about double the forecasted figure for the fifth year.

Marketing expense was about twice the forecasted figure, partly reflecting heavy competitive conditions and the inability to establish Corfam strongly in the market.[3]

Certainly one of the reasons for the demise of Corfam was the inability to lower production costs enough to penetrate a wider market. Eighty percent of the total shoe market at the time of Corfam's inception was in the eleven dollar and below price. Corfam was aimed at the 15 to 20 dollar and up market, which comprised only 10 percent of the total shoe market.

An alternative to the marketing strategy of Du Pont would have been to lower the price to penetrate this lower 80 percent and gain acceptance there rather than try to build an image as a prestige shoe material. While Du Pont would have lost money initially since manufacturing costs were high, the increased demand from this market might have offset early losses and resulted in a substantial market share. However, such a penetration pricing policy would have had to be effected before low-priced imports had acquired market dominance. Production at the Old Hickory plant would have had to be increased significantly (or another plant opened). With the production problems that were incurred under the more modest expansion of demand, Du Pont could hardly have handled a much heavier demand during the first few years of the Corfam introduction. Consequently, the practicality of a strikingly different marketing policy for Corfam must be suspect.

Certainly, by opting for the high-price market, Du Pont repudiated the mass market comprising large families with limited purchasing power but burgeoning needs. In fact, Corfam was not even offered in children's sizes.

In the 1950s, before the introduction of Corfam, Du Pont analysts had estimated that by 1982 there would be a 30 percent shortage of real leather. The most popular leather substitute at that time was vinyl-coated fabric, with the serious flaw of impermeability—it did not "breathe." Therefore, the opportunity for a profitable substitute material for leather seemed clear. However, how well did Corfam substitute for leather?

The marketing research study in which some 15,000 pairs of shoes made from Corfam were consumer tested before the full-scale introduction of Corfam, may have been misinterpreted. While the reaction of the wearers was enthusiastic, especially regarding the ease of caring for Corfam shoes, 8 percent of those tested indicated they experienced some discomfort; this compared with 3 percent of those wearing leather. Since 24 percent of the users of vinyl-coated fabric shoes also felt discomfort, the 8 percent for

[3]W. D. Lawson, "History and Analysis of Corfam," unpublished in-house report for Du Pont Company, November 1972.

INFORMATION SIDELIGHT

SKIMMING vs. PENETRATION PRICING

A firm, when it has a sufficiently different product to introduce to the market, may take two opposite approaches to pricing it. A relatively high price may be charged (a skimming price aimed at taking the "cream" of the market), or a relatively low price (a penetration price).

The temptation in introducing a highly differentiated product is to use a skimming price that will yield maximum profit per unit sold—and this essentially is what Du Pont did. This is also a rather easy approach to pricing since the price may be lowered later if the initial one proves unattractive to consumers. Furthermore, skimming permits a natural approach to market segmentation: the high initial price attracts the upper portion of the market, those consumers interested in highest quality and perhaps in the prestige of having something distinctive; later, as production expands, the price can be periodically reduced to appeal to other segments.

There are, however, limitations to skimming. Usually it is most practical when a firm either faces a relatively inelastic demand curve, in which sales will not be appreciably affected by price, or else has a limited market. If the price elasticity of demand is at least moderate, greater total profits may be gained by pricing lower, and expanding production. But the major deterrent to skimming is competition. A high price encourages competitors to enter the market because they see good profit opportunities where prices are held at a high level and productive capacity expands slowly. If imitation is easy (while direct imitation of Corfam was not a factor, substitute materials were), then a skimming price may be forced down quickly and/or competitors become firmly entrenched.

Conditions favoring penetration pricing are more common. Such a policy assumes an elastic demand with sales increasing substantially if prices can be lowered; therefore a large market must also be expected. By gaining maximum sales, a firm has the opportunity to build an unassailable position. A penetration pricing situation is a necessity if the initial product differentiation is not ample, or is easily matched, or if there is no elite market that would take higher-priced offerings. While penetration pricing, with its low unit profits, may force a firm to accept some losses at first, the expectation is for economies of scale and reduced costs as volume expands.

Corfam was not considered bad at all. But perhaps the factor of comfort was not given proper consideration. Corfam shoes had to fit properly in order to be comfortable; they did not stretch and mold to one's feet after even prolonged wearing. While Du Pont tried to train and motivate its retail dealers to do a good job of fitting, practically speaking, this was not always accomplished.

Du Pont also underestimated the response of the leather industry. In markets of low growth, which described the shoe market, competitive reactions tend to be vigorous because of the threat a newcomer offers to established firms. The generally superior qualities of leather, in the estimation of many people, prevailed over Corfam, especially when backed by heavy industry advertising and generally lower prices.

Even vinyl-coated fabrics were too tough a competitor for Corfam. While vinyls were of less quality, they were priced far below Corfam, and considerably less than leather. Although the vinyls were not durable, high-style shoes made from this material would look good for three to six months. With styles changing rapidly, this was all consumers felt necessary.

Errors were also made in forecasting how cheaply Corfam could be made. The production was highly complicated; Du Pont felt no one would even attempt to copy them for years. But the very complexity of processing and producing Corfam resulted in costs remaining higher than anticipated and added to the difficulty of competing with leather manufacturers and their price cuts. Despite Corfam sales going from 1 million pairs in 1964 to 20 million in 1967, the cost of producing was not substantially reduced.

And so the promise of Corfam was buried under years of red ink.

Update

By 1981, Corfam was far from dead. Poland, which bought the process from Du Pont, was not only selling Corfam, or PolCorfam as they call it, in its own country, but was exporting it to the U.S. for such shoe makers as Edison Brothers and Brown Shoe (whose shoes are stamped "man-made material"). The price of leather, 50 cents to 60 cents a foot when Corfam was first introduced, was now $1.50 a foot and rising, thereby making Corfam a more attractive alternative. The 1980–1981 selling season was particularly strong for Corfam since alligator and lizard-like products were fashionable. Real alligator skin was selling for $138 a foot and Corfam provided a realistic and much less expensive imitation. While total production figures for PolCorfam are impossible to obtain, its versatility is such that it was even being sold to U.S. semiconductor firms which were using it to make silicon wafers.[4] Could Du Pont have made a even bigger mistake in selling Corfam?

For Thought and Discussion

1. With the benefit of hindsight, do you think Du Pont should have ever introduced Corfam? Why or why not?
2. Would you say that Corfam's debacle represented primarily marketing mistakes, or production and engineering ones?
3. The advantages of Corfam over leather were that Corfam was more scuff resistant, water repellant, and durable. However, many consumers did not perceive these advantages as being worth the additional cost in dress shoes. Do you think Du Pont should have aimed its efforts at another target market? How successful would you estimate this would have been?
4. In view of the success of Poland with Corfam, do you think Du Pont should have sold the process to Poland? Evaluate as many facets of this decision as you can.

Invitation to Role Play

Assume the role of the Du Pont executive responsible for the Corfam marketing effort. What marketing strategy would you have used? Be specific, and defend your rationale, using the facts known from the case.

[4]Maurice Barnfather, "Polish Joke," *Forbes* March 2, 1981, p. 46.

15

A & P's WEO—A Price
Offensive Backfires

A common failing of large and long-established organizations is a reluctance to take aggressive action. To remain with the tried and true, the established ways of doing things, is much easier. No undue friction is thus created, and the trauma of change and severed little empires can thereby be avoided.

Once in a while a person comes into such an organization and upsets things, gets it moving again, makes major and even risky decisions. In so doing, a giant may be shaken from its lethargy, and a new spirit of innovation and rejuvenation implanted.

This is what happened to the Great Atlantic and Pacific Tea Company, some 113 years old, in the spring of 1972. But sometimes dramatic and forceful decisions do not always turn out for the best; they may reflect poor judgment, or they may be affected by detrimental environmental factors impossible to predict at the time the decision was made.

Is no action better than a major profit-destroying bad decision? Judge for yourself in the following description of the WEO strategy of A & P.

THE DECISION

William J. Kane, 59, took over as chairman and chief executive of A & P in 1971 at a time when sales had leveled and profits were shrinking. In early 1972 he made the decision to convert the chain to superdiscount stores: "We have to start the growth factor in this company right now," Kane was quoted by *Business Week.* "This is a business based strictly on volume, with sales measured in tonnage."[1]

Overnight in various cities across the country, stores were converted to something called "Where Economy Originates" or WEO for short. While stores were not remodeled, two major changes were made:

> Prices were lowered on 90 percent of the merchandise. While some of the reductions were only a few cents, still, percentagewise, they were not insignificant for grocery items where the markup percentage might only be 20 percent.

> The variety of merchandise was pared—from an average 11,000 items in the conventional A & P to around 8,000 in a WEO conversion. This meant less sizes and kinds of certain items.

New signs and a profusion of banners were used to acquaint customers with the new policies. Heavy advertising, not only the traditional newspaper advertising of supermarkets, but also radio and television were used to broadcast food prices lower than competitors'.

The decision to convert thousands of A & P stores to the WEO concept did not come easily, especially in a tradition-bound 113-years-old company. Kane, in breaking with the company reluctance to change, ordered a store in Pennsauken, N.J., modified to a low-price discount food operation a month after he took office. It was called a "WEO" store, meaning a "Warehouse Economy Outlet." This first trial WEO store lacked all frills; merchandise stood in open cartons and customers bagged their own groceries, but prices were slashed and the store's volume "increased fantastically."

The second experimental WEO store was opened in Braddock, Pennsylvania, an old economically depressed steel mill town near Pittsburgh. S. R. Thompson, the store manager, reported: "We were ready to close back in June 1971. We wanted to bring the store back to life again, and WEO did it."[2] For the first six months the store operated as a WEO, average weekly sales rose more than 500 percent over the year before. During 1971, A & P opened ten more WEOs and went back to regular shelf displays and more regular services in them.

The success of the WEO experiments, coupled with the company's first quarterly loss since 1961, helped to make the decision to switch all the stores to the WEO concept.

---

[1]"A & P's Ploy: Cutting Prices to Turn a Profit," *Business Week*, May 20, 1972, p. 76.
[2]Ibid., p. 78.

INFORMATION SIDELIGHT

ADVANTAGES OF CHAINS: OPPORTUNITY FOR EXPERIMENTATION

A & P's testing and modifying of its WEO idea in 1971 shows one of the big advantages multi-store organizations have over firms with only a few stores. Prospective strategy changes can be experimented with in a few stores, any desirable adjustments determined, and the success of the strategy ascertained from concrete sales and profits results. All this can be done with relatively little risk since only a few outlets of the total chain are involved, and the strategy can be adopted throughout the company only if the results are good. Experimentation is hardly possible for the firm with one or a few stores, and there is substantial risk in making major strategy changes.

How much were prices really reduced in the WEO stores? The real impact is best seen in the effect on margins. Margins or markup percentages for most supermarkets, including the regular A & Ps, are around 20 to 22 percent; the WEO margins were estimated to run between 9 and 13 percent. This translated into a can of beef stew being reduced from 67 to 59 cents, for example, while plastic sandwich bags went from 53 to 49 cents. Even if sales volume were to increase dramatically, the question in the fall of 1972 was whether volume would rise fast enough to yield profits at such low margins. But Kane expressed his basic food merchandising philosophy:

> I want to get us back to good, sound, basic fundamentals. This company was build on quality foods sold at low prices.[3]

BACKGROUND

George Huntington Hartford started what was to become A & P in 1859, when he was 26. Tea was selling in New York City at $1 a pound, and Hartford thought this could be reduced to 30 cents by eliminating middlemen. He persuaded his employer, George Gilman, to join him. Wild hoopla was used to promote the first store, such as eight dapple-gray horses pulling a tremendous red wagon through the streets of New York. Gradually spices, coffee, and then other staple grocery items were added, with middlemen bypassed whenever possible. More stores were opened: five by 1865 and

[3]Ibid., p. 76.

Table 15.1   A & P Changeover to Supermarkets

	Total Number of Stores	Number of Supermarkets
1936	14,446	20
1937	13,058	282
1938	10,671	771
1939	9,021	1,119
1940	7,073	1,396
1941	6,042	1,594

Source: U. S. v. The Great Atlantic and Pacific Tea Co., U. S. Circuit Court of Appeals, 7th district, Docket 9221, Records and Briefs, Vol. 1, p. 323.

eleven by 1869 when the name, The Great Atlantic & Pacific Tea Company (to signify the intention to expand coast-to-coast), was adopted.

Cash and carry, a major innovation by A & P, was introduced in 1912. Doing away with charge-account paper work and thousands of delivery horses and wagons enabled "economy" stores to sell a large volume at a low markup. (This sounds reminiscent of the 1972 WEO strategy.) For the next two years, economy stores were opened at the rate of one every three days. By 1916 there were 1000 A & P stores, each laid out exactly the same. By 1930 there were 19,422 stores, and sales passed the billion-dollar mark.

But in 1930 a "revolution" began in food retailing that would profoundly affect A & P and all the other food chains. The first King Kullen supermarket was opened by Michael Cullen, an ex-chain-store executive, in August 1930. By the end of 1932 he had eight outlets. More "supermarkets" soon followed as other innovators came on the scene. These first supermarkets often were opened in abandoned warehouses, barns, empty garages and factories; they had crude floors, bare ceilings, unpainted fixtures, and merchandise was piled everywhere. Big compared to regular grocery stores of that time, they were self-service and usually had abundant free parking. Since they had lower operating costs they could offer lower prices than the chain groceries. They also commonly used loss leaders, and customers came from as far as fifty miles to shop in these stores for the bargains they afforded. By 1935, more attractive supermarkets were being opened.

A & P and the other major grocery chains did not respond to this new challenge until 1937. But by then these innovative supermarkets were beginning to dominate the market. Table 15.1 shows the conversion to supermarket operation made by A & P within six years; in the process, thousands of its smaller unprofitable units were abandoned.

After World War II ended, A & P lagged behind in the use of two merchandising ideas that were sweeping the rest of the industry. Nonfood items, ranging all the way from health and beauty aids to toys and certain apparel, were being widely stocked. Goods with high volume and impulse-buying potential that could yield high markups were especially selected. While A & P did not ignore nonfood items, this business was not developed as fully as with most other food chains.

Trading stamps also became extremely popular after World War II. Here again, A & P was slow to act, doing so only after most of its competitors. Finally Plaid Stamps were brought into some stores.

Grocery retailing experienced two additional innovative approaches in the last decade or so: discounting, and the convenience store. While the latter did not directly affect A & P, discounting had considerable influence.

Discounting of general merchandise swept into the retail scene in the 1950s and 1960s. During most of this time it was not a significant factor in food, although some independent stores had tried across-the-board low-margin, high-volume selling with varying degrees of success. The big chains for the most part ignored the discount approach until 1970.

Several things accounted for the slowness to move into food discounting. Grocery margins were low to begin with—for the most part around 20 to 22 percent, versus 38 to 42 percent for nonfood. Even when expenses were pared to the limit, it was difficult to reduce grocery markups to much less than 15 percent and still make money; in nonfood items, discount margins were sometimes as low as 20 to 22 percent, or almost half those of regular retailers. This meant that discount prices for appliances, sporting goods, and many other nonfood items could be significantly lower than regular prices and consequently have a strong impact on demand. Since food prices could not be reduced as much, discounting had less impact. Furthermore, the common use by all supermarkets of attractively priced leader items to lure customers into a store often disguised the fact that other items might be proportionately higher.

Besides minimum expenses, another facet of discount operations is lean stocks. Such a decreased assortment ideally consists only of fast-moving items and sizes. But the typical supermarket was geared to offering customers the widest possible variety and so had hundreds of feet of shelf space to fill.

The major chains in the early 1970s finally began moving into discounting either with separate discount operations or with company-wide low-margin policies. Safeway, the second largest chain (next to A & P) in mid-1970, gradually moved into price leadership or price matching in most markets where it was already dominant. A & P moved more from a position of weakness in a rather desperate attempt to solve a long-standing decline in average store performance. A gradual approach to discounting would not produce results as quickly as needed. Consequently the decision was made for a more drastic and exciting program in order to achieve a shift in its share of the market.

Convenience food stores were also spreading rapidly during the 1960s. These were in marked contrast to discount stores in that they offered higher prices than conventional food stores. They were originally developed in the southwest during the 1930s and were a more sophisticated version of the mom-and-pop neighborhood groceries.

Convenience food stores typically are open seven days a week and often from 7 a.m. to 11 p.m. (the largest convenience food chain is called 7-Eleven, reflecting this). They cater to shoppers between their regular trips to the supermarket and are designed to make shopping quick and convenient. Consequently they are small, afford close-to-the-door parking, and have no long waits at checkouts. There is only a limited selection of merchandise, and this is carefully chosen to yield high turnover. These stores charge at least 15 to 20 percent more than other food stores. But the factor of convenience is a powerful shopping inducement; the number of such food stores grew from 500 in 1957 to 17,000 in 1973. As indirect competitors, convenience food stores were a force to be reckoned with by conventional supermarkets such as A & P.

PRELUDE TO THE WEO DECISION

After being for decades the largest supermarket chain, A & P was finding its position seriously challenged by Safeway; indeed, in 1971 A & P barely nosed out Safeway in total sales. But sales had reached a plateau in the 1960s and were even falling a little in 1970 and 1971, along with a serious erosion of market share. Profits also were faltering during this period and fell drastically in 1971. The following tables show sales, profit, and market share position of A & P and those of its two largest competitors, Safeway and Kroger, since 1963.

The worsening dilemma of A & P by 1970 reflected a history of bad decisions and reluctance to make aggressive moves. Many years before, A & P decided not to go into major shopping centers but stuck mostly with free-standing neighborhood stores. A major reason for this policy was a reluctance to pay the higher rents demanded by shopping centers. There was also the belief that A & P was so big and powerful that it could attract people regardless of location. Furthermore, management hesitated to build the bigger stores that were becoming the accepted mode of much of the industry. For example, in 1970 A & P stores averaged only 14,000 square feet compared with an average of more than 20,000 for other major chains.

Not the least of A & P's failings had been carelessness with store

Table 15.2 The Long Slide of A & P

	Sales	Income	Market Share[a]
1963	$5,189,000,000	$57,489,000	20.9
1965	5,119,000,000	52,339,000	19.0
1966	5,475,000,000	56,239,000	18.8
1967	5,458,000,000	55,897,000	17.6
1968	5,436,000,000	45,247,000	15.8
1969	5,753,000,000	53,302,000	15.4
1970	5,664,000,000	50,129,000	13.1
1971	5,508,000,000	14,619,000	12.1

[a] Percentage of A & P sales to total grocery chain (11 or more units) sales.
Sources: Based on U. S. Dept. of Commerce reports, and *Moody's*.

maintenance and customer service. Many stores were old and poorly lit; displays were unattractive and disordered. Staffing was often so minimal that customers waited for an unduly long time at checkouts. Stores might have cluttered aisles, shelves in need of dusting, and cartloads of sale items might crowd ends of aisles. For example:

> One display with a "Reduced for Quick Sale" sign, included badly dented cans of Ann Page tomato juice and corn, cream cheese with bits of macaroni sticking to the package bottom, packages of breakfast food with already opened pour spouts, and a large box of oatmeal with the lid partly ripped off.[4]

Table 15.3 Comparative Statistics for Safeway and Kroger

	Safeway			Kroger		
	Sales	Income	Market share	Sales	Income	Market share
	(000,000)			(000,000)		
1963	$2,649.7	$44.82	10.7	$2,102.1	$22.08	8.5
1965	2,939.0	48.18	10.9	2,555.1	31.30	9.5
1966	3,345.2	59.75	11.4	2,660.0	29.38	9.1
1967	3,360.9	50.89	10.8	2,806.1	25.72	9.0
1968	3,685.7	55.06	10.7	3,160.8	34.00	9.2
1969	4,099.6	51.31	11.0	3,477.2	37.39	9.3
1970	4,860.2	68.89	11.2	3,735.8	39.77	8.6
1971	5,358.8	80.18	11.8	3,707.9	36.27	8.1

Sources: U. S. Dept. of Commerce reports, and *Moody's*.

[4]Ibid., p. 77.

This situation of small, often badly located stores, careless display and housekeeping, and sometimes inadequate service brought an inevitable consequence to A & P—a dowdy, dull, and old-fashioned image. Several other things also conspired to bring this about. Any company over a hundred years old would probably have to fight extra hard to escape this image. Furthermore, many of the employees of the company were old—they didn't help counter such a pervasive image.

What kind of customers are attracted to a store with this kind of image? The young suburban families with increasing purchasing power and burgeoning needs? Hardly. A profile of customers would more likely find the preponderance to be old or retired people who grew up on the A & P economy appeal. Is this a healthy type of customer segment to appeal to? It is hardly compatible with growth.

Some of the disaffection toward A & P has been attributed to its emphasis on private labels, including goods produced in its own twenty-four manufacturing and processing plants and twenty-two bakeries. Those customers who come to A & P stores looking for nationally advertised brands may find them unavailable and turn to other stores. Undoubtedly, if the quality image of the chain's private label had been successfully sold, this would not be a disadvantage. But there were questions as to how successful A & P had been in selling its private label program.

So the groundwork was laid, the cause established, for drastic action by A & P in the spring of 1972 to generate a new spark in company policies and initiate strong and aggressive action to reverse a stagnant trend of sales and a declining trend of profits. The resulting militant price-cutting was to cause industrywide concern and countermoves, and was to result in deteriorating profits for many firms of the industry, most of all for A & P.

COMPETITIVE REACTION

Competitors could not afford to ignore the aggressive price cutting and promotion of A & P. Of course, smaller supermarket chains without the financial resources of an A & P found difficulty trying to match prices with the behemoth of the industry. But most attempted to do so and hoped to weather the storm.

For example, Pantry Pride, an eastern chain, advised customers in advertisements to bring in copies of A & P's ads showing their price leaders, and Pantry Pride would match the prices. Profits dropped drastically. Kroger reported a 63 percent decline in profits for the first three months of 1973, after a 36 percent profit drop for 1972. Food Fair reported profits down 50 percent in two quarters of 1972. The battle raged hardest in Baltimore, Philadelphia, Boston, Chicago, and the state of New Jersey.

But while many chains sought to combat A & P's price assault by matching their prices and by boosting advertising, some also sought new ways to boost earnings. Two in particular found favor: opening longer hours and stocking more nongrocery items.

Some competitors, particularly Jewel, Pathmark, and Arlan's, went to round-the-clock service, open 24 hours a day. The intent, of course, was to attract customers when A & P was closed. But how many customers really are going to shop at midnight? Apparently quite a few. Stuart Rosenthal, assistant to the president of Supermarkets General, said, "We get all kinds of people late at night or early in the morning—couples unable to shop together during regular hours, or the wife who trusts her husband to babysit only when the kids are asleep."[5]

But even if only a handful of customers shopped during these extended hours, the cost of maintaining 24-hour operations was not that formidable. Ralph Krueger, vice president of Allied Supermarkets, noted: "It doesn't add much to our labor expense because we must have people in to stock at night anyhow. Certain other expenses, like rent, remain the same whether we stay open or not."[6]

In order to increase profits, more supermarkets turned to additional nonfood items. We know that scrambled merchandising has long been a phenomenon in food retailing, with hosiery, housewares, and even toys being stocked with regularity by many stores. Now guitars, plants, wine shops, sports-clothes boutiques, and even pharmacies began finding space in supermarkets. Such nonfood items were safe from the cut-price actions of A & P; in addition they carried a much higher markup than the typical food item. If an adequate volume could be generated, such nonfood merchandise was well worth carrying.

Competitive Reaction of Jewel

Jewel Companies, a Chicago-based supermarket chain now the fifth largest in the United States, successfully bucked the WEO campaign, without really trying to match A & P's prices. In fact it did just the opposite. Shopping hours were extended from 8 a.m. to midnight. Various frills, such as bus transportation for the elderly, were added. A small number of items were sold at discount prices, but the great majority were sold at normal or higher-than-normal prices.

However, Jewel had rather smoothly acquired the image of a discount

[5]"War in the Supermarkets," *Time*, August 14, 1972, p. 60.
[6]Ibid.

chain without really being one—and this undoubtedly helped with the price-conscious customers A & P was seeking to win away. In the summer of 1971, when prices were skyrocketing and two days after President Nixon froze prices, Jewel announced its own "Phase I" program. With heavy advertising, the company rolled back its prices to lower than prefreeze levels and did not increase them until months after the 90-day freeze ended. While the price cuts were only token, the publicity value was substantial.

In the late 1960s the company had spread into hard goods and fashion items, drugs, and snack-type restaurants. Many of Jewel's supermarkets are located next to or in the same building as one of its other retailing operations, so that traffic is funneled between. And Jewel's per-store sales volume outstripped A & P's by almost three to one. So, competing with service, integrated retailing, aggressive promotion, and an image of innovativeness but also of low prices (even if hardly justified), the price-cutting assault of A & P was neatly thwarted.

CONSEQUENCES OF THE WEO CAMPAIGN

The WEO strategy was inaugurated early in 1972, although it took some months for all stores to be converted. By August, 3700 of the 4200 stores were ready, with the rest expected to be by fall. All that remained was to watch for the sales and profits results.

Sales gains were achieved, an increase of $800 million. But A & P also suffered a serious deficit (what would have been catastrophic for many firms) of $51.3 million, the worst in recent history for the company. The following table updates Tables 15.2 and 15.3, and shows the comparative results of A & P, Safeway, and Kroger for 1972 as well as the preceding two years.

You can see from Table 15.4 that A & P did reverse the falling trend in sales and market share, even though the cost was high. Safeway, despite the aggressive tactics of A & P, not only posted a significant sales gain of $700 million and a major gain in market share, but also substantially increased an already healthy profit base. For a time during 1972, Safeway became the nation's biggest food retailer, as A & P closed more than 400 stores in the name of efficiency while opening up 80 larger units. Kroger was badly affected profitwise by the WEO campaign, although it still had a sales gain. What was of deeper concern to Kroger was the steadily eroding market share.

Because of the loss, A & P was forced to omit a quarterly dividend for the first time since 1925. This broke the proud chain of continuous dividends managed even through the depression of the 1930s. Stockholders were understandably unhappy, and Huntington Hartford, heir to an A & P fortune, criticized management as inefficient.

Table 15.4 Comparative Statistics for A & P, Safeway, and Kroger, 1970–72

	Sales	*Income*	*Market Share*
A & P:			
1970	$5,664,000,000	$50,129,000	13.1 percent
1971	5,508,000,000	14,619,000	12.1
1972	6,307,000,000	def. 51,280,000	13.1
Safeway:			
1970	4,860,000,000	68,890,000	11.2
1971	5,359,000,000	80,180,000	11.8
1972	6,058,000,000	91,060,000	12.5
Kroger:			
1970	3,736,000,000	39,770,000	8.6
1971	3,708,000,000	36,270,000	8.1
1972	3,791,000,000	23,180,000	7.8

Sources: U. S. Dept. of Commerce reports, and *Moody's*.

To add to the woes of A & P, a battle of ownership commenced. Management was challenged by Gulf & Western Industries, an acquisition-minded conglomerate. Gulf & Western sought to win disaffected stockholders to its side with an attractive offer for 3.75 million shares. Others were also interested. But in extended legal maneuvers, Kane and his associates were able to win a court order against the tender offer becoming effective.

Heavy losses were not unexpected by A & P management during the start of the WEO campaign. With margins reduced on thousands of items, increased advertising and refurbishing of stores, and the hiring and training of more employees to handle increased business, some pressures on profits were inevitable. But with virtually no debt, the company was in a position to stick with reduced profits until the WEO strategy had time to prove itself. A dramatic turnaround in profitability was expected by the close of 1972 as greater sales volume and improved market share was achieved.

Unfortunately, an external factor entered the picture and reduced the full impact of A & P's pricing actions. The WEO campaign was begun almost simultaneously with an explosion of food prices. In February 1973, the Consumer Price Index rose 3.9 percent—in one month's time—over 1972, and wholesale food prices increased across the board.

Beset on all sides—by rising food prices, by tremendous stockholder pressure to cut losses, and by the takeover attempt by Gulf & Western—A & P began hiking its prices. The real price war was over by early 1973, even though WEO signs and advertising continued prominently.

Aside from what *Business Week* called a "Pyrrhic victory"[7] (that is, a victory won with staggering losses, based on a victory by Pyrrhus over the Romans in 279 B.C.), what other consequences can be seen in the WEO campaign? Undoubtedly A & P gained the enmity of its competitors and a reputation as a bully in an industry that already had slender profit margins.

As to the efforts to improve market share in some key cities, the results were not very portentous. In Chicago, where A & P had an estimated 7 percent of the market, no lasting advantage was gained, although some business was initially taken from smaller independents and from National Tea Company, which had problems of its own before A & P's price war. In Washington, D.C., where A & P also had 7 percent of the market, there was no change, although some thought A & P had been less aggressive there where most of its stores were old and where little money had been spent on new construction. In Pittsburgh, A & P even lost ground, with market share falling from 10 percent to 8.9 percent. But in Philadelphia, a significant gain was initially scored, as market share rose from 13 percent to 16 percent in one year.

While A & P eased its price-cutting tactics early in 1973, the perception of low prices in the minds of some customers appeared to be more lasting. For example, a limited study by *Business Week* of customers interviewed in WEO stores found 32 were there because of cheaper prices, while 17 of these said they had switched from other chains in the last nine months in order to pare their food costs.[8] This was at a time when several independent studies had found that A & P prices were no longer lower than competitors. For example, a Philadelphia study of fifty key grocery items at WEO and major competitors found only five that cost less at WEO. Another study found that of ten items advertised in March 1973, seven were the same as competitors', two were slightly higher, and only one was cheaper.[9]

The major question facing A & P in 1973 was whether the hard won gains would last. Would customers who had been wooed to A & P because of supposed lower prices stay with A & P? Or would they quickly shift when they discovered that WEO prices were comparable with those of other stores?

Time proved the failure of the WEO strategy. The $51 million loss due to severe price cutting was a wasted effort. While sales rose to $6.7 billion in 1973, and the company went into the black on its higher prices with a $12.2 million profit, this was small compared to past years (see Table 15.2); of even

[7]"A & P Counts the Cost of Its Pyrrhic Victory," *Business Week*, April 28, 1973, pp. 117–119.
[8]Ibid., p. 117.
[9]Ibid., p. 118.

more concern, A & P lost its top spot in sales to Safeway. In 1974 the situation worsened; while sales nudged up 1.9 percent to $6.9 billion, the company plunged to a loss of $157.1 million. To add to its problems, the company was hit with a price-fixing suit and assessed $32.7 million in damages.

In December of 1974, Jonathan L. Scott, chief executive of Albertson's, the fifteenth largest food chain, became the first outsider to head A & P in its entire history. In one of the biggest retrenchments in retailing history, Scott began closing one-third of A & P's 3500 stores at a total write-off of some $200 million. This involved renegotiating hundreds of local labor contracts and weakening employee morale. In place of the small, marginal stores, Scott planned to follow the examples of Safeway and other front-running chains and open large stores stocking a wider assortment of foods and nonfoods with higher markups. The prescription for correcting the ills of A & P also included refurbishing other stores, more emphasis on national brands, better displays, and insistence on clean and uncluttered stores.

A & P probably will never regain its lead over arch-rival Safeway. Results for the two chains for 1974 were as follows:

	Sales	Net Income
Safeway	$8,185,200,000	$79,200,000
A & P	6,874,600,000	−157,100,000

WHAT CAN BE LEARNED?

Where basic weaknesses exist in a company, any strategy not directed to correcting these weaknesses can only be a short-term solution. In A & P's case, a smug, imbred management, too many small inefficient stores in decaying central city locations, and minimum penetration in affluent suburban markets had to be corrected before price cutting, heavier emphasis on advertising, or any other strategy could have any lasting impact.

The strategy of severe price cutting is especially ill-advised in the supermarket industry where markups are small to begin with and where competition is keen.

While A & P increased sales by $800 million during the WEO campaign, this was not nearly enough to compensate for the lower prices, so major losses were incurred. Volume likely cannot be raised sufficiently to compensate for drastically reduced prices and markups, since competition will retaliate and usually attempt to match prices in self-defense.

Update

The new management did not solve A & P's problems. Chairman Jonathan Scott "swung a cruel ax," closing 1700 stores, releasing 10,000 employees, and borrowing heavily to revamp and enlarge the remaining supermarkets. He hired nineteen new executives, including Grant Gentry, who left the flourishing Jewel chain to become A & P president. Scott said: "I have a philosophy that you should surround yourself with people better than yourself."[10]

An expensive and self-critical ad campaign, "to put price and pride back together again," was instituted, aimed both at luring shoppers and also at bucking up store employees. But results remained dismal. For the second quarter of fiscal 1977, profits dropped 88 percent below the previous year, and they were hardly breathtaking then. With the release of this news, President Gentry resigned.

By 1978, sales had risen to $7.2 billion; but now Kroger had also surpassed A & P. The company had either lost money or barely made a profit in every year since 1971. Part of the problem was the many center-city stores that were stuck in deteriorating neighborhoods. This situation could not be remedied quickly. Scott made an identifiable mistake in electing to close unprofitable stores one by one in the 36 states serviced, with the result that A & P did not get the distribution savings of quitting an entire region.

Unexpectedly, in early 1979, one of West Germany's largest food retailers, the Tangelmann Group, offered to pay $7.50 a share, a small premium over the market price of $6.75, and far below the book value, for A & P. Thus A & P fell into foreign hands, after 120 years. At first the future looked better for A & P as the German company could supply much-needed capital. It had 2000 stores in Germany and Austria and annual sales of about $3 billion.

But the problems were not to disappear. Jonathan Scott quit in 1980—to start a real estate investment firm in Dallas—and Tanglemann replaced him with James Wood who was running Grand Union food stores, a subsidiary of English-owned Cavenham Ltd. A & P again reverted to heavy losses, recording $53 million in red ink over five quarters in 1980–1981.

For Thought and Discussion

1. With the situation facing the new management of A & P in 1971, what alternative actions might have been taken to shake the giant food chain from its waning competitive position? How desirable are these alternatives, rather than the severe price cutting that was decided on?

[10]"Price and Pride on the Skids," *Time*, December 12, 1977, p. 79.

2. Surveys of customers' motives for shopping particular stores have usually found that lowest prices ranks rather far down the list. For example, one study in 1965 found "low prices" to be 20th on the list, with such things as high quality, reliability, large selection, and friendly employees being much more important.[11] If these surveys have any validity, how wise do you think the reaction was of Kroger, Food Fair, and other supermarket chains matching the price cutting of A & P, with the result that their profits also dropped drastically in 1972 and early 1973?
3. Did the WEO campaign have any advantageous results?

Invitation to Role Play

1. Place yourself in the role of Jonathan Scott. What specific actions would you initiate to bring the A & P chain back to satisfactory profits as quickly as possible?
2. Place yourself in the role of manager of a fairly run-down A & P store in a deteriorating neighborhood. You have been asked by your district and regional managers to come to the home office to present your views as to how best to bring such stores into profitability. Develop your recommendations carefully and with sound reasoning; your future advancement will undoubtedly depend on the judgment and persuasion you display. (Make any assumptions you need to for this problem, but keep them reasonable and state them clearly.)

[11]F. F. Brown and George Fisk, "Department Stores and Discount Houses: Who Dies Next?" *Journal of Retailing*, Fall 1975.

CHAPTER 16

Osborne Computer— The Illusion of Product Uniqueness

Only rarely may a new firm hit the jackpot: a meteoric rise surpassing even the most optimistic expectations of founders and investors. In the heady excitement of great growth anything seems possible. It is tantalizing to think that such an enterprise is invincible to competition. Alas, sometimes such stars can come tumbling back to earth, and reality. Perhaps no better example can be found in modern business annals than the almost vertical rise and collapse of Osborne Computer Corporation. Founded in 1981, the business was booming at a $100 million clip—in barely 18 months. But on September 14, 1983, the company sought protection from creditors under Chapter 11 of the Bankruptcy Code.

ADAM OSBORNE

Adam Osborne was born in Thailand, the son of a British professor, and spent his earliest years in India. His parents were disciples of a maharishi, although Adam was educated in Catholic schools. Later he was sent to Britain for schooling, and in 1961 at the age of 22 he moved to the United States. He obtained a Ph.D. in chemical engineering at the University of Delaware and then worked for Shell Development Company in California.

Osborne and Shell soon parted company, the bureaucratic structure frustrating him. He became interested in computers, and in 1970 he set up his own computer consulting company. The market for personal computers began to mushroom in the mid-1970s and he emerged as a guru. He had a computer column, "From the Fountainhead," for *Interface Age,* and he began making speeches and building a reputation. He wrote a book geared to the mass market, *Introduction to Microcomputers,* which was turned down by a publisher. Osborne published the book himself and it sold 300,000 copies. By 1975 his publishing company had put out some 40 books on microcomputers, nearly a dozen of which Osborne had written himself. In 1979 he sold the publishing company to McGraw-Hill, but agreed to stay as a consultant through May 1982.

Osborne was thus in a position to take full advantage of the growth of the microcomputer industry. But he had also angered many in the industry by his stinging criticisms and bold assertions. In particular he spoke out sharply against the pricing strategies of the personal computer manufacturers, contending that they were ignoring the mass market by constantly raising prices with every new feature added.

Osborne himself came to be the subject of some of the most colorful copy of the industry. Tall and energetic, he possessed a strong British accent to go along with his volubility, his charm, and his supreme confidence. He seemed to epitomize the new breed of entrepreneurs drawn to the epicenter of new high-tech industry, the so-called Silicon Valley in California.

Early in 1981, Osborne put his criticisms and assertions to the test. To a chorus of skeptics he announced plans to manufacture and market a new personal computer; one priced well below the competition. His first machines were ready for shipping by that July, and before long the skeptics were running for the hills. Now Osborne could prove that he was a doer, and not merely a talker.

INDUSTRY BACKGROUND

In the early 1970s, computers ranged from small to very large units, with prices reaching limits only affordable by the well-heeled firms. The industry was dominated by one company, IBM, which held 70 percent of the market. All the other firms in the industry were scrambling for small shares. IBM seemed to have an unassailable advantage because it had the resources for the heaviest marketing expenditures in the industry as well as the best research and development. The firm with the masterful lead in a rapidly growing industry has ever-increasing resources over its lesser competitors who can hardly hope to catch up and seemingly must be content to chip away at the periphery of the total market.

The computer industry had been characterized by rapid technological changes since the early 1960s. By the early 1970s, however, the new technology being introduced generally involved peripheral accessories, and not major changes in main units.

Before the advent of microelectronics technology, which makes smaller parts possible, computers were very costly and complicated. It was not economically feasible for one person to interact with one computer. The processing power at that time existed only in a central data processing installation, and for those who could not afford to have their own computer, time-sharing services were available.

The "small" or minicomputer industry began in 1974 when a few small firms began using memory chips to produce small computer systems as do-it-yourself kits for as low as $400. These proved popular and other companies began to build microcomputers designed for the affluent hobbyist and small businessperson.

In 1975 microcomputer and small business computer shipments went over the $1 billion mark. As the mainframe market began to mature, the microcomputer industry was starting its rocketing ascendancy. In 1975 the first personal computer reached the market.

Personal computers can be defined as easy-to-use desktop machines that are microprocessor based, have their own power supply, and are priced below $10,000. By using various software packages, these computers can be customized to serve the needs of businesses and a variety of professionals such as accountants, financial analysts, scientists, and educators, as well as the sophisticated individual at home. It should be noted that the minicomputer grew up without IBM, the company that dominated mainframe computers and accounted for two-thirds of all computer revenues in the mid-1970s. And one of the great success stories of the century had occurred with personal computers. Apple Computer was started in a family garage on $1300 capital in 1976. By 1982 sales were $583 million, and Steven Jobs, a college dropout who was the co-founder at age 21, had become one of the richest people in America with a net worth exceeding $225 million.[1]

Portable computers are a subset of personal computers, being as the name implies, lightweight and relatively easy to carry. Actually, three categories of portable computers are recognized by the industry: (1) hand-held computers; (2) portable, which have a small display screen, limited memory, and weigh between ten and twenty pounds; and (3) transportable, which have bigger screens and memories, and weigh more than twenty pounds. Osborne computer was in the third group.

---

[1]For more details of the Apple success story, see Robert F. Hartley *Marketing Successes,* (New York: John Wiley & Sons), 1985, pp. 200–213.

THE OSBORNE STRATEGY

Osborne had discerned a significant niche in the portable computer market: "I saw a truck-size hole in the industry, and I plugged it," he said.[2] He hired Lee Felsenstein, a former Berkeley radical, to design a powerful unit that weighed only 24 pounds and could be placed in a briefcase small enough to fit under an airline seat. It was the first portable business computer; the other portable computers being of much more limited sophistication. And it sold for $1795, which was hundreds of dollars less than other business-oriented computers, and half the price of an Apple. He was able to sell for this price by running a low-overhead operation. For example, he hired Georgette Psaris, then 25, and made her vice president of sales and marketing. Her office was in a chilly, former warehouse. He was able to achieve economies of scale, and also capitalized on the declining prices of semiconductor parts. The computers were assembled from standard industry components. The display screen was small, only 5 inches across, and there was no color graphics capability. Osborne himself admitted, "The Osborne 1 had no technology of consequence. We made the purchasing decision convenient by bundling hardware and needed software in one price."[3]

To cut costs on software, no programmers were employed. This was a drastic departure from other personal computer makers. Instead, independent software companies were relied upon entirely to provide programs written in the popular programming language. To reduce software costs still further, Osborne gave some software suppliers equity in the company. The result was that Osborne was able to provide almost $1500 worth of software packages as part of the $1795 system price.

Osborne had a flair for showmanship. One of his first triumphs was in the 1981 West Coast Computer Faire in San Francisco. In place of the rather ordinary booths and displays of the other computer makers, he took a substantial part of his venture capital to build a plexiglas booth that towered toward the ceiling. The Osborne Company logo, the "Flying O," dominated the show.

He believed that mass distribution was a key to success. By 1982 he had signed an agreement with Computerland Corporation, the largest computer retailer. This extended Osborne's distribution by doubling in one swoop the number of retail stores carrying his computer. The Osborne 1 was proving to be a hot item, with sales hitting $10 million by the end of 1981, the first year of operation in which the first computer had not even been shipped until

[2]"Osborne: From Brags to Riches," *Business Week*, February 22, 1982, p. 86.
[3]"Osborne Bytes the Distribution Bullet," *Sales & Marketing Management*, July 4, 1983, p. 34.

July. By the end of 1982, after only 18 months of operation, annual sales were soaring to $100 million. Predictions were made that "most of the Osborne management team would be millionaires by the time they're 40 or even 30,"[4] and their earlier bare-bones operating style was forsaken.

By 1983 some 750 retail outlets were stocking the company's portables: the Computerland chain, Xerox's retail stores, Sears' business centers, and such department stores as Macy. And early in 1983, 150 office-equipment dealers with experience in selling the most advanced copiers also were added, thus enabling Osborne to reach small- and medium-sized businesses.

In summary, Osborne was certainly not the originator of the portable computer, but he was the first to sell such computers in mass quantities and his efforts expanded the market greatly.

MARCHING INTO 1983

By early 1983 Osborne began to loosen his grip on the company, under pressure from his investors. It was felt that the growing operation—it already had 800 employees—required a professional management that Osborne and his early hirees were not. Osborne was an entrepreneur and not an administrator, and the two abilities are quite different. To protect the company's front-running position—estimated at an 80 to 90% market share—Robert Jaunich II, president of Consolidated Foods, was hired to head up Osborne Computer as president and chief executive officer. Adam Osborne moved up to chairman. Jaunich had turned down offers at Apple and Atari because he felt that these firms would not give him enough control. He also sacrificed a $1 million incentive to remain at Consolidated Foods, so he must have felt strongly that the opportunities and potential of Osborne far surpassed his other options.

Jaunich moved quickly to decentralize the management structure. Georgette Psaris, vice president of marketing, was moved into a newly created position as vice president of strategic planning. She was replaced by Joseph Roebuck, lured from Apple Computer, where he had been marketing director. Fred Brown, the director of sales for Osborne, was elevated to vice president of sales, and David Lorenzen, a consultant for Osborne, was made director of marketing services, with responsibility for dealer-support programs.

The distribution strategy, which Adam Osborne had prided as one of the strengths of the venture, was refined. The computer-store outlets were continued, but some alternative channels were instituted as well. A major addition was an affiliation with Harris Corporation's computer systems

---

[4]Steve Fishman, "Facing Up to Failure," *Success*, November 1984, p. 48.

division to act as a national distributor for contacting major firms. Harris was a $1.7 billion minicomputer firm whose computer systems division had some 70 salespeople and 1200 support personnel, including systems analysts. To protect Osborne's smaller clients, Harris agreed to handle only large orders of 50 units and over.

Other sales targets were United Press International (UPI), the news service, where Osborne planned to sell portables to the 1000 subscriber newspapers as personal workstations. Brown, the vice president of sales, also began exploring other distribution possibilities, including independent sales organizations, airlines, and hotel chains.

As competitors started to enter the portable market, offering cheaper and fancier machines than the Osborne 1, the firm began readying itself to broaden its product line. An even cheaper version of the Osborne 1, the Vixen, was being prepared. And an Executive 1 was unveiled in the spring of 1983, with an Executive 2 planned for late summer. These offered more storage capacity and larger screens than Osborne 1. The Executive 1 could serve as a terminal to communicate with a mainframe, thereby enabling users to work with larger data bases and to handle more complicated jobs. This was to have a $2495 price tag with some $2000 worth of software, including word processing, an electronic spread sheet, and data base management. The Executive 2, at $3195 was to be promoted as compatible with IBM's hot-selling personal computer, the IBM PC.

In 1982 Osborne spent $3.5 million on advertising. This included $1.5 million in consumer magazines and $500,000 on spot TV, with $1.5 million in business publications. Plans were laid to continue heavy advertising in order to reinforce the product differentiation. The sales force was also being expanded to keep pace with the growing firm. An eight-person salesforce was to be supplemented by an additional 30 to 40 people, thereby permitting more specialized selling. Instead of being generalists selling to all types of customers, sales was to be organized by specialists concentrating either on retail or nonretail accounts. Brown explained this rationale: "Retailers . . . need help on such things as point-of-sale displays to stimulate the guy who comes in off the street. Dealers call on purchasing and data-processing departments and need advice on direct mail campaigns.[5]

The sky seemed to be the limit. Osborne was predicting revenues of $300 million for 1983. And when he made one of his frequent trips abroad, he was received by ambassadors and prime ministers, most of whom wanted stock in his company. He was the head of the fastest-growing company Silicon Valley had ever seen—even faster growing than Apple.

[5]"Osborne Bytes . . ." p. 36.

PREMONITION

The first premonition of trouble came to Adam Osborne on April 26, 1983. He was giving a seminar in Colorado when he received a call. "Over the weekend considerable losses were discovered," he was told. "That's not possible," he is reported to have said.[6]

The news of earlier profit figures being in error was particularly ominous because of its timing. On April 29 a public stock offering was planned. This was designed to raise about $50 million, and would have made the top executives of Osborne rich. How would this news of losses instead of profits affect the stock offering? Adam Osborne had to wonder.

Actually, in the few days Adam had been away from the office, the bad news had been building up. In the first two months of the fourth fiscal quarter (the fiscal year ended February 1983), pretax profits had been reported that ran $300,000 ahead of company projections. And in February the company racked up an all-time high in shipments, all these with supposed very high profit margins. Projections had been that profits in February would be in the neighborhood of $750,000 for that month alone, and the future seemed even brighter.

But the heady optimism was to rapidly disappear. By late March the results for February showed instead of a profit, a loss of more than $600,000 for the month, reflecting charges against new facilities as well as very heavy promotional spending. For the entire fiscal year a loss of $1.5 million was incurred, this despite revenues of slightly more than $100 million.

The worst was still to come. On April 21, Jaunich, the CEO, had learned that later data showed that the company would have a $1.5 million loss for the February quarter, and a $4 million loss for the full year. The chief reasons seemed to be excessive inventories of old stock that the company did not even realize it had, liabilities in software contracts, and the need for greater bad debt and warranty reserves. Jaunich still planned to move ahead with the filing for the stock offering, although certainly the attractiveness of stock in the company was rapidly diminishing.

On April 24, Jaunich was informed that the losses would be even greater: $5 million for the quarter and $8 million for the year, thanks to further unrecorded liabilities and more inventory problems.

That same day Jaunich decided to scrap the offering, despite heavy pressure to find another underwriter to bring the stock to market. Now every report blackened the situation still further. The final report for the year showed a loss of more than $12 million. Heavy losses continued over the

---

[6]Fishman, "Facing Up to Failure," p. 51.

next months, as further adjustments in inventories and reserves became necessary. Adam Osborne's house of cards was close to collapsing.

Osborne had had no trouble attracting seed money from venture capitalists before—indeed, venture capital firms had been clamoring to participate. But now that the company's earnings problems had come to light, such funding was drying up. A few investors still had hopes, and Osborne found another $11 million in June. But an additional $20 million which the company considered necessary to speed a competitive product from drawing board to market could not be found.

Black Friday

Sporadic employee layoffs had been occurring since late spring as the company desperately tried to improve its cash flow. The climax came on Friday, September 16. On the previous Tuesday the company had filed for protection from creditor lawsuits under Chapter 11 of the federal Bankruptcy Code. The company filed its petition after three creditors filed two lawsuits saying Osborne owed them a total of $4.7 million. Osborne's petition stated that it owed secured and unsecured creditors about $45 million while its assets were $40 million.

Osborne's employees had to expect the worst when a meeting was abruptly called in the company cafeteria. Top management then announced that more than 300 workers, about 80 percent of the company staff still remaining, were to be immediately "furloughed." Final paychecks were issued and the workers were given two hours to empty their desks and vacate the company offices.

News of the company's Chapter 11 filing and near total shutdown shocked the industry, even though Osborne's recently sagging sales and the consequent need for cash were well known. The company had made strenuous efforts to raise money, especially after July shipments had turned soft and the banks were pressing it to improve its shrinking capital base. But venture capitalists appeared to have fled the industry as a serious shakeout was occurring, not only for Osborne but for other personal computer firms as well. The market was just not able to support some 150 plus microcomputer companies.

POST MORTEM

Internal Factors

Adam Osborne was an entrepreneur, not a professional manager. Perhaps this accounted for most of the problems that were to befall his company. So often it seems that the entrepreneurial personality is incompatible with the manager-type of person who must necessarily be engrossed with the nitty gritty of details and day-to-day controls over operations. Osborne had never managed more than 50 people, and the organization had grown to almost 20 times that size. He operated under a "fire fighting" perspective, with no advanced planning and with problems being dealt with as they arose. "I had no professional training whatsoever in finance or business management," Osborne admitted.[7]

The board of directors of Osborne and the venture capitalists who had contributed mightily to the fledgling enterprise certainly brought about sufficient pressure to persuade Adam Osborne to step aside and turn over the operating responsibilities to a professional manager, Robert Jaunich, early in 1983. But this was apparently too late to rectify the damage that had already been done. Perhaps six months earlier . . . ?

Some of the mistakes made are inexcusable from the standpoint of any prudently-run operation. Perhaps they can be explained as due to the heady excitement that can accompany rapidly rising sales and the subsequent euphoria that clouds rational judgments and expectations. Other mistakes can be credited to simple miscalculations—to which any firm could be guilty of—as to the impact of competitors of all kinds, and particularly the rapidity with which the awesome IBM could enter the market and dominate it.

Lack of controls was the most obvious failing of the company. It had no efficient means of monitoring inventories of finished products. Consequently, managers did not know how much inventory they had. They did not know how much they were spending, or needed to spend. Information management was sorely lacking—and this in a company whose product was primarily geared to aiding information management. While rapid growth can be accompanied by growing pains and some difficulty in keeping abreast of booming operations, in Osborne's case the lack was abysmal and accounted for supposed profits suddenly being revealed instead as devastating losses. Other examples of incompetence were: unrecorded liabilities, with some bills never handed over to the accounting department; no reserves established for the shutdown of a New Jersey plant that was producing computers with a 40 percent failure rate; and not enough capital was set aside to pay for a new European headquarters on Lake Geneva in Switzerland.

Lack of controls permitted expenses to run rampant. "Everybody was trying to buy anything they wanted," said one former Osborne employee.[8]

[7]Jaye Scholl, "Osborne's Back Byting," *Barron's*, July 26, 1984, p. 26.

[8]"Shaken Osborne Computer Seeking Suitor in the Face of Possible Failure," *Wall Street Journal*, September 12, 1983, p. 35.

INFORMATION SIDELIGHT

THE PRODUCT LIFE CYCLE

Just as people and animals do, products go through stages of growth and maturity, that is, life cycles. They are affected by different competitive conditions at each stage, ranging often from no competition in the early stages to intense competition later on. We can recognize four stages in a product's life cycle: introduction, growth, maturity, and decline.

Figure 16.1 depicts three different product life cycles. #1 is that of a standard item in which sales take some time to develop, and then

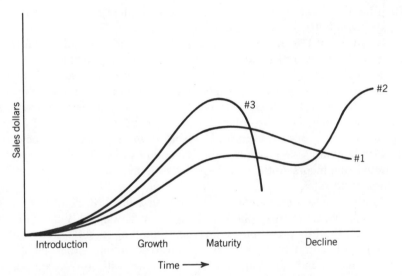

Figure 16.1. The product life cycle.

eventually begin a slow decline. #2 shows a life cycle for a product in which a modification of the product or else the uncovering of a new market rejuvenates the product so that it takes off on a new cycle of growth (the classic examples of such *remarketing* are Listerine, originally sold as a mild external antiseptic, and Arm & Hammer Baking Soda, which was remarketed as a deodorizer). #3 shows the life cycle for a fad product or one experiencing rapid technological change and intense competition. Notice its sharp rise in sales and the abrupt downturn.

In certain industries the competitive environment is volatile enough that some products quickly become obsolete—this is more a characteristic of young industries, such as microcomputers, than of mature industries like steel. A host of competitors, drawn into the industry by the growing market and the relative ease of getting started, contribute to the short life cycle. Short life cycles can severely test any management. The organization must constantly be working on new product ideas, technological improvements, and greater production efficiency. But inventories must also be closely monitored so that they not be allowed to build up faster than the rate of sale. Otherwise, severe inventory writeoffs may become necessary because of obsolescence.

When Jaunich finally took over the managerial reins, he clamped down hard on expenses, but perhaps it was too late.

By spring of 1983 marketing miscalculations had reduced cash flow to a trickle. Osborne had planned to introduce a new computer, the Executive, but he made the grievous mistake of announcing it too soon. While the Executive was not supposed to compete against the original Osborne 1, many dealers saw it as doing just that. Upon learning of the new machine in April, many canceled their orders for the Osborne 1. This in itself necessitated heavy inventory writeoffs as the Osborne was not planned to be phased out. Compounding the problems, the Executive was delayed and not ready for initial shipments until May. April was a month, consequently, with practically no sales.

Another major mistake was failing to realize just how short the product life cycle could be in this volatile industry, and how quickly a competitive advantage—the low price, portability, and bundling of software—could be countered by competitors and even improved upon. Other companies, notably Kaypro and Compaq, entered the market with low-priced portable computers and at least as much bundled software. But the biggest impact was that of IBM. Its personal computer was introduced in late 1981 and it quickly became the industry standard against which other computers were judged. Osborne turned out to be slow in reacting and adopting IBM's state of the art technology. Furthermore, Osborne was slow in coming up with a model that was compatible with the IBM personal computer at home or in the office. Scores of other computer companies jumped to produce IBM-compatible computers, while Osborne lagged, and suddenly its product was not selling. Hardly a year after coming to market, the formerly popular Osborne computer with its tiny screen was practically obsolete.

One new product developed by Osborne was obsolete before it was even introduced. The Vixen was originally scheduled for introduction in

December 1982. It was 10 pounds lighter and an even cheaper version of the Osborne 1. A poorly designed circuit board caused production delays, and the project was finally scrapped as company resources were at last redirected to an Executive model, an IBM-compatible unit with a larger screen. The Osborne production delays and the speed with which IBM took over the personal computer market were tough to cope with.

External Factors

The environment for personal computer makers was rapidly becoming unhealthy by 1983. A major shakeout for the more than 150 small manufacturers in this industry was inevitable. A major factor behind the proliferation of firms was a tidal wave of venture capital. Early winners such as Apple Computer had dazzled investors and led to the perception of a "can't lose" industry. It became almost too easy to start a new computer company. "As a result, a whole series of 'me too' companies have been started. They are developing products that do not have a unique feature or competitive advantage. They don't stand a chance," one venture capitalist said.[9] Only the strongest firms were likely to survive. And yet, in size and with its headstart, Osborne should have been one of the survivors.

While demand by businesses and consumers alike for small computers was rapidly increasing, so was cutthroat competition. Price-cutting and shrinking profit margins were inevitable. And certainly dealers' shelves could hardly accommodate more than a few brands.

The first presentiment of worsening problems for the industry came early in 1983 when three big manufacturers of low-priced home computers, Atari, Texas Instruments, and Mattel, reported first-half losses totaling more than half a billion dollars. Makers of higher-priced computers tried to dissociate themselves from this low-end calamitous environment. But other well-known companies such as Victor Technologies, Fortune Systems, and Vector Graphics all reported shocking losses for the second quarter. Even Apple Computer saw its stock price sink nearly 34 points between June and September 1983.

Indicative of the price-cutting going on, Texas Instruments' 99/4A home computer which sold for $525 when introduced in 1981, was retailing for $100 by early 1983. Yet, each 99/4A cost about $80 in parts and labor, to which must be added TI's overhead expenses, dealer profits, and marketing costs.[10]

[9]"Trouble in Computer Land," *Newsweek,* September 26, 1983, p. 73.
[10]"Behind the Shakeout in Personal Computers," *U.S. News & World Report,* June 27, 1983, pp. 59–60.

Other computer-makers were desperately struggling to revamp their production and marketing efforts. For example, Vector Graphic after losing $1.7 million in the second quarter of 1983 obtained a new $7 million line of credit to help it tailor its computers to such specialty markets as meeting the accounting needs of farmers.[11]

Now the problems of the industry dried up venture capital. Osborne was partly the victim of an external situation of which it had no control. The external factors were unforgiving of its internal mistakes.

AFTERMATH

Under Chapter 11 of the federal Bankruptcy Act, a company continues to operate, but has court protection against creditors' lawsuits while working out a plan for paying its debts. By the end of 1984, Osborne was emerging from bankruptcy with most of its debts paid and two new machines to sell. Its retail network had shrunk from 800 dealers to about 50. Suppliers now demanded cash on delivery. And the firm was anathema to venture capitalists who lost $31 million when the company collapsed. Gone were the factories, the 1000-worker payroll, and the posh executive offices. But the lean, trimmed-down company had $10 to $30 million worth of tax-loss carryforwards. And its name and still-extant dealer network in Europe was a plus. Perhaps the biggest challenge it then faced was redeveloping its retail network: "Competition for shelf space is hot even for companies with no strikes against them. Retailers were left with a bad taste when the company went Chapter 11," noted the president of a 40-store chain.[12] The new president was Ronald J. Brown, the former vice president of international operations who engineered the company's restructuring.

Adam Osborne had left the company. He was now trying his entrepreneurial talents in the marketing of software, as well as organizing a defense against investor lawsuits. He wrote a book (publishing it himself, since major publishers were reluctant to), *Hypergrowth: The Rise and Fall of the Osborne Computer Corporation* (with John Dvorak) soundly criticizing Robert Jaunich. Georgette Psaris, Osborne's former vice president noted: "I've gone from being a multimillionaire to being in the hole."[13] But she joined Adam Osborne in his new entrepreneurial endeavor.

[11]"Trouble in Computer Land," p. 73.
[12]"Osborne Tries for Comeback in Computers," *Wall Street Journal,* October 12, 1984, p. 27.
[13]"Trouble in Computer Land," p. 74.

WHAT CAN BE LEARNED?

The rapid rise, and even more rapid fall, of Osborne has to be sobering to investors, executives, and employees alike—as well as to dealers and customers who may find themselves with no recourse for warranty and parts service. But inexperienced entrepreneurs tend to fall into the quicksand of expanding operations as fast as they can, without building up the organization and controls necessary for larger enterprises. As a result, costs get out of hand, inventory buildup becomes an albatross, customer accounts may imprudently be allowed to become excessive and overdue, and in the excitement of increasing sales, profits may be assumed when in reality losses are being incurred. The caution is plain: beware of uncontrolled growth. Tight controls, especially over inventories and expenses, is essential.

New and rapidly growing industries present dangers far greater than those facing the entrant to more mature industries. Unless entry to the industry is exceedingly difficult because of high startup costs or secure technological expertise, the new, rapidly growing industry is attractive to all kinds of firms and a host of investors. Such new industries are usually characterized by rapid product improvements and by severe price-cutting. A firm in such an industry must beware the shakeout. It may well have to resist expanding so fast as to leave itself vulnerable to overcapacity and excessive inventory when the trauma of price-cutting begins. Competition is almost surely going to be heavily involved on a price basis, as production efficiencies and technological improvements are advanced by the competing firms. Where a large number of firms have entered the industry, it requires no great insight to expect many marginal ones to fall by the wayside, with the field left only to the more able firms with better management and greater resources. Yet, during the shakeout period virtually all firms may find themselves losing money because of the severe price competition and the dumping of excessive inventories. A stayer must be prepared to weather some rough times before the industry stabilizes.

In such a new industry we often find the transience of uniqueness. Osborne certainly had a unique product offering in its early months. But the firm vastly underestimated how quickly the uniqueness would be matched, and even surpassed, by competitors. Research and development efforts must not be delayed simply because a firm now has a successful product. The product life cycle can be very short in the turmoil of such new industries. Such short product life cycles necessitate very careful monitoring of production and inventories that these do not expand faster than current sales warrant.

Finally we see in the Osborne example the dangers of cannibalization carried to the extreme. Cannibalization refers to one product of the firm taking away sales from another or other products of the firm. Generally a new product's success will to some extent be at the expense of other products in the line, but hopefully there will be enough new business to increase total sales. In Osborne's case, the foolish announcement of the new Executive computer—before it was even ready to go to market—practically killed sales for the older Osborne 1. Encountering a month and more of virtually no sales is more than most firms could endure. Competition made the new product necessary, but its market impact could have been far better anticipated. The threat of cannibalization should not preclude new product introductions, but it should be anticipated and prepared for.

For Thought and Discussion

1. What factors account for the surge of competitors in the portable computer field? Should this have been anticipated by a prudent executive?
2. What kind of controls would you advise Osborne to have set up to prevent the debacle that befell it?
3. Did Osborne Computer have any unique strengths that could have enabled it to survive in this hotly competitive industry?

Invitation to Role Play

1. Place yourself in the role of Adam Osborne in late 1982. Sales are exceeding the wildest expectations. Yet you sense that IBM will soon be a factor in this market, as well as many smaller firms. Plan your strategy for 1983 to protect the viability of your enterprise and pave the way for further growth.
2. As a management consultant you have been called in by Robert Jaunich in late spring of 1983. Company losses are mounting. You have been charged to develop recommendations to save the company.

17

Adidas—Letting Market Advantage Slip Away

In the early 1970s, Adidas dominated the running-shoe industry. It had done so for decades. It stood on the threshold of one of the biggest surges of popularity for its market that any recreational pursuit had even known. Millions of people were to take up running or jogging in the next few years; other millions of nonrunners would be buying and wearing running shoes because they were comfortable, and because they conveyed an aura of fitness and youth—an image that most people were not averse to emulating.

Did Adidas cash in on this recreational boom of the century? In one of the classic errors of miscalculation, it underestimated the U.S. market. (It still was to dominate in other parts of the world.) Even worse, it underestimated the entry and the aggressiveness of U.S. competitors. Most of these competitors were to be upstart firms that had not even been around at the beginning of the decade. In just a few years, Adidas was to be pushed aside by one of the fastest growing firms outside the computer industry: Nike.

HISTORICAL BACKGROUND

Rudolf and Adolf Dassler began making shoes in Herzogenaurach, West Germany, shortly after World War I. Adolf, known as Adi to his family, was the innovator, and Rudolf was the marketer who sold his brother's creations. The brothers achieved only moderate success at first, but then in 1936 a big breakthrough came. Jesse Owens agreed to wear their shoes in the Olympics and won his medals in front of Hitler, the German nation, and the world. The lucrative association of shoes with a famous athlete was to trigger a marketing strategy that Adidas—and other athletic shoe manufacturers—was to practice from that point on.

In 1949 the brothers had a falling out and never again spoke to each other outside of court. Rudolf took half the equipment and left his brother to go to the other side of town where he set up the Puma Company. Adolf established the Adidas Company from the existing firm ("Adidas" was derived from his nickname and the first three letters of his surname). Rudolf and his Pumas never quite caught up with Adolf's Adidas, but they did become number two in the world.

Adolf was constantly experimenting with new materials and techniques to develop stronger, yet lighter shoes. He tested thorny sharkskin in attempts to develop abrasive leather for indoor flats. He tried kangaroo leather to toughen the sides of shoes.

The first samples of Adidas footwear were shown at the Helsinki Olympic Games of 1952. Then in 1954 the German soccer team, equipped with Adidas footwear, won the World Cup over Hungary. The shoes were definitely a factor in the win, as Dassler had developed a special stud to screw into the shoes that allowed good footing on the muddy playing field that day; Hungary's shoes did not give the same traction.

Dassler's many innovations in the running-shoe industry included four-spiked running shoes, track shoes with a nylon sole, and injected spikes. He developed a shoe that allowed an athlete to choose from 30 different variations of interchangeable spike elements that could be adapted to an indoor or outdoor track as well as to natural or artificial surfaces.

With its great variety of superior products, Adidas dominated in the widely publicized international showcase events. For example, at the Montreal games, Adidas-equipped athletes accounted for 82.8 percent of all individual medal winners.[1] This was tremendous publicity for the company, and sales rose to $1 billion worldwide.

But competitors were entering the marketplace. Prior to 1972, Adidas and Puma had practically the entire athletic shoe market to themselves. Although this was changing, Adidas seemingly had built up an insurmountable lead, providing footwear for virtually every type of sporting activity as well as diversifying into other sports-related product lines: shorts, jerseys, leisure suits, and track suits; tennis and swimwear; balls for every kind of

---

[1]Norris Willett, "How Adidas Ran Faster," *Management Today,* December 1979, p. 58.

sport; tennis racquets and cross-country skis, and the popular sports bag that carried the Adidas name as a prominently displayed status symbol.

MARKETING STRATEGY

The marketing strategy originated by the Dassler brothers became the guiding influence for the entire industry. The Dasslers had long used international athletic competition as a testing ground for their products. Many years of feedback from these athletes led to continual design changes and improvements. Agreements were entered into with professional athletes to use their products. However, Adidas' strength was in international and Olympic events in which the participants were amateurs, and such endorsement contracts were more often made with national sports associations rather than the individuals.

Following the lead of Adidas and Puma, endorsement contracts with athletes have become commonplace. For example, every player in the National Basketball Association is under contract to at least one manufacturer. The going rate for an endorsement contract today ranges from $500 to $150,000. The athlete must wear a certain brand and appear in various promotional activities. It has become an industry practice to spend about 80 percent of the advertising budget for endorsements and 20 percent for media advertising. The distinctive logos that all manufacturers have developed is key to the effectiveness of these endorsement contracts. Such logos permit immediate identification of product; fans and potential customers can see the product actually in use by the famous athlete. These logos also permitted effective product diversification into apparel, bags, and so on.

To increase volume quickly, production facilities were sought where shoes could be made cheaply and in great quantities, in areas such as Yugoslavia and the Far East. Medium-sized firms in such countries were therefore signed up as licensees, and goods were produced to specifications. Great outlays for plants and equipment were thus avoided, and costs could be kept low.

Finally, Adidas led the running-shoe industry into offering a very wide variety of shoe styles—shoes to fit all kinds of running activities, from various kinds of races to training shoes. Shoes were also offered for every type of runner and running style. The great variety of offerings, more than a hundred different styles and models for Adidas, was to be exceeded only by Nike as it charged to capture the U.S. market.

THE 1970s RUNNING MARKET

During the late 1960s and early 1970s the environment affecting the running-shoe industry changed dramatically and positively. Americans were increasingly concerned with physical fitness. Millions of previously unathletic people were searching for ways to exercise. The spark that ignited the booming interest may have been the 1972 Munich Olympics. Millions of television viewers watched Dave Wottle defeat Russian Evgeni Arzanov in the 800-meters and Frank Shorter win the prestigious marathon. But the groundwork for the running boom was laid before. The idea of fitness perhaps first came to the attention of the general public in a trailblazing book by Dr. Kenneth Cooper, *Aerobics,* which sold millions of copies and gave scientific evidence of the physical benefits of a running (or jogging) regimen. A little less than 10 years later, another book with monumental impact, *The Complete Book of Running* by James Fixx, also sold millions of copies and was on the best selling list for months.

Through the decade of the 1970s the number of joggers increased. Estimates by the end of the decade were that 25 million to 30 million Americans were joggers, while another 10 million wore running shoes around home and town.[2] The number of shoe manufacturers also increased. The original three of Adidas, Puma, and Tiger were joined by new U.S. brands: Nike, Brooks, New Balance, Etonic, and even J. C. Penney, Sears, and Converse. To sell and distribute these new shoes, specialty shoe stores such as Athlete's Foot, Athletic Attic, and Kinney's Foot Lockers sprouted up nationwide. New magazines catering to this market were starting up and showing big increases in circulation: for example, *Runner's World, The Runner,* and *Running Times.* These provided the advertising media to reach runners with no wasted coverage.

COMPETITION

The Beginning of Nike

Phil Knight was a miler of modest accomplishments. His best time was a 4:13, hardly in the same class as the below 4:00 world-class runners. But he had trained under the renowned coach Bill Bowerman at the University of Oregon in the late 1950s. Bowerman had put Eugene, Oregon on the map in the 1950s when year after year he turned out world-record-setting long-distance runners. He was constantly experimenting with shoes, because of his theory that an ounce off a running shoe might make enough difference to win a race.

In the process of completing his MBA at Stanford University, Phil wrote a research paper that was based on the theory that the Japanese could

---

[2]"The Jogging-Shoe Race Heats Up," *Business Week,* April 9, 1979, p. 125.

do for athletic shoes what they were doing for cameras. After receiving his degree in 1960, Knight went to Japan to seek an American distributorship from the Onitsuka Company for Tiger shoes. Returning home, he took samples of the shoes to Bowerman.

In 1964 Knight and Bowerman went into business. They each put up $500, and formed the Blue Ribbon Shoe Company, sole distributor in the United States for Tiger running shoes. They put the inventory in Knight's father-in-law's basement, and they sold $8,000 worth of these imported shoes that first year. Knight worked by days as a Cooper & Lybrand accountant, while at night and on weekends he peddled these shoes mostly to high school athletic teams.

Knight and Bowerman finally developed their own shoe in 1972 and decided to manufacture it themselves. They contracted the work out to Asian factories where labor was cheap. They named the shoe, Nike, after the Greek goddess of victory. At that time they also developed the "swoosh" logo, which was highly distinctive and subsequently was placed on every Nike product. The Nike shoes' first appearance in competition came during the 1972 Olympic trials in Eugene, Oregon. Marathon runners persuaded to wear the new shoes placed fourth through seventh, whereas Adidas wearers finished first, second, and third in these trials.

On a Sunday morning in 1975, Bowerman began tinkering with a waffle iron and some urethane rubber, and he fashioned a new type of sole, a "waffle" sole whose tiny rubber studs made it more springy than those of other shoes currently on the market. This product improvement—seemingly so simple—gave Knight and Bowerman an initial impetus. The marketing strategy that propelled Nike to tops in the U.S. market was more imitative than innovative, however. It was patterned after that of Adidas. But the result was that the imitator outdid the originator.

Nike's Charge

The new "waffle sole" developed by Bowerman proved popular with runners, and this, along with the favorable market, brought 1976 sales to $14 million, up from $8.3 million the year before, and only $2 million in 1972.

Nike stayed in the forefront of the industry with its careful research and development of new models. By the end of the decade Nike was employing almost 100 people in the research and development section of the company. Over 140 different models were offered in the product line, some of these the most innovative and technologically advanced on the market. This diversity came from models designed from different foot types, body weights, running speeds, training schedules, sexes, and different levels of skill.

By the late 1970s and early 1980s, demand for Nikes was so great that

Table 17.1   Nike Sales Growth, 1976–1981

Year	Sales (millions of dollars)	Percent Change from Previous Year
1976	$14.	
1977	29	107%
1978	71	145
1979	200	182
1980	370	35
1981	458	70
1982	694	34

Source: Company annual reports.

60 percent of its 8000 department store, sporting goods, and shoe store dealers gave advanced orders, often waiting six months for delivery. This gave Nike a big advantage in production scheduling and inventory costs. Table 17.1 shows the phenomenal growth of Nike, with sales rising from $14 million in 1976 to $694 million only six years later. Table 17.2 shows the market shares in the U.S. market for the beginning of 1979. By then Nike was the market leader with 33 percent of the market; within two years it had taken an even more commanding lead, with approximately 50 percent of the total market.[3] Adidas' share was falling, well below that of Nike, and it had U.S. firms such as Brooks and New Balance also to worry about.

In 1980 Nike went public, and Knight became an instant multimillionaire, reaching the coveted *Forbes'* Richest Four Hundred Americans, with a net worth estimated at just under $300 million.[4] Bowerman, age 70, had sold most of his stock earlier, and owned only 2 percent of the company, worth a mere $9.5 million.

In the January 4, 1982 edition of *Forbes,* in the "Annual Report on American Industry," Nike was rated number one in profitability over the previous five years, ahead of all other firms in all other industries.[5]

Ingredients of Nike's Success

Unquestionably, Nike faced an extraordinarily favorable primary demand in the decade of the 1970s. Nike was positioned to take advantage of this, and indeed most of the running-shoe manufacturers had impressive gains during

[3]"Jogging's Fade Fails to Push Nike Off Track," *Wall Street Journal,* March 5, 1981, p. 25.

[4]"The Richest People in America—The *Forbes* Four Hundred," *Forbes,* Fall 1983, p. 104.

[5]*Forbes,* Jan. 4, 1982, p. 246.

Table 17.2   U.S. Running-Shoe Market Shares, 1978

	Percent of Total U.S. Market
Nike	33%
Adidas	20
Brooks	11
New Balance	10
Converse	5
Puma	5

Source: Compiled from various published material, including "The Jogging-Shoe Race Heats Up," *Business Week*, April 9, 1979, p. 125.

these years. But Nike's success went far beyond simply coasting with a favorable primary demand. Nike outstripped all its competitors, including the heretofore dominant Adidas. Nike was able to overcome whatever aura or mystique such foreign producers as Adidas, Puma, and Tiger had.

Nike, as it began to reach its potential, offered an even broader product line than Adidas, which had pioneered with a great variety of shoe styles. A broad product line can have its problems; it can be overdone, hurt efficiency, and greatly add to costs. Most firms are better advised to pare their product line, to prune their weak products so that adequate attention and resources can be directed to the winners. Here we see the disavowal of such a policy, and yet Nike was one of the great successes of the decade, largely at the expense of Adidas. What is a prudent product mix?

Although Nike may have violated some product mix concepts, let us recognize what they accomplished and at what cost. By offering a great variety of styles, prices, and uses, Nike was able to appeal to all kinds of runners; it was able to convey the image of the most complete running-shoe manufacturer of all. In a rapidly evolving industry in which millions of runners of all kinds and abilities were embracing the idea, such an image became very attractive. Furthermore, in a rapidly expanding market, Nike found that it could tap the widest possible distribution with its breadth of products. It could sell its shoes to conventional retailers, such as department stores and shoe stores, and it could continue to do business with the specialized running-shoe stores. It could even be only moderately concerned about discounters getting some Nike shoes since there were certainly enough styles and models to go around—different models for different types of retail outlets, and everyone could be happy.

Short production runs and many styles generally add to production costs, but perhaps in Nike's case this was less of a factor. Most of the shoe production was contracted out—some 85 percent to foreign, mostly Far

Eastern, factories. Short production runs were less of an economic deterrent where many foreign plants were contracting for part of the production.

Early on Nike placed a heavy emphasis on research and technological improvement. It sought ever more flexible and lighter weight running shoes that would be protective but also give the athlete—world-class or slowest amateur—the utmost advantage that running-shoe technology could provide. Nike's commitment to research and development was evident in the approximately 100 employees working in this area, with their many holding degrees in biomechanics, exercise physiology, engineering, industrial design, chemistry, and related fields. The firm also engaged research committees and advisory boards, including coaches, athletes, athletic trainers, equipment managers, podiatrists, and orthopedists who met periodically with the firm to review designs, materials, and concepts for improved athletic shoes. Activities included high-speed photographic analyses of the human body in motion, the use of athletes on force plates and treadmills, wear testing using over 300 athletes in an organized program, and continual testing and study of new and modified shoes and materials. Some $2.5 million was spent in 1980 on product research, development, and evaluation, and the 1981 budget was approximately $4 million. For such an apparently simple thing as a shoe, this was a major commitment to research and development.

Nike attempted no major deviation from the accepted and successful marketing strategy norm of the industry. This norm was established several decades before by Adidas. In summary, it primarily involved testing and development of better running shoes, a broad product line to appeal to all segments of the market, a readily identifiable trademark of motif prominently displayed on all products, and the use of well-known athletes and prestigious athletic events to show off the products in use. Even the contracting out of much of the production to low-cost foreign factories was not unique to Nike. But Nike used these proven techniques better and more aggressively than any of its competitors, even Adidas.

ADIDAS' MISTAKES—WHAT WENT WRONG?

Adolph Dassler died in 1978. Perhaps this was a factor in Adidas' lessening of its aggressiveness, although the management transition after his death appeared to have gone very smoothly. And actually Nike had made its big inroads by this time. No, perhaps we have to seek further to find a suitable explanation of a frontrunner stumbling to give the lead to someone coming from far back in the pack.

Undoubtedly, Adidas underestimated the growth of the market for running shoes. For a firm that had been four decades in this business, and had always seen the stability of slow growth during these years, a skepticism about the extent and duration of the "boom" would have seemed most reasonable. And Adidas was not alone in misjudging the market opportunity. Some of the U.S. firms that were traditionally strong in the lower-priced athletic shoe industry, notably Converse and Uniroyal's Keds, were caught flatfooted in the race to bring new and technologically improved models to the market. These major producers of tennis shoes and sneakers (Converse made two-thirds of U.S. basketball shoes) also vastly underestimated the potential and did not direct strong efforts toward this market until they were completely outclassed by Nike and several other U.S. manufacturers.

In gearing an operation for rapid growth, sales forecasting becomes a vital element of the planning and preparation for handling the opportunity at hand. All aspects of a firm's operation are necessarily based on the sales estimates for the coming period(s); for example, production planning, facilities, inventories, sales staff, and advertising efforts. But when sales are reaching uncharted territory, the firm faces the dilemma of optimistic versus conservative sales projections, as the following "Information Sidelight" discusses.

It seems evident that Adidas, in addition to underestimating the market potential, also underestimated the aggressiveness of Nike and the other U.S. manufacturers. Perhaps this was a natural consequence after being the market leader with a seemingly unassailable position. After all, foreign brands in many product lines command a mystique and attraction that no domestic brands can. And then, how could small U.S. manufacturers, starting practically from scratch, pose any serious threat to the more than three decades of seasoned experience of Adidas? So, the perception of U.S. firms as mere weak opportunists seemed not unreasonable.

But we know that the U.S. manufacturers were not weak opportunists striving for a stray bone. Nike among others saw an opportunity, seized it, and charged. Perhaps this happening is less a reflection of Adidas' deficiencies than it is a credit to Nike. But we can still raise doubts about Adidas' role in the Nike inroads. Should Adidas not have been more alert in such an easy to enter industry? After all, neither the technology nor the plant investment requirements were enough to preclude other firms from entering the arena. Should not the front runner have recognized this ease of competitive entry and acted aggressively to discourage it—especially in a market that was increasing geometrically? Strong promotional efforts, new product introductions, a stepup in research and development, sharper pricing practices, expanding the channels of distribution—these actions might not have prevented competition, but given the resources of the market leader they should have lessened the inroads. But Adidas did not take aggressive counteractions until its dominance had been severely breached.

INFORMATION SIDELIGHT

OPTIMISTIC VERSUS CONSERVATIVE SALES FORECASTS IN RAPIDLY EXPANDING MARKETS

The sales forecast—the estimate of sales for the period(s) ahead— serves a crucial role, since it is the starting point for all planning and budgeting. When markets are volatile and rapidly growing, it presents some high risk alternatives: should we be optimistic or conservative?

If the forecasts are conservative, the danger that the firm faces when its market begins to boom is that it cannot keep up with demand and cannot expand its resources sufficiently to handle the potential. It simply does not have enough manufacturing capability and sales staff. The result, invariably, is to abdicate a good share of this growing business to competitors who are willing and able to match their capability and marketing efforts to the demands of the market.

On the other hand, for the firm facing burgeoning demand, the judgment should be made whether this is likely to be a short-term fad or a more permanent situation. You can see how easily a firm can permit itself to become overextended in the buoyancy of booming business, only to see the collapse of the market actually jeopardizing its viability.

When a firm is operating under extreme conditions of uncertainty, forecasted and actual results should be carefully monitored and the forecast adjusted upward or downward as indicated by empirical sales data.

WHAT CAN BE LEARNED?

This case provides learning experiences both from the success of Nike and from the mistakes of Adidas.

The success did not come primarily from an innovative approach to marketing, recognizing a marketing opportunity that no one else had, or plowing more resources into promotion and advertising than hapless competitors were able to muster. The key ingredient of Nike's success was *effective imitation.*

Of course, imitation must be judicious. A marketing strategy to be imitated should be the most effective approach; it should be historically successful. In the case of the running-shoe market, the long-time strategy of Adidas in offering many models, in associating its brand with major athletic events and athletes themselves, in constantly seeking product improvement—these could hardly have been improved on, and all running-shoe manufacturers followed the same strategy—only Nike did it better.

In the effort to be imitative, a firm still needs to develop its own identity. By imitation we do not mean a slavish effort to be identical. Only the successful policies, standards, and actions are imitated. There is still room to develop the distinctive image, the trademark or logo, and an organization and management ever alert to new opportunities.

Finally, we see in this case how fragile market dominance and being first in the market can be. No firm, market leader or otherwise, can afford to rest on its laurels, to disregard a changing environment and aggressive but smaller competitors. Adidas had as commanding a lead in this industry as IBM has in computers. But Adidas let its guard down, and its aggressiveness lagged at a critical point.

A front runner tends more toward complacency in the situation we have seen here. A sharply rising primary demand is reassuring and lulling. Sales will be increasing sharply for the industry leader during such a time, and this is conducive to complacency. But such increasing sales may mask a declining market position, in which competitors are making major gains at the expense of the dominant firm. Eventually the momentum shifts to one or more of the now significant competitors. The once dominant firm may not be able to regain its position. Success for one firm can come from the mistakes of another—not so much of commission as omission—in which needed actions were not taken or at least were not until too late.

The critical lapse of Adidas, faced with the growing strength of Nike and its American contemporaries, as well as the greatly increasing market potential, suggests the need for a closer attuning to the marketplace, a better sensoring of demand and competitive factors. As we noted specifically in the Gilbert case and alluded to in other cases, an extensive marketing research program is not essential for such sensoring. Alert executives should be able to detect nascent changes by encouraging systematic feedback from those closest to the market such as sales representatives, dealers, suppliers alike; by keeping abreast of the latest trade journal statistics and commentaries; and by working with such control or measuring tools as market share analysis and trend data. There must be a willingness to act on significant changes in market conditions—and this is something that veteran firms in any industry have a difficult time in doing: that is, disassociating themselves from the perspectives and practices of a different past.

For Thought and Discussion

1. Do you think Adidas could have successfully blunted the charge of Nike? Why or why not?

2. In what ways does the age and experience of a firm tend to induce myopia and resistance to change?

3. "The success of Nike was strictly fortuitous and had little to do with a powerful marketing strategy." Evaluate this statement.

4. Discuss the pros and cons of optimistic versus conservative sales forecasts for a hot new product.

Invitation to Role Play

1. As an Adidas executive, how would you propose to counter the initial thrusts at your market share by Nike and other U.S. running-shoe manufacturers?

2. As an executive for a medium-size U.S. running-shoe manufacturer, you recognize that the long overdue lessening of the popularity of running is beginning to take place. What strategy recommendations would you make now that the primary demand curve is moving down?

PART Five

DISREGARD OF SOCIAL CONSTRAINTS

18

STP Corporation—The Successful Marketing of "Mouse Milk," Until . . .

This is the story of a notable marketing success that came from developing an image of those who used the product and a reference group that many car owners thought worthy of emulating—all this brought about and supported by heavy advertising. Almost a classic marketing success. Except for one thing. The product really offered consumers no benefits—the experts who knew spoke of it in derogatory fashion as "mouse milk," and what could be more impotent than that? Eventually, bad publicity surfaced about the product, and the Federal Trade Commission took action against the company for misleading advertising.

THE PRODUCT

The principal product of the STP Corporation in the 1960s was STP, a brand of lubricating oil additive supposed to improve car performance (in addition the firm marketed STP Gasoline Treatment and STP Diesel Fuel Treatment). The name STP means "Scientifically Treated Petroleum." It was sold in 15-ounce cans at around $1.50 a can, and was poured into the crankcase of a car, preferably with every oil change, as a supplement to the motor oil itself.

While the ingredients of STP remain a closely-guarded secret, the major component of all additives is a polyisobutylene polymer dissolved in petroleum oil. Such a polymer-oil solution is called a viscosity-index (VI) improver. This helps motor oil retain its normal thickness despite the large temperature changes that result from hard driving. In other words, with a VI improver, hot oil thins less than it normally would, thus helping lubrication over a wide temperature range.

So far so good. STP promotional messages stressed that the additive would help reduce oil consumption, free sticking valves, make engines run more smoothly, and prevent many other repairs. There was even the strong intimation that the use of a can of STP with every oil change would forestall the expense of a valve and ring job. So intriguingly simple it all seemed: only pour this elixir in the crankcase of a car and make its ailing engine healthy and powerful again.

Unfortunately, there were those who disputed such claims, among them most petroleum engineers who had labeled these additives "mouse milk." These experts were in general agreement that there was rarely any benefit for a normal engine. The auto firms likewise were critical of STP and similar additives: "No one has ever presented any scientific data to prove that additives do anything good," noted Ray Potter, supervisor of fuels and lubricant research at Ford.[1] The automakers had even found that regular use of the polyisobutylene compounds could sometimes clog small oil passages and cause engine damage, and they refused to recommend the use of additives in their owners' manuals.

So, what do we have here? A product of dubious benefit, and one with experts in almost complete agreement of its worthlessness, at least under normal driving conditions. How can such a product wrest a niche in the marketplace? But it did, and with gusto.

ANDY GRANATELLI

The success of STP is really the story of Andy Granatelli, who became president of STP Corporation in 1963. How he moved STP from a smallish $9 million in sales in 1963 to sales of $85 million and profits of almost $12 million by 1970 has to make him one of the most astute marketers to come around—or one of the best promoters.

Granatelli had gained a public reputation as a race driver and a person closely connected with racing. When he was only in his early thirties he made his first million with a company called Grancor, which developed and sold parts and supplies for racing cars. In 1958 he sold Grancor and became owner of Paxton Products, which made superchargers and similar items. In 1961 he sold Paxton to the Studebaker Company (later to become Studebaker-Worthington in a 1967 merger). He stayed on to run the

[1]Quoted from "Big Profits in Little Cans," *Time*, August 8, 1969, pp. 70–71.

subsidiary, but then in 1963 was persuaded to take over as president of the STP Division of Studebaker.

Heretofore, additives had been marketed as something to keep "clunkers" operating a little longer. And this was a limited market segment, one with little growth potential in an era of prosperity. Granatelli changed this image for STP. He surmised that if speed could sell cars and tires, it should be able to sell additives as well. "One of the first things Andy realized," said a company executive, "is that to expand sales he had to expand the market . . . Andy changed the image of STP from an additive to a performance product by promoting it through racing, on the theory that if race drivers used it on $50,000 cars to keep engines cool and maintain lubrication, the general public would buy it for the same reason."[2]

Granatelli offered extra money to race drivers who would paste STP decals conspicuously on their cars, and even on their jackets and coveralls. He subsidized cars at major races, of course well-publicized as STP cars. A major coup came when an STP-sponsored car driven by Mario Andretti won the Indianapolis 500 on May 30, 1969. The implication was that STP was the vital ingredient enabling Andretti to achieve the extra performance. Publicity gained for STP from the decal-decorated car and pictures of Granatelli alongside Andretti was worth millions to the company.

Something more subtle than simply a performance product was operative under Granatelli's management: the mystique of fast cars and of the machos who drove them—a reference group that a certain segment of the car-driving public looked up to and psychologically wished to emulate. Hence, these customers could easily be persuaded to buy a product indelibly identified with this group.

Granatelli poured on the advertising to promote the race-driver image, the "Racer's Edge," as STP publicity called it. The 1969 advertising budget was $10 million. This was an amount equal to 20 percent of the previous year's sales, an advertising-to-sales ratio matched by only a handful of firms, and these chiefly in the drug and cosmetics industry, such as Colgate-Palmolive, J. B. Williams, and Alberto Culver. The advertising hit three radio networks, two TV networks, and some thirty auto buff magazines, with ads featuring the STP motto—the "racer's edge"—and pictures of Granatelli and race cars and drivers. Even Dolly Granatelli, his wife, participated in very successful radio and TV commercials. By 1969 STP was spending 18 cents more per can for advertising than it spent on the can and the contents.

The great sleeper in all of this was the STP logo. It helped to fuel the

---

[2]As quoted in "The Wheeler Who Deals in STP," *Business Week,* May 31, 1969, p. 57.

INFORMATION SIDELIGHT

REFERENCE GROUPS

Reference groups, according to consumer behavior researchers, are those groups, or, less commonly, those individuals, with whom a person identifies. The group then becomes a standard or a point of reference; an individual looks to these people when forming or evaluating his or her norms, personal values, status, and behavior, both purchasing and otherwise. A person's reference groups may be those to which he or she belongs; these are called membership groups. But a reference group may also be those types of persons the individual aspires toward, or admires, but does not belong to and perhaps never can, such as athletes, or astronauts, the jet-set, or race drivers. As we can see with STP, these "referents" may have considerable influence on purchase behavior and brand preference.

---

burgeoning popularity of the product. In its ads starting in 1966, STP offered the little decals free with the coupon. And kids by the thousands began swamping the company for this the newest status symbol. The appeal spread to adults, with stickers being plastered on trucks, passenger cars, tractors, and even limousines. By the end of 1967, STP had to hire six secretaries solely to answer 4000 requests a day for the free stickers. By 1969, the company was giving away 50 million a year. Requests were pouring in from toy makers, confectioners, electronics firms, clothiers, and others to use the STP logo on products. Granatelli readily gave his permission to use the logo without charge, seeing this as a powerful way to broaden recognition of the product and brand. Eventually, the opportunity to tap some of the demand for the logo was realized, and the company established a mail-order marketing organization to handle a full line of STP jackets, caps, coveralls, t-shirts, and such.

Sales sprinted ahead. See Table 18.1 for the sales and profit performance from 1963, when Granatelli first took over, to 1970, when the zenith was reached. Note the almost 50 percent spurt in sales in one year, 1969, and the over 50 percent gain in profits, a phenomenal achievement.

The identification of STP with speed resulted in an unwanted by-product that developed in California early in 1968. A particularly potent hallucinogenic drug widely used by hippies was dubbed STP.

As the decade of the '60s drew to a close, Granatelli could not help but be optimistic about the future. He could see great potential in expanding the product line, first with a cooling system additive, and then spreading into

Table 18.1 Sales and Profit Growth of STP Corporation, 1963–1970

Year	Sales (000)	Percent Change	Net Income (000)	Percent Change
1963	$ 9,340		$ 1,733	
1964	12,781	36.8%	2,439	40.7%
1965	18,475	44.6	3,537	45.0
1966	20,828	12.7	4,037	14.1
1967	30,886	48.3	4,807	19.1
1968	44,000	42.5	6,000	24.8
1969	65,335	48.5	9,052	50.9
1970	85,936	31.5	11,601	28.2

Source: STP annual reports.

other markets, particularly the industrial and marine markets. Furthermore, Granatelli saw tremendous opportunities abroad, and overseas sales indeed had tripled in a single year. In Japan, sales of STP exceeded the sales of any single state of the Union, while selling at more than twice the price in this country. Granatelli could happily observe: "There's only one other symbol used more than STP, and that's Coke. But they've been around longer than we have."[3]

COMPETITION

Were there any competitors of STP? There were, but they had all been left far behind. Wynn and Bardahl were the two oldest firms in the field. Bardahl advertised its product as a preventative of repairs, although compared to STP it did little advertising. The Bardahl product image was that of a steady, dependable product, but without glamour. Wynn's Friction Proofing was similar to Bardahl in image and market position. Wynn was founded by a lawyer in 1939; he had mixed a home-brew "friction proofing" in a 55-gallon drum and sold bottles of it to local garages. Both Wynn and Bardahl had broad product lines, with Wynn having twenty-six related products and Bardahl eighteen.

PHA Hi-Performance Oil Treatment was the least well known of the four major oil additives, although the company tried to project a top quality performance image. Stud, a Union Carbide product, was the latest entry into the oil additive field. It had rapidly climbed to the No. 2 market position behind STP, primarily on the strength of an aggressive advertising campaign "guaranteeing to equal or exceed the performance of any oil treatment or

[3]Ibid., p. 57.

your money back.'' While the formula for each additive was a closely guarded secret, the major ingredient, polyisobutylene, was the same, and the results were similar.

WHY THE STP SUCCESS?

How can we account for the phenomenal success of STP? Was it primarily due to the willingness to spend heavily on mass-media advertising? Was it primarily due to race drivers publicly promoting it? What role, if any, did the popularity of STP decals have on the success of the product?

In order to test certain hypotheses regarding the image and appeal of STP, one researcher asked students and other car owners to write down the two or three associations that most readily came to mind upon seeing the letters "STP." The following responses predominated:[4]

Granatelli	Racing
Racer's edge	Indianapolis 500
Speed	High performance
Sports cars	Names of various high
Andretti (who won the	performance and sports cars,
1969 Indianapolis 500)	such as Charger, Corvette, etc.

Clearly STP had succeeded in developing an association of its product with the professional racing community and with higher performance cars—in other words, with a reference group that a significant segment of younger car-owning consumers admired or wished to emulate. The overwhelming and unexpected popularity of the STP logo became a highly visible indication of an individual's wish to be identified with this reference group.

That the product itself, offered at a premium price many times higher than the cost of production, was of dubious benefit remained disregarded in the glamour associated with the aura of professional racing. So, STP furnishes tangible evidence that reference group influence, when carefully chosen and strongly promoted, can be a significant marketing tool.

CLOUDS ON THE HORIZON

By the late 1960s, despite a rate of sales and profit growth that seemed not only to be continuing, but even intensifying, some communications began

---

[4]Research conducted by Sidney C. Wooten, Jr., "Self-Concept Theory, the Symbolic Value of Products, and Consumer Behavior: A Study in Interrelationships." Unpublished MBA thesis, George Washington University, January 1971, pp. 84–86.

appearing that revealed the general uselessness of STP and other oil additives for most passenger car engines. For example, *Time* and *Business Week* had articles about this in 1969.[5] While these publications were directed to people not typical customers of STP, still they presaged more adverse publicity to come.

Then in July 1971, *Consumer Reports,* the respected consumer advocate magazine, made a harsh indictment against STP.[6] Not only did it charge that STP oil additive was a useless concoction, but it also warned that the product could be harmful to engines and might even void a new car warranty.

While *Consumer Reports* agreed that STP helped engine oil retain its normal thickness despite large temperature changes, it noted that major oil refiners had already taken care of this with their multiviscosity oils (labeled 5W-20, 10W-30, and so on), and that adding STP tended to make the oil thicker than desirable. For example, a 20W motor oil was found by testing to have been changed to a 40 with the addition of the recommended amount of STP. While admitting that this would help with an old, oil-burning clunker of an engine by making loose mechanical joints and fittings quieter and seemingly tighter and perhaps even cutting down on oil consumption, *Consumer Reports* stated that any 40 or 50 oil would do this, and would be far cheaper. With a normal engine, such a thick oil mixture would cause hard starting and noticeable drag in cold weather and the engine would not be properly lubricated. Furthermore, *Consumer Reports* noted that because STP can change the viscosity of a new car's oil to a much thicker grade than auto manufacturers recommended, a new car warranty could be voided. General Motors and Ford officials were quoted specifically as to how the use of additives would affect a new car warranty:

General Motors: If in the analysis of a warranty repair there is evidence that the use of additives is responsible for, or has contributed to the vehicle malfunction or part failure, this fact would be taken into consideration in determining General Motors' responsibility.

Ford: If supplementary additives . . . modify the properties of the lubricants so that they no longer meet Ford specifications, then warranty terms may be affected.[7]

[5]"Big Profits in Little Cans," pp. 70–71; and "The Wheeler Who Deals in STP," pp. 31–32.
[6]"STP, Does Your Car Really Need It?" *Consumer Reports,* July 1971, p. 422.
[7]Ibid.

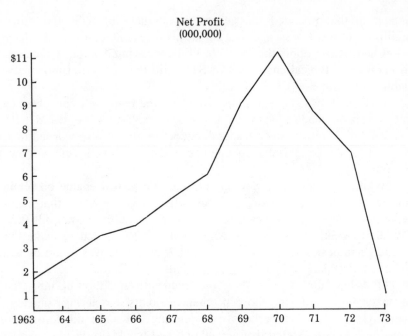

Figure 18.1. STP Corp. profits during Granatelli, 1963–1973. (Source: Company published reports.)

Granatelli quickly responded. He called the *Consumer Report* article "an attempt to sabotage the successful business of our company with a twisted set of alleged facts assembled by incompetents."[8]

STP on the Ropes

Despite Granatelli's counterattack, both earnings and stock prices of STP plunged. The stock, which had peaked at almost $60 early in 1971, was down to $3 in 1973. Profits by 1973 had fallen to barely $1 million from the $11.6 million of 1970. Figure 18.1 shows the rise and then the collapse of income during the Granatelli years of 1963 through 1973.

To add to Granatelli's troubles, now the Federal Trade Commission (FTC) began looking into a 22-page petition filed early in 1973 against STP by the Center for Automotive Safety, a Ralph Nader-inspired consumer group. The petition asked the FTC specifically to order the company to:

[8]As quoted in "FTC Tries to Dull the Racer's Edge—STP," *Iron Age,* June 21, 1973, p. 17.

1. Stop asserting unfair and deceptive claims for STP oil treatment.
2. Substantiate all future advertising claims relating to STP oil treatment.
3. Refund to buyers of the product funds obtained through unfair and deceptive advertising.

Granatelli stated: "We believe this unknown group (the Center) is simply seeking publicity by the device of bringing totally unfounded and irresponsible charges against us."[9] When asked whether STP Corp. planned to issue scientific data to support its advertising claims, Granatelli responded: "I take offense at having to defend myself against an unknown group of two or three guys out to get publicity."[10]

In 1973 the Federal Trade Commission finally charged the company with deceptive advertising. And in 1973 Granatelli left STP.

Coming Back

While the reign of Granatelli was over, and the glory days gone, the company doggedly began making a comeback from the lows of 1973. The comeback, however, was not without more charges of deceptive advertising and false and unsupported claims. Sales and profits rose somewhat in 1974 and began climbing steadily after that, although they were still well below the peaks attained in 1970.

The complaint initiated by the FTC in 1973 was settled in September of 1976 with the company agreeing with the consent order not to use false and misleading advertising and to support any claims for the oil additive with competent and reliable scientific tests or other objective data. Two of the FTC commissioners, including the chairman, dissented from accepting the consent order. Chairman Engman criticized the acceptance by the FTC:

> I dissent because this order is too weak. Though the consent order prohibits claims that are not substantiated, I have the statutory "reason to believe" that STP Oil Treatment is of no significant value to the majority of cars which regularly use the proper grade of oil. I accordingly have difficulty in accepting an order which does not explicitly require STP to qualify its future claims.[11]

However weak the consent order was seen to be, STP still did not abide by it. The FTC was forced to sue the company in 1978 for violation of the

---

[9]Ibid.
[10]Ibid.
[11]"Legal Developments," *Journal of Marketing,* October 1976, p. 119.

two-year-old cease and desist order. The new complaint charged as false STP's advertisements that its oil treatment reduced oil consumption by 20 percent in certain road tests. An agreement concerning this was negotiated by the FTC and STP Corp. and made public in February 1978, with STP agreeing to a $500,000 record-setting fine plus another $200,000 to be spent for a corrective advertising campaign. Under the terms of the settlement a notice was to be placed in 14 publications, most of them with heavy business readership, such as *Wall Street Journal, Business Week, Forbes,* and *Harvard Business Review*; the only more consumer-oriented magazines on the schedule were *Esquire, Guns & Ammo, National Geographic, Newsweek,* and *People.* The ads were to be mostly full-page, reading as follows:

> FTC Notice. As a result of an investigation by the Federal Trade Commission into certain allegedly inaccurate past advertisements for STP's Oil Additive, STP Corporation has agreed to a $700,000 settlement.

The notice also included a statement by STP that:

> Agreement to this settlement does not constitute an admission by STP that the law has been violated.[12]

The new STP chairman, Craig A. Nalen, said that he doubted the corrective ads would have any impact at all on STP sales. "Nowhere is there any challenge to the efficacy of the product," he said. "It's merely a question of some defective tests done years ago."[13] Despite the critical limelight, the FTC did not probe into whether or not the products worked, but was only concerned with the lack of documentation for STP's advertising claims. The products of STP were not reformulated, and *Consumer Reports* did not change its negative position.

Nevertheless, Nalen brought STP back to increasing profits. Nalen himself was a former marketing executive with General Mills. He at first shunned an offer to run STP: "I was skeptical about the products as much as anybody else. It took a lot of head scratching for me to decide to go to STP."[14] However, he was finally persuaded to take the job as a result of studies made by an independent laboratory and several "lubrication ex-

[12]As reported in "Legal Developments in Marketing," *Journal of Marketing,* October 1978, p. 91.
[13]"Corrective Ads for STP Publicize Settlement Costs to Business Execs," *Advertising Age,* February 13, 1978, p. 1.
[14]As quoted in "What Craig Nalen Did to Turn STP Around," *Business Week,* January 10, 1977, p. 38.

INFORMATION SIDELIGHT

CORRECTIVE ADVERTISING

In recent years the Federal Trade Commission has been taking a militant stand against ads that smack of deception or of unfounded claims. One of the alternatives the FTC has in dealing with such unsatisfactory advertising is corrective advertising.

Corrective advertising may be required in order, theoretically, to eliminate the "residue" effects of misleading advertising in the past. The first such order was issued against ITT Continental Baking Company, and required that 25 percent of Continental's advertising budget for one year be given to FTC-approved advertisements that Profile Bread was *not* the effective weight reducer that previous ads had represented. The makers of Ocean Spray Cranberry Juice were also required to correct possible misrepresentations of their product as having the food energy of orange or tomato juice, and 25 percent of the budget was specified for this purpose. Listerine was also required to "correct" advertising claims that it had made for over 50 years that it was a cold and sore-throat remedy, with $10.2 million worth of ads stating that "Listerine will not help prevent colds or sore throats or lessen their severity."

While one would think that corrective advertising aimed at nullifying false impressions would severely penalize a firm, evidence suggests that the firm is not really harmed. Perhaps this is partly due to the innocuous wording of many of these ads; furthermore, any advertising promotes the name of the company, and the fine print is often not read.

---

perts" about whom Nalen said: "Their analysis showed that STP oil treatments result in a reduction of oil consumption and wear rate."[15] The next steps were to sign the consent agreement with the FTC and begin the slow job of rebuilding the company's battered image.

Costs were substantially reduced by trimming the sales force from 180 to 100, and by eliminating a policy of giving discounts to dealers for shelf space. A number of new products were test marketed and then introduced, including a multigrade diesel oil claimed to be good for at least 50,000 miles, a passenger-car oil good for 12,000, and a synthetic compression oil for machinery. The channel of distribution was shifted from service stations and garages to supermarkets, with 65 percent of STP products sold in super-

[15]Ibid.

Table 18.2   STP Corp. Sales and Profits, 1973–1976

Year	Sales	Net Profit
1973	$54,605,000	$1,033,436
1974	62,377,000	3,453,000
1975	65,269,000	3,882,000
1976	69,737,000	6,627,000

Source: Published company reports.

markets by 1977, compared with only 30 percent five years before. Extensive advertising was continued—for example, a $200,000 four-page ad in *Readers Digest*—using test results to document the claims made for the additive. Actor Robert Blake, who played the role of a supercop on the TV show "Baretta," replaced flamboyant Granatelli as the company's television pitchman. Table 18.2 shows the gains in sales and profits during this rebuilding period.

In 1978, giant Esmark, Inc., offered to acquire STP from parent Studebaker-Worthington, which owned 60 percent of the stock, for about $117,000,000, paying $22.50 for each share of STP stock. Studebaker-Worthington agreed to vote its holdings for the merger. Philip Thomas, vice president, corporate communications for Esmark, called STP "a fantastic company and a perfect fit" for Esmark. He said Esmark had conducted intensive tests on STP oil treatment before it began serious negotiations on the acquisition and, as a result, was convinced "the product works."[16]

About the time the merger was finalized, STP began national advertising for a new product, "Son of a Gun," a pump spray that it claimed would restore and beautify vinyl, rubber, leather, and wood. Carrying a suggested $2.95 price, Son of a Gun was promoted via 30- and 60-second network commercials, and promoted to both male and female audiences—a first time for the company that a product was promoted other than to men. STP Oil Treatment, which had not been advertised for about a year, also began to be backed by new TV ads, with Robert Blake in his continuing role as STP's spokesman. The company had fully recovered from the dark days at the turn of the decade.

[16]"STP Presents Its New Parent with a New 'Son'," *Advertising Age,* March 27, 1978, p. 50.

WHAT CAN BE LEARNED?

We can consider the STP case from two perspectives: as consumers, and as company executives. From both viewpoints we see rather awesome implications, as well as cautions.

The effectiveness of advertising and proper image building is manifested beyond doubt. That the product itself may be of little, if any, good, and may even be harmful, makes the power of the advertising all the more significant. Can it be that if the marketer chooses the proper reference group and image for a brand, and advertises it heavily and confidently, virtually anything can be marketed, whether good or not?

We know that advertising can induce people to try a product for the first time. But unless it is satisfactory and meets their expectations, they will not buy it again: this is practically a marketing truism. Surely it is valid. Yet, the STP example seems to disprove it. The answer lies in the user's inability to correctly assess the effectiveness of STP. Who could say that one's car was helped or hindered by it? Certainly any judgment could only be made over a long period of use. But many products are like this: their performance and quality cannot be easily and quickly assessed because of their complexity or hidden ingredients.

Is effective promotion more important than a good product in the marketing mix? If so, this becomes somewhat scary to us as consumers; it makes us leery, destroys our confidence, puts us at the mercy of the marketplace. At the same time, for marketers, the challenge of finding the best image, the most effective promotional appeal, can be an intriguing one. Even the best product needs the proper promotional effort to induce people to try it and be satisfied with it.

About the FTC and the general stance against deceptive practices. Where do we draw the line? Is the action of the FTC against STP (as well as against other firms) too harsh? Are the regulators too zealous? Does every advertising claim have to be supported with unimpeachable test results? Are hard sell and image building to be completely ruled out so that the helpless consumer can be protected, even from a careless purchase of a $1.50 can of oil additive? Or, to take the other side, does the action of the FTC in permitting a rather innocuous consent agreement—soon to be violated—and a less than million dollar settlement for doing so, represent a cop-out? Does such have any deterrent value? As you can see, the issues are hard to resolve, and cannot be to everyone's satisfaction.

So, what can we conclude from the STP example? If simply leading consumers on with alluring advertising claims and macho images is so bad, when do we draw the line—at every exaggeration, at every optimistic statement? We must also be somewhat sobered by the realization that almost anything under the sun can be proven: that STP is good for cars, that cigarettes do not induce lung cancer, that a certain dentifrice retards tooth decay.

The possibility of corrective advertising being required as a "remedy" for past advertising abuses ought to be considered by firms in making careless unsubstantiated claims. While it appears that corrective advertising heretofore has not had much adverse effect for the firms involved, the possibility still remains. The marketing environment today prescribes more honest practices, even though there appear to be those who can somehow circumvent them. The environment for honest marketing benefits both consumers, in being able to rely on more honest claims and more effective products, and firms, in being somewhat protected from unscrupulous efforts of competitors.

A final thing to learn from the STP example is that a firm can come back. It can be on the ropes yet bounce off and still be viable and even successful. Criticism can be short-lived. Adversity is not forever.

For Thought and Discussion

1. Critique the FTC corrective advertising resolution.
2. How would you, as an STP executive, answer the charge that STP was only mouse milk?
3. Do you think another oil additive firm could have successfully pursued a different image for its brand from STP's?
4. Do you think STP decals should have been dispensed as freely as Granatelli did? Why or why not?
5. Discuss the association of the Stud brand of oil additive versus the STP image.
6. Was the success of STP in the 1960s attributable primarily to its willingness to spend much more on advertising than its competitors? Why or why not?
7. To what degree should advertising claims be regulated by the FTC or other governmental agencies? Be as specific as you can and defend your position.

Invitation to Role Play

As an STP company spokesperson, how would you answer the charge before the Federal Trade Commission of deceptive advertising? Defend your position as persuasively as possible.

CHAPTER 19

Boise Cascade— Social Pressure Defeats Vigorous Growth

In the 1960s, growth by merger and acquisition, fostered by astute financial manipulations, focused attention on certain business wizards. These captured the public fancy and the adulation of investors and bankers as corporate growth in sales and profits—and the prospects of more of the same—seemed unbounded. Not the least of these "geniuses" was Robert V. Hansberger, who transformed a $35 million lumber operation into a $1.8 billion conglomerate in thirteen years.

The management style of Hansberger in his overseeing of diverse operations was to let each division or mini-company have wide scope, thus creating a highly decentralized organization. Boise Cascade had been cited as "a spectacular example of 'free form' management . . . relatively free from job descriptions, organization charts, and other inhibiting restrictions."[1] Such a situation was particularly attractive to bright young MBA's who flocked to the company that was rapidly growing and that could offer them wide latitude to use their knowledge and talents in dozens of near-autonomous operating groups.

Unfortunately, Boise Cascade, in its quest for rapid growth, built on a precarious base. Like a structure of cards, its diverse ventures began collapsing in the early 1970s as marketing mistakes, combined with critical

---

[1]"Boise Cascade Shifts Toward Tighter Control," *Business Week,* May 15, 1971, p. 86.

environmental scrutiny, brought its fastest-growing division to the block, caused severe retrenchment and divestment of many of the acquisitions, and led the corporation itself to the brink of bankruptcy.

HANSBERGER AND THE METEORIC GROWTH OF BOISE CASCADE

Robert Hansberger was born in 1920 on a farm near Worthington, Minnesota. He took engineering at the University of Minnesota and later received a master's degree in business administration (with great distinction) from Harvard Business School. He joined Container Corporation of America in 1947 as assistant to the executive vice president and had risen to corporate director of the budget by 1953. He left in 1954 to become vice president of Western Kraft Company, where he played a major role in the design and construction of the industry's first economical pulp and paper mill with a relatively small capacity of 120 tons/day. This mill completely changed existing ideas of economies of scale, which had assumed that only mills of much larger size were economically practical. This led directly to Hansberger's appointment as president of the then Boise Payette Lumber Company in 1956. He was 36 years old.

At the time Hansberger became president of Boise Payette (founded in 1913), it owned three sawmills, all located in the state of Idaho. The company produced slightly more than 100 million board feet of lumber in 1956. By 1959 it had ten sawmills scattered across the states of Washington, Idaho, and Oregon and produced 504 million board feet (thus becoming one of the three largest softwood lumber producers in the United States). Between 1956 and 1959, the company also entered into a number of new operations, including a millwork plant, a paper bag factory, and concrete plants. One of the first mergers of Hansberger was with the Cascade Lumber Company, at which time the name was changed to Boise Cascade. In the first three years of Hansberger's presidency, sales rose 250 percent to $126 million, and earnings were up 370 percent to $5.6 million. This was only an inkling of what was to come.

By 1970 Hansberger has made some 35 acquisitions, and Boise Cascade had equaled or passed in sales its major competitors, Georgia-Pacific, Weyerhaeuser, International Paper, U.S. Plywood-Champion, and Johns Manville, with revenues of $1.7 billion and earnings of $76 million. Unlike these giant competitors, Boise did not dominate any single market, such as plywood, lumber, paper, pulp, or building materials. Rather, the company represented an integration from raw material to end product, as Hansberger sought to develop a broad-based, forest-products company with strong marketing. He shrewdly borrowed against timber lands acquired by merger in order to get into paper and packaging, lumber, and other things.

In the 1960s, diversification was fashionable and often viewed as the way to keep a company growing vigorously in earnings per share. So Hansberger turned his sights beyond the basic forest-products business of Boise. He went into what seemed at the time to be great growth areas. A batch of acquisitions were made between 1966 and 1969 in real estate, especially recreational land and housing. Divco-Wayne, the largest producer in the fast-growing mobile homes industry, was bought. Boise went into urban renewal and modular housing. More unrelated diversifications were Princess Cruises, a charter pleasure cruise operation, and CRM, which published *Psychology Today* magazine. Hansberger defended his hodge-podge:

> From the outside we may look like a conglomeration. But the process is certainly not. Today, we are an idea company, with the only limitation being that we engage in things that have a definite relation to something in which the company has experience.[2]

Such expansion was costly, and a high ratio of debt to equity (for example, in 1966–67, there was $1.25 of debt for every $1 of equity) suggested that the company was becoming overextended. However, through several mergers and accounting manipulations, the figure was brought down to 50 cents of debt per equity dollar by 1970.

In 1966, after Boise entered the recreational land development field, there was a more urgent need for cash than ever before, since expenditures are incurred for things like roads, sewers, golf courses, and other facilities before installment sales can generate much cash flow. In 1969 the answer to the need for an immediate source of money appeared to be found. Boise acquired Ebasco (formerly Electric Bond & Share), primarily a holding company engaged in the construction and design of heavy industrial facilities and office buildings in the United States. Ebasco had $237 million of Latin American bonds payable in U.S. dollars from the sale of some utility holdings to foreign governments, and these could be borrowed against. The Ebasco merger also brought substantial tax credits so that Boise's taxes could be reduced.

With the substantial and successful growth of the past decade, an aggressive and enthusiastic young management, a strong position in some of the seemingly most rapidly growing areas of business for the coming years, and now with the chronic liquidity problem apparently corrected, the future looked very good for Hansberger and his company as they entered the decade of the 1970s.

[2]"Cinderella," *Forbes,* November 15, 1972, p. 72.

THE RECREATIONAL LAND COMMITMENT

Boise entered the land development business in a 50 percent joint venture with R. A. Watt, a land developer and home builder in the greater Los Angeles area. Watt had built 17,500 homes during the preceding 20 years, as well as many industrial, commercial, and apartment buildings. Further acquisitions in this area continued in 1967 with the acquiring of a San Francisco area contractor, Perma-Bilt Enterprises, which had projects underway having a total value of $45 million.

U.S. Land Company of Indianapolis was acquired shortly after. This was a major developer of lake-oriented resort properties. Five major developments were in operation: a 1700 acre project near Gary, Indiana, a 1500 acre one near Chicago, 1300 acres near Cleveland, 2500 acres near Washington, D.C., and a 3200 acre project in the foothills of the Sierra Nevada Mountains, not far from San Francisco. The lots ranged in price from $2000 to $20,000, and each development surrounded a 200- or 500-acre man-made lake.

Lake Arrowhead Development Company was also acquired in 1967. This was a year-round and second home developer in the San Bernardino-Los Angeles area.

Two new developments were also started in the fall of 1967: a lakeland homesite development called Lake Los Angeles, a 4000 acre project about 75 minutes from Los Angeles; and a $38 million development on the Palos Verdes Peninsula of California.

By 1968, sales of recreational land were $90 million; in 1969, this had spurted to $165 million. Profits also began building rapidly, since in real estate accounting, sales and profits are booked in the year a property is sold, even though the money may not be collected for some years. How are profits determined? Future development costs are estimated, and then prorated to the various parcels of land. While not a very conservative method of accounting, this is the standard procedure. To bring a bit more conservatism into its accounting, Boise set up larger reserves for possible defaults on land sales than in 1966 and 1967.

As the real estate expansion continued, Boise acquired a total of 126,000 acres, in tracts of 700 to 31,000 acres. This land consisted of twenty-nine projects scattered over a dozen states from the East Coast to Hawaii. The net investment in realty was $142 million by the end of 1970, about 70 percent being in recreational communities. Between 1967 and July 1972, Boise sold over $360 million of recreational land.

The growth potential for such developments seemed unmistakable. In a nation with more leisure time, good and relatively cheap transportation, and more affluence, a second home became the dream of many families. Planned recreational communities, with choice amenities available such as lakes, country clubs with golf courses and "Olympic-size" swimming pools, other facilities such as skiing at certain sites, and offering security against vandalism and theft, seemed the answer. The growth of land sales and profits since 1966 seemed proof that this was a premier growth industry.

No Boise executive in the late 1960s would have believed that anything could destroy the golden future of the company, spearheaded now by its land development operations. In 1969 its stock climbed to $75 a share.

But in just a few short years the stock was to fall to $9 a share, and there was concern that Boise might follow Penn Central into the corporate graveyard. The land development operation led the company into its debacle.

The Downfall

Two things conspired to destroy the recreational land commitment. Neither would have been a factor a decade earlier. But Boise and other land developers were facing an environment of far more social criticism of marketing methods and also of stronger ecological concern than had ever been experienced before.

In the rush to acquire firms active in recreational land development, Boise also obtained some of their executives and salesmen. At first, Boise, with its management policies of loose control and maximum decentralization, was content to let the land companies run themselves. But these land developers tended to be of the old school, unconcerned with consumer satisfaction as long as a sale could be made quickly. Their attitude toward land was also selfish: ". . . cut it up, develop it, sell it, and get out. If the buyer was unhappy later, the developer and his salesmen were long gone."[3] These acquisitions were paced by fast-talking salesmen who promised far more than Boise could deliver in the way of access roads and highways, recreational facilities, and investment potential. In order to create a feeling of urgency and the belief that lots were selling fast, high-pressure sales personnel used two-way radios by which they could radio the central "communications" office to tensely ask whether such and such a lot is still "available."

However, public attitudes and policies were rapidly changing nationwide, and particularly in California, where Boise's recreational developments predominated. Reflecting environmentalists' and consumerists' inputs, practices that would have been uncontested a decade before now became subject to virulent criticism and legal and governmental regulation.

[3]"Boise Cascade Shifts," p. 86.

INFORMATION SIDELIGHT

HIGH PRESSURE vs. SOFT SELL: WHICH IS MORE EFFECTIVE?

We can recognize a wide range of selling techniques, ranging from a laissez faire approach, which we sometimes encounter in retail stores with bored clerks almost having to be forced to ring up the purchase, to such high-pressure techniques that unethical and illegal practices result. The continuum below reflects this range.

High Pressure	Medium Pressure		No Pressure
deceptive	strong	soft	laissez
tactics and	selling	sell	faire
false statements	efforts		

What degree of pressure or lack of pressure is the most effective? To a considerable extent this depends on the audience of the sales presentation. If the prospect is a sophisticated and professional purchasing agent or buyer, obvious efforts to high pressure would be anathema. On the other hand, effective salesmanship requires some pressure, even though this may be kept very subtle: the salesperson should be persuasive and at least ask for the order and encourage the prospect to make a decision. With a naive consumer, high pressure can be very effective and there is the temptation to misuse it. Selling practices in the ghetto have often involved high pressure and dishonest tactics. With educated and sophisticated consumers, it is doubtful that strong high pressure makes for very effective selling. The shrewd pressure tactics and misrepresentations of Boise Cascade sales representatives proved short-term effective, but long-term disastrous as consumers refused to put up with this and complained bitterly to receptive governmental agencies.

Mayer and Greenberg, after seven years of field research, concluded that ego drive and empathy were the key ingredients in the most effective selling.[4] Ego drive makes the salesperson want and need to make the sale—it becomes a conquest and a powerful means of enhancing the ego. But empathy—the ability to feel as the other person does—must complement this. Otherwise, the salesperson will tend to bulldoze the way through to close a sale and thereby drive off many prospects. So we can conclude that some middle ground between no pressure and high presure is best for most selling situations and with most prospects.

[4]David Mayer and Herbert M. Greenberg, "What Makes a Good Salesman," *Harvard Business Review*, July–August, 1964, pp. 119–125.

The marketing tactics of Boise led to lawsuits against the company and its subsidiaries charging misrepresentation in the sales of recreation land in 19 California subdivisions and one in Nevada. Civil actions were filed by the California attorney general's office and the Contra Costa County district attorney, and class action lawsuits were filed in state and federal courts. In Maryland, the state's Real Estate Board halted sales for 90 days on Boise's 3500 acre Ocean Pines project, charging that the company was using unlicensed salespeople. Boise eventually had to spend $60 million to settle the lawsuits.

Other problems were also confronting some of the projects. Ecologists were mobilizing public opinion against communities planned for a Puget Sound shoreline, a Hawaiian beach, and other locations. The bad publicity was front page news.

Amid increasing public pressure, Boise was forced to reevaluate its land operations. Moving toward a heavier investment in recreational facilities, the company also attempted to meet local demands for more open spaces, underground utilities, and full sewage-treatment facilities. None of these came cheap: on a 3000 acre project, a sewage system might cost $4 million.[5] Such higher costs lowered the profit margin, unless lot prices could be raised substantially. But sometimes this was not possible. For example, demand tended to dry up as lot prices were raised from $8000 to $12,000.

Despite efforts by Boise to improve acceptability of its selling methods and its ecological impact, the bad image gained as the most visible land developer ripping off consumers and raping the environment was difficult to overcome. Sluggish sales were resulting, and its customer default ratio was one of the worst in the industry (a situation not helped by an estimated 5 percent of sales to its own salespeople speculating on quick investment profits).

In 1970, after almost a decade-and-a-half of climbing steeply, sales for Boise Cascade fell 1 percent below the 1969 level. Worse, profits plummeted 55 percent. Then in 1971 the ax fell. The company reported a staggering $85.1 million loss, of which $74 million was accounted for by the beleaguered land development operation.

Plagued by deficits and lawsuits, Boise began to work its way out of the land business. Getting out did not come easily or cheaply. Real estate is a difficult business to pull out of, since if contractual obligations on the numerous projects are not fulfilled, customer receivables disappear; and if a customer sees no neighbors in his recreational community, he is likely to stop payment. The company swallowed write-offs and losses of $100 million

[5]Ibid., p. 90.

in 1971 and $200 million in 1972. Some projects were sold to other firms. For example, projects in New Jersey were sold to Kaufman & Broad, a housing producer; Larwin, a land developer-builder subsidiary of CNA, bought a Boise project in the Pennsylvania Pocono Mountains and land sites in Chicago—all these at "fire sale prices."

Now the huge debt of Boise—$916 million—was becoming a serious factor. Bankers and insurance companies who had lent the money were in a position of dictation. They forced Boise to begin selling off assets to reduce the heavy debt load. And in October of 1972, Robert Hansberger, the "genius" who had built the huge conglomerate from three small lumber mills in 1957, was forced out of management of the company.

THE STRUGGLE BACK

Boise's troubles did not end with its land development business. The Ebasco merger of 1969, made to generate badly needed current assets, turned sour. The $237 million worth of Latin American bonds acquired with the merger turned out to be illiquid. These bonds had been obtained by Ebasco from the sale of utility operations in Argentina, Brazil, Chile, Colombia, and Costa Rica. Changes in governments in these countries jeopardized the investments. In 1972, for political reasons, Boise sold two Latin American utilities at prices below book value.

Other acquisitions also were faltering. The Divco-Wayne acquisition of the largest producer of mobile homes was suffering as the two top people left within months, and Divco began making mistakes in production planning. The Princess Cruises Boise had bought in 1968 lost $2.5 million in 1970, and was sold.

The debt-ridden conglomerate continued to retrench and sell off diversifications in an attempt to return to its business of the 1950s, forest products. However, in order to raise cash to pay down on its long-term and realty debt, even some of the basic forest products operations went to the block. In 1973 the Union Lumber operation was sold to Georgia Pacific Corporation for $120 million. Union had earned a respectable $8 million on sales of $29 million in 1972. However, this and other divestments reduced Boise's debt to close to 33 percent of equity by the end of 1973. Virtually all of its construction and engineering group, which generated sales of $378 million in 1970, was now gone. Of the land sales projects, only two remained in 1973, and these the company hoped to be rid of in a few years.

Except for the Union divestment, the mainstay of Boise, its timber, building materials, and paper-packaging groups remained intact. The company still had some 7 million acres of timberlands. Whereas in 1971, 44 percent of its $1.8 billion sales came from nonforest products, by 1973 almost zero revenue came from this.

John B. Fery presided over this rapid divestment of Boise's far-flung operations. After Hansberger was ousted, Fery, one of his proteges and an executive vice president, was chosen to revive the company. Fery was the first major executive to identify the serious nature of Boise's real estate woes, and he pressed for the company to rid itself of this operation despite the cost. He was Boise's chief spokesman with creditors during the dark days of 1972, and he engineered the retrenchment that put Boise on a much sounder footing, albeit hundreds of millions of dollars smaller in sales.

The basic soundness of the company was manifested in 1973, when Fery moved Boise back into the black. While sales dropped to $1.3 billion, it registered a profit of $90 million as opposed to a $171 million deficit in 1972, and an $85 million deficit in 1971. With a tighter, more centralized control, and a planned diversification strictly within Boise's basic line of business, the future became again promising for Boise Cascade.

ANALYSIS

In an interview in 1974, after time to view the Boise situation from a more objective and distant vantage point, Hansberger said that the major problem was to be able to switch quickly enough to a changing social clime in California: ". . . we were the biggest land developer in California . . . but tremendous changes were taking place there, and California has the tendency to be one of the first states to effect changes, especially social changes . . . environmental issue was hot there, and came suddenly upon the company . . . we could not change quickly enough."[6]

When queried about the questionable practices of Boise salesmen of making promises that could not be kept and ultimately causing dozens of lawsuits, Hansberger noted that in acquiring companies in the land business, Boise had kept their personnel and their sales practices, ". . . while their loose ways of doing business were very rapidly becoming obsolete, it was difficult to find the expertise that would be viable in the future." He admitted that at first these subsidiaries were perhaps too autonomous, were given too much latitude, but ". . . it takes a while to change a massive sales force, replace it, retrain it, or reorient it."[7] He noted that he did try to impose stiff controls by sending out company people to represent themselves as customers, with salespeople knowing this was taking place.

> One of our problems was our visibility—we were a prime target because of our size, so we restricted our salespeople . . . strict controls with tougher terms of

[6]"Interview with Robert Vail Hansber," *Dun's*, September 1974, pp. 12–14.
[7]Ibid.

sale, down payment requirements, what they could represent to customers in terms of products . . . this made it tougher to sell against competition which wasn't so visible . . . a lot of our salesmen just went down the street and got a job with someone else who didn't impose these rigid controls on them. When you begin to lose your sales force, you begin to lose your sales volume. And that's when the viability of the land projects began to evaporate.[8]

Hansberger placed the blame for the problems that confronted Boise primarily on outside factors, such as the changing milieu of California. But any firm has to operate and adjust to an ever-changing environment. Today, governmental regulations and public policies are changing rapidly, reflecting public pressures due to consumerism and ecological concerns. These are social constraints to be contended with for a long time to come. The successful firm is responsive to such changes and anticipates and/or quickly adjusts to them. Boise fell down here on two counts. Unconcerned at first about the questionable marketing practices taking place in its name, the company was slow to recognize the seriousness of customer complaints and ecological pressures. When the critical nature of the problem was finally recognized, drastic action was taken, but too late.

Boise's solution at that point was to repudiate and get rid of the part of the business that was coming up against environmental problems, despite the cost. Although perhaps the best solution, given the late awareness of the problem, there was another alternative. The company could have moved more slowly in land development projects, guided by a firm commitment to honesty of marketing and an ecological compatibility—in other words, more responsive marketing. Instead of disavowing the situation, Boise might have adjusted.

Certainly a large part of the internal problems of Boise was the consequence of the rapidity of expansion through highly diversified acquisitions in the late 1960s. In those days such a strategy was heralded and was characteristic of other wildly growing conglomerates. Most of these also found themselves overextended financially and managerially and had to cut back drastically and even fatally, and the value of their stocks tumbled. A highly decentralized or "free form" management such as Hansberger had at one time thought to be the key to corporate success was really a consequence of acquiring such widely divergent companies that no one in the parent organization had the expertise to closely manage and control them. Consequently, the running of such acquisitions was left to the original executives. If they were capable, things usually turned out well; if they were less than scrupulous, unresponsive to social and ecological demands (as

[8]Ibid.

Table 19.1   Boise Cascade Sales and Profits, 1971–1978

Year	Sales (billions)	Net Profits (millions)
1971	$1.8	deficit $85
1972	1.15	deficit 171
1973	1.3	90
1974	1.45	103.6
1976	1.9	97
1978	2.6	136

Source: Company published data.

most of the land development subsidiary executives of Boise turned out to be), or not very competent, serious damage had often been done before this was detected. Then the parent company had the formidable task of replacing them, usually without the management resources to do so quickly and effectively. Therefore, the plight of Boise with its land development operations was not unique; it reflected the fallacy of heedless and reckless growth, growth beyond the assimilation abilities of a parent firm.

Even today, investors remain skeptical of highly diversified companies, the conglomerates. Some such companies are doing an excellent job, although their stock market prices scarcely reflect this; others are still trying to cope with unwise and poorly structured diversifications. The retrenchment of Boise in repudiating almost all the acquisitions made in the 1960s left a solid base from which to build more carefully and more compatibly in the future.

Update

To see how a company can bounce back from adversity should be inspiring. And Boise Cascade did that, streamlining its operation, cutting almost to the bone, but emerging a stronger and more profitable company. Table 19.1 shows the revenues and profits for the bad years and for the recovery years.

By 1983, sales had reached $3.45 billion. And interestingly, John Fery was still chief executive.

For Thought and Discussion

1. Why do you think high pressure tactics were considered necessary for selling recreational land? What pros and cons do you see of such marketing efforts?
2. What potential do you presently see for recreational land development? Is this likely to change in the 1980s? Why or why not?
3. Do you think Boise was wise to have divested itself so completely of the land operation?

Invitation to Role Play

1. Place yourself in the role of Robert Hansberger in the late 1960s. What are some specific ways in which you would have built a more responsive marketing strategy in the land operations?
2. As a sales manager for the recreational land division, how would you have developed and supervised a sales force so that it would be both effective in generating sales and high in integrity and fair dealing? What problems, if any, would you expect to encounter in achieving this?

20

Conclusions—What
Can Be Learned?

In considering mistakes, two things are worth noting: (1) even the most successful organizations make mistakes, but can and do survive as long as they can maintain a good batting average; and (2) making mistakes can be an effective teaching tool. The difference in overall success or failure is what is learned from these errors to avoid the repetition of similar mistakes.

A number of generalizations can be drawn from the mistakes described. Of course, we need to recognize that marketing, as all the social sciences, is a discipline that does not lend itself to laws or axioms. Examples of successful exceptions to every principle or generalization can be found. But the marketing executive does well to heed these generalizations.

IMPORTANCE OF PUBLIC IMAGE

As we discussed at some length in Chapter 2 and in the cases in Part I, the image that people (that is, the various publics an organization is involved with) have of the organization and its products or services is of major importance. In particular, we singled out four firms with serious image problems: Coors, Nestle, Korvette, and Gilbert.

The Coors image of mystique proved to be vulnerable under a nonaggressive marketing strategy and the onslaught of strong competitors. Nestle tried to ignore a damning reputation having to do with only one part of its diverse and worldwide operation, but alas found this image problem to be both durable and transferable to all other aspects of its operation. Korvette lost its positive image as a reliable discounter offering greater values than most other firms when its food and furniture operations became questionable. When it tried to upgrade, the low-price, discount image remained and diluted efforts to move up successfully to a higher quality operation. Finally, we saw how very quickly a superior image, a quality image, such as Gilbert had built up from decades of well-conceived toys, could be cut down. In Gilbert's case, two or three years of an image-destructive marketing strategy destroyed the positive image.

But other cases in the book also had image problems. For example, the rather negative, old-fashioned image of A & P helped to thwart its price offensive aimed at regaining market share. Grant's lack of a specific image— whether as a discounter, a 5-and 10-cent store, or a department store— impeded its aggressive efforts to expand. Burger Chef's lack of a distinctive image placed it at a major disadvantage vis-a-vis McDonald's and other successful fast-food operations. Adidas' image as the major factor in the athletic shoe industry was not enough to protect it when it let its guard down during a few crucial years of market expansion.

Image can be a lodestone for the organization wishing to expand or to upgrade its reputation. Improving an image can be a long process requiring great patience and strong resources. Penney was able to change its image of a small-town, soft-line retailer; but it took a decade or longer, and the firm is still struggling to upgrade its fashion image. For many firms the best course may be to go with the present image rather than radically try to change it. An alternative is to introduce a different brand or a different division, anything to escape the negative or fuzzy image.

A favorable image can be an offensive weapon, insulating the organization from most of the rigors of competition, permitting it to charge higher prices, to recruit better employees, to obtain more favorable financing, as well as smoothing the way for product expansion or diversification. But we are concerned here with mistakes, not with successes.

SUCCESS DOES NOT GUARANTEE CONTINUED SUCCESS

That success does not guarantee continued success or freedom from adversity is a sobering realization that must come from examining these cases. Almost all the organizations described—except for the World Football League and to some extent Burger Chef—were notably successful. Most of them had exhibited enviable growth records; some had grown to such a large size that they dominated their industry. Yet they succumbed to grievous mistakes, some at the very pinnacle of their growth and success. How could this possibly have happened to these firms, firms with such experience, such momentum, and such resources, both financial and managerial, behind them?

We are forced to conclude that, far from assuring continued success and mastery of the marketplace, success may actually promote vulnerability, may leave a firm more easy prey to hungry competitors. The reason for this? Complacency. It is difficult for a successful firm not to become smug about its position and disdainful of lesser competitors. Such an organization is usually resistant to drastic changes—because these can be traumatic and disruptive to what has heretofore been successful. Success encourages the viewpoint that the future is a mirror of the past. With such attitudes permeating an organization—even though they may not be overtly communicated—then a changing environment can go undetected for far too long.

The environment is dynamic. It is changing, sometimes subtly, other times more drastically and recognizably. This fact needs to be realized by all organizations. To rest on laurels is perilous. In view of a changing environment, which opens up opportunities as well as problems, a firm can be an innovator, a leader. Not all firms are willing to accept the rewards and risks of this. But a firm must at least be adaptive if it is not to be wounded by the changing environment. We have examples of a number of firms that were far too long oblivious to the changes around them: Penney's, Adidas, Coors, A. C. Gilbert, Boise Cascade, the roller coaster ride of Osborne. In Gillette's case, it was aware of change—the popularizing of the stainless steel blade— but was reluctant to cannibalize its highly profitable Super Blue blade, and so procrastinated for an unduly long time.

The two terms—*adaptive* and *innovative*—are somewhat different although related. For our discussion we will consider them as different degrees of responsive behavior on the same dimension. *Innovative* may be defined as originating significant changes, implying improvement. *Adaptive* implies a better coping with changing circumstances, but a response somewhat less significant than an innovative reaction.

A useful perspective of the dynamics of marketing can be gained by considering a continuum of behavior, such as:

Degree of Responsiveness to Environmental Change		
inflexible, unchanging	adaptive	innovative

Thus a firm can be judged as occupying a certain point along this continuum: the more conservative and rigid firm toward the left, the more progressive one that is constantly developing new ideas, toward the right. Even the historical trend of a firm can be viewed on such a scale. For example, the Ford Motor Company in its early years was extremely innovative, as it was one of the pioneers in the effective use of the assembly line; however, the long adherence to a single unchanging product, the Model T, in the face of changing consumer wants and more aggressive competition would have placed the firm eventually at the other extreme on the scale.

NEED FOR GROWTH ORIENTATION—BUT NOT RECKLESS GROWTH

The opposite of a growth commitment is a status quo philosophy, not interested in expansion and the problems and work involved. We saw three cases where a growth orientation was lacking. With Montgomery Ward, growth plans were shelved under the mistaken belief that expansion would be less costly sometime in the future. With Penney, there was an unwillingness to change old traditional ways of doing things that were stifling growth. For Gilbert, contentment with the status quo seemed to have reached an extreme until a drastically worsening sales and profit picture and a takeover by new management hastened the company on its path of ill-conceived expansion efforts.

In general, how tenable is a low-or-no-growth philosophy? While at first glance it seems workable, upon closer inspection such a philosophy can be seen as sowing the seeds of its own destruction, unless reversed before too late. More than two decades ago Wroe Alderson pointed out:

> Vitality is required even for survival; but vitality is difficult to maintain without growth, at least in the American business climate. The vitality of a firm depends on the vigor and ambition of its members. The prospect of growth is one of the principal means by which a firm can attract able and vigorous recruits.[1]

Consequently, if a firm is obviously not growth-minded, its ability to attract able people diminishes so that it is vulnerable to competition. Customers see a growing firm as reliable, eager to please, and getting better all the time. Suppliers and creditors tend to give preferential treatment to a growth-oriented firm, since they hope to retain it as a customer and client when it reaches a large size.

On the other hand, as we have seen with Grant and Korvette, with Osborne, Boise Cascade, and Burger Chef, growth can be too extreme, can exceed the abilities of the organization to assimilate, control, and provide sufficient managerial and financial resources. Consequently, we may conclude that a firm's objectives might best be directed neither to reckless

---

[1] Wroe Alderson, *Marketing Behavior and Executive Action* (Homewood, Illinois: Irwin, 1957), p. 59.

headlong growth, nor to simply maintaining the status quo. Both extremes are dangerous.

DESIRABILITY OF SYSTEMATIC EVALUATION

Organizations need feedback to determine how well something is being done, whether improvement is possible, where it should occur, how much is needed, and how quickly it must be accomplished. Without feedback or performance evaluation, a worsening situation can go unrecognized until too late for corrective action. That was apparently the situation with Gilbert. For some reason, sales declines and market share erosion up to 1961 did not arouse any particular concern; certainly no serious attempt was made to find the causes and to take corrective action. With Boise Cascade, serious emerging problems of overall marketing performance were hidden in sales and profit figures. Operations apparently were not carefully monitored for the recreation land division until a plethora of customer and environmentalist complaints brought the company to the realization that drastic action was needed; this came too late to save the division, as well as the president of the company.

As firms become larger, the need for better controls or feedback increases, since top management can no longer personally monitor all aspects of the operation. This was where Eugene Ferkauf found the Korvette operation getting too much for him, but he was unable to install adequate controls in time to prevent overwhelming problems. The trend toward diversification and mergers, which often results in loosely controlled decentralized operations, such as Boise Cascade's, also makes timely feedback on marketing performance critical.

While any introductory marketing management textbook[2] describes the various measures of overall marketing performance in some detail, we will briefly list them here:

Total sales and profits, and comparison with preceding years

Market share—a measure of performance relative to that of competitors

Sales analysis—comparing sales variations from plans by such breakdowns as geographical, salespeople, customers, and products

Distribution cost analysis—determining the relative profitability of the present ways of doing business

[2]Such as Robert F. Hartley, *Marketing Fundamentals (New York: Harper & Row, 1983)*, Chapter 18.

Measures of customer satisfaction—through surveys, customer panels, and other market feedback

Marketing audit—an overall total evaluation of marketing objectives and performance

With these tools, a firm can determine if operations are proceeding according to plans, can identify problem areas, and can determine suitable courses of action.

NEED FOR MARKET SENSORS

Marketing research is desirable for most firms of medium or large size if for no other reason than to keep them abreast of changing conditions in the marketplace. A formal research function is not always necessary, however. Company executives, through observation and through feedback from customers, salespeople, and other sources such as creditors and suppliers, can often obtain a rather good feel for basic changes occurring in competition, in consumer preferences, in governmental restrictions, and the like. Mainly a firm needs to be alert to changes, to encourage good communications and feedback from the marketplace, and to be willing to react or respond to these emerging changes. Yet we have seen a number of examples of firms unheeding of changes, even though they should have been obvious. The Gilbert Company failed dismally in this area; the Penney Company for a lengthy period was myopic; Boise Cascade had its fatal period of faulty marketing sensing, as also did Coors, Adidas, and the STP Corporation. Such a common failing, the lack of marketing sensing! But it goes with the success syndrome described earlier.

If a firm is to practice responsive marketing, it must not only keep abreast of competitive and environmental changes, but also be in a position to cope with them, not only from the firm's viewpoint but also that of society. For example, if Boise Cascade had been better attuned to the growing consumer resentment of high pressure and deceptive selling practices, as well as the environmentalist fear of careless land use that was beginning to affect all recreational land development, it might not only have escaped consumer and government censure and lawsuits, but also have been able to muster a strong positive approach to these matters and become a bellwether of the recreational land industry. Similarly with STP: the clues as to a harsher public and governmental stance against unsupported advertising claims should have been obvious. But the feeling "they won't pick on us" was unrealistic and poor judgment.

LIMITATIONS OF ADVERTISING

Several cases have illustrated that heavy advertising expenditures do not assure marketing success. The Edsel and DuPont's Corfam failed despite substantial advertising. If the product advertised is contrary to consumers' expectations, if it somehow fails to satisfy their wants, or is not sufficiently different from other generally accepted products, advertising will not win market penetration.

In the Gilbert case, a $1 million commitment was made for another type of promotion, point-of-purchase displays furnished free to retailers. Few used them, and the extravagant expenditure edged Gilbert further to the brink of bankruptcy. Point-of-purchase displays often have less impact than advertising, since if dealers do not use them—and many retailers are surfeited with manufacturer-supplied displays—the effort is wasted.

Other aspects of a marketing strategy are needed—product desirability, an attractive price, reasonable distribution outlets—in addition to adequate expenditures for advertising and an attractive message. In the case of the Edsel, massive advertising brought consumers to dealer showrooms, but what they saw did not impress them, and there was little positive effect. The poor quality products and their back-breaking merchandise returns wasted the heavy promotional expenditures of Gilbert.

On the other hand, lest we are left with a false impression of the efficacy of advertising, the STP case shows that even a useless product can achieve high success if enough money is spent and the right appeals used. (However, the useless or poor product must be such that this is not readily evident, as with an oil additive to make engines last longer or a toothpaste to make whiter teeth. If the product deficiencies are clearly evident upon use, then there will be no repeat business despite massive advertising.) We also have to wonder whether a more competitive advertising stance would have enabled Coors to maintain image and market dominance.

LIMITATIONS OF MARKETING RESEARCH

Marketing research is usually proposed as the way to make better marketing decisions, and the mark of sophisticated professional management. A common perception is that the more money spent for marketing research, the less chance for a bad decision. Yet, we have seen several examples where extremely heavy use of marketing research did not help the situation: for example, the Edsel and Corfam.

Marketing research does not guarantee a correct decision. The most that can be expected is that it will increase the batting average of correct decisions—maybe by only a little, sometimes by quite a bit. However, research needs to be current and unbiased. This lack was the basic flaw in the several million dollars spent on the Edsel marketing research. Most of the research on consumer preferences and attitudes was done several years before the Edsel came on the market. Consumer attitudes changed greatly in that time, particularly in preferences toward smaller cars. The choice of the name, Edsel, which to many consumers had negative connotations, also showed an unwise use of research, in this instance by not alerting top management to this negativism.

Viewing all marketing research as useless, however, is as bad as unhesitatingly accepting all research findings. Research does not produce auguries from Delphi. But neither is it valueless. There is both good and bad research. Some of the flawed studies might have been worthwhile with another researcher and a better interpretation of the problem.

In at least one case, marketing research was sorely needed: the World Football League. Swept up in enthusiasm and a sales pitch that was hardly realistic, the crucial need to determine market potential for the new venture—whether there was a reasonable chance to break even—was ignored. Carefully designed research here should have disclosed the poor likelihood of success, so that a no-go decision was called for. But that would have been unacceptable to the promoters and the investors eager for a tax shelter. With the Coors case, it would hardly have taken strenuous research to discover that customers did not like the hard-to-open cans and were increasingly preferring low-caloric beer.

The examples of marketing failures despite heavy expenditures for marketing research should caution the marketer to use it with care, plan how it can help, and recognize its limitations. At the same time, we must recognize that some problems do not lend themselves to valid research conclusions with the available tools and techniques. There may be too many variables. They may be intangible and incapable of precise measurement. This is often the case where an optimum allocation is sought for marketing efforts. When is the optimum reached? How can it be obtained? How is it to be measured? The answers to these questions defy us. Some analyses rest on the shaky foundation of subjectivity. Consumer preference statements often are not translatable into actual sales, without judicious imagination. Much research consists of collecting data of past and present. While this is helpful in predicting the future, such predictions do not always come to pass.

IMPOTENCE OF PRICE AS AN OFFENSIVE WEAPON

We generally think of price promotions as the most aggressive form of marketing and the one most desirable in the eyes of society. Yet we have seen here an example of the misguided use of price as a marketing weapon. The A & P WEO campaign had strong repercussions in the food marketing industry. Food prices were reduced by A & P to almost intolerable low markups. A & P hoped to win a much greater share of the market for itself; if it drove some of its weaker adversaries out of business in the meantime, A & P would not have cared. However, the strategy had only negative consequences for A & P and the rest of the industry. A & P lost over $50 million in the first year of its WEO campaign; most other grocers also lost money. And what was gained? While consumers enjoyed somewhat lower prices, most were scarcely aware of this since wholesale prices were relentlessly going up during this time. As for winning substantial market share and holding it, this did not happen for A & P. Its problems were not solved by merely lowering prices for a few months or a year.

The major disadvantage of price as an offensive weapon is that other firms in the industry are almost forced to meet the price-cutter's prices—such a marketing strategy is easy to match. Consequently, prices for an entire industry fall; no firm has any particular advantage and all suffer the effects of diminished profits. Competitive advantage is therefore seldom won by price cutting. Other marketing strategies more successfully enable a firm to better its competitors—strategies such as better quality, better product and brand image, better service, improved warranties. All are aspects of nonprice rather than price competition.

At the same time, we have to recognize that in new industries, which are characterized by rapid technological changes and production efficiencies, severe price competition can be expected—and is even necessary to weed out the host of marginal operations that entered in the expectation of cashing in on a rapidly growing market. Alas, as Osborne learned, even a substantial position in such an industry does not necessarily protect a firm from such severe price competition that its very viability may be jeopardized.

DESIRABILITY OF JUDICIOUS IMITATION

Some firms are reluctant to adopt successful practices of their competitors; they want to be leaders, not followers. In the example of Gillette, even when a highly successful new product was practically forced upon it, there was resistance. Partly this was because of fear that existing products would be adversely affected. But there was also a psychological basis: top management's reluctance to admit that the industry leader was in this instance only a follower.

There are good arguments for systematically observing the operations of successful competitors (and even similar, but noncompetitive, organizations), evaluating them and identifying those aspects that contribute most to the success, and then adopting these if compatible with the resources of the imitator. Let someone else do the experimenting and take the risks of innovating. While there can be some risk for an imitator to wait too long, this is usually far less than the risk of an untested product or operation failing. Theodore Levitt, in a classic article, "Innovative Imitation," notes:

> No single company, regardless of its determination, energy, imagination, and resources, is big enough or solvent enough to do all the productive first things that will ever occur in its industry and to always beat its competitors to all the innovations emanating from the industry . . . each organization [should] look to imitation as one of its survival and growth strategies.[3]

In few firms was the need for judicious imitation more pronounced than with Burger Chef. Confronted with the outstandingly successful and highly publicized operation of McDonald's, it did not attempt to improve its own faltering operation by imitating the success that had been analyzed in trade journals and even in the public press for years.

By imitation, we do not mean a slavish effort to be identical. Burger Chef still needed to develop its own identity. But the standards of performance, the training and selection of franchisees, and the imposition of strict controls to assure that performance was up to prescribed standards—these could certainly have been closely duplicated.

And we saw the great success of Nike, and to a lesser extent the other U.S. athletic shoe manufacturers, who simply imitated the strategy of the dominant firm, Adidas, but somehow managed to do this more aggressively and with better timing than their mentor.

ROLE OF SOCIAL AND ENVIRONMENTAL INFLUENCES

The Nestle case and the last two cases in the book illustrate the new milieu of marketing: the role that the general public and their agents can play in curbing what critics claim are undesirable practices. The wrath of activists focused on Nestle and its aggressive marketing practices in Third World countries. And while the issue was not as black as the protestors maintained, Nestle was eventually forced to retreat from its stand and bow to the demands of the protestors and boycotters. In the STP example, the undesirable practice was what some saw as misleading, deceptive, or, at the least, unsupported advertising claims. With Boise Cascade, the concern was both environmental degradation and unacceptable selling methods.

There is an important lesson for all marketers to be gained from these cases. No longer can social and environmental issues be disregarded by

---

[3]Theodore Levitt, "Innovative Imitation," *Harvard Business Review*, September–October 1966.

today's marketers; no longer can the consumer be viewed as malleable and easily influenced.

GENERAL CONCLUSIONS

From mistakes we learn. Yet every marketing problem seems cast in a somewhat different setting, requiring a different strategy. One author has likened marketing strategy to military strategy:

> . . . strategies which are flexible rather than static enhance optimum use and offer the greatest number of alternative objectives. A good commander knows that he cannot control his environment to suit a prescribed strategy. Natural phenomena pose their own restraints to strategic planning, whether physical, geographic, regional, or psychological and sociological.

And:

> Planning leadership recognizes the unpleasant fact that, despite every effort, the war may be lost. Therefore, the aim is to retain the maximum number of facilities and the basic organization. Indicators of a deteriorating and unsalvageable total situation are, therefore, mandatory . . . No possible combination of strategies and tactics, no mobilization of resources . . . can supply a magic formula which guarantees victory; it is possible only to increase the probability of victory.[4]

Thus we can pull two concepts from military strategy to help guide marketing strategy: the desirability of flexibility due to an unknown or changing environment, and the idea of a basic core that should be maintained under all circumstances. The first suggests that the marketer should be prepared for adjustments in strategy as conditions warrant. As we have seen, most of the cases ultimately reached such adjustments, although not always promptly. The second suggests that the basic core of a firm's business should not be tampered with; it should be the final bastion to fall back to for regrouping if necessary. Boise Cascade was able to do this, to fall back to its basic business of forest products and again begin expansion from that point; Gilbert and Korvette abandoned their basic strengths, one drastically and with finality, the other to a degree.

In regard to the basic core of a firm, let us go back to Wroe Alderson.

---

[4]Myron S. Heidingsfield, *Changing Patterns in Marketing* (Boston: Allyn and Bacon, 1968), p. 11.

He sees every viable firm as having some distinctive function or "ecological niche" in the marketplace:

> Every business firm occupies a position which is in some respects unique. Its location, the product it sells, its operating methods, or the customers it serves tend to set it off in some degree from every other firm. Each firm competes by making the most of its individuality and its special character.[5]

Woe to the firm that loses its ecological niche.

For Thought and Discussion

1. Design a program aimed at mistake avoidance. Be as specific, as creative, and as complete as possible.
2. How would you build into an organization the controls to assure that similar mistakes will not happen in the future?
3. Which would you advise a firm to be: an imitator or an innovator? Why?

Invitation to Role Play

You have been assigned the responsibility of assuring that your firm has adequate sensors of the marketplace. How would you go about developing such sensors?

[5]Alderson, p. 101.